Peach Girl
Change of Heart

by Miwa Ueda

TOKYOPOP

Los Angeles • Tokyo • London • Hamburg

Translator - Ray Yoshimoto
English Adaptation - Jodi Bryson
Retouch and Lettering - Peter Sattler
Cover Layout - Anna Kernbaum

Editor - Nora Wong
Digital Imaging Manager - Chris Buford
Pre-Press Manager - Antonio DePietro
Production Managers - Jennifer Miller & Mutsumi Miyazaki
Art Director - Matt Alford
Managing Editor - Jill Freshney
VP of Production - Ron Klamert
President & C.O.O. - John Parker
Publisher & C.E.O. - Stuart Levy

E-mail: info@TOKYOPOP.com

Come visit us online at www.TOKYOPOP.com

A  Manga

TOKYOPOP Inc.
5900 Wilshire Blvd. Suite 2000
Los Angeles, CA 90036

Peach Girl: Change of Heart Vol. 9

ISBN: 1-59182-498-2

First TOKYOPOP printing: July 2004

10 9 8 7 6 5 4 3 2 1

Printed in the USA

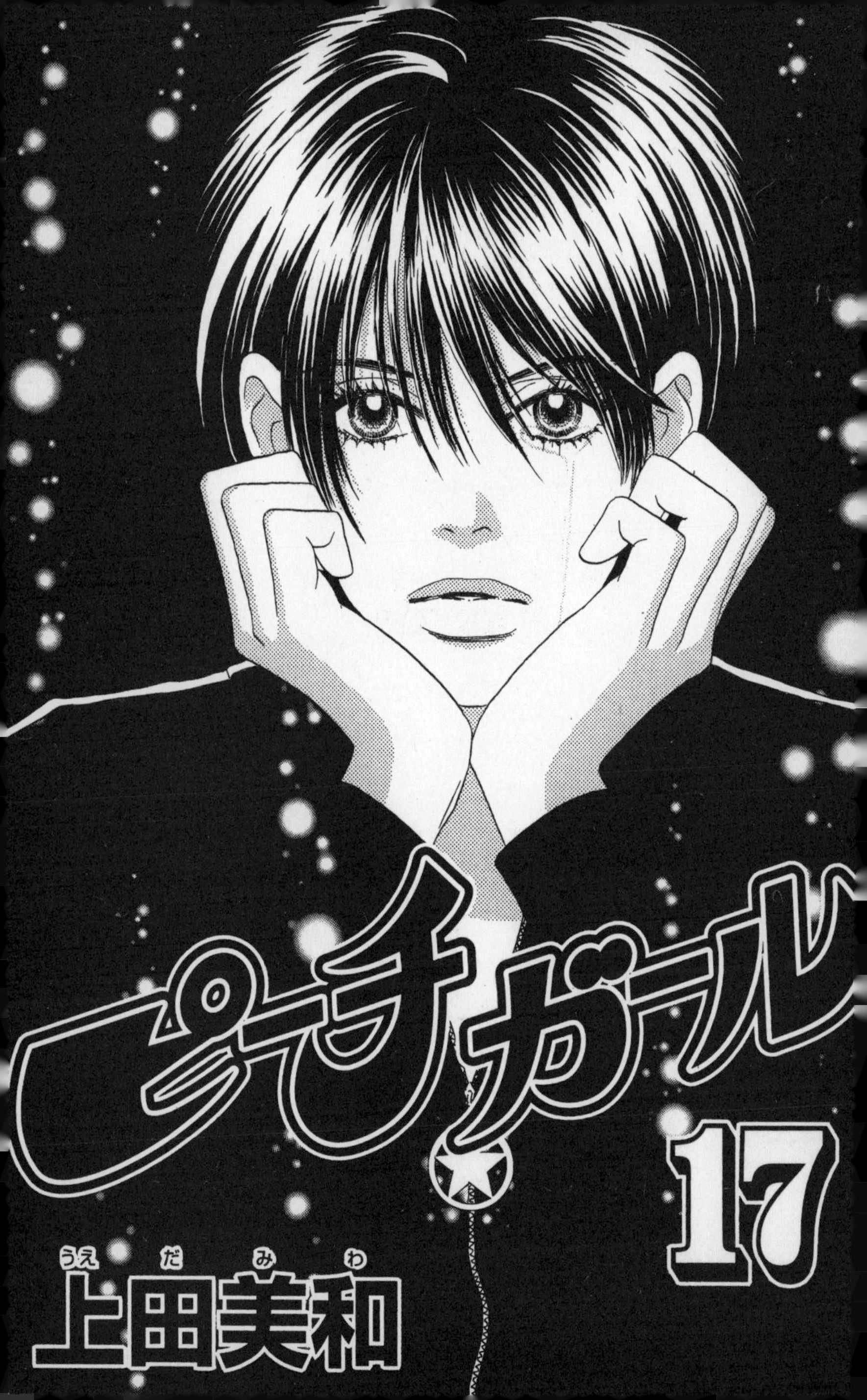
ピーチガール
17
うえだみわ
上田美和

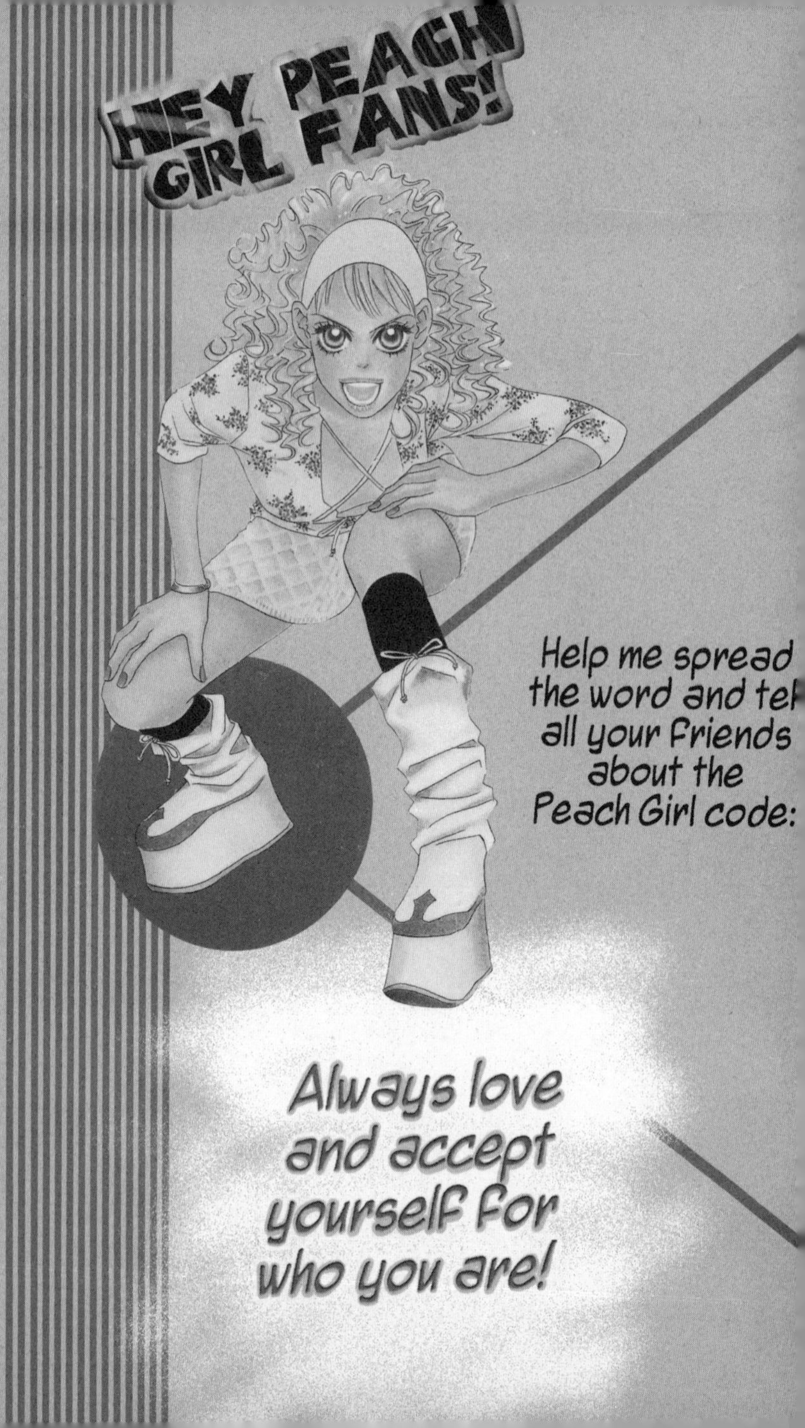
HEY PEACH GIRL FANS!
Help me spread the word and tel all your friends about the Peach Girl code:
Always love and accept yourself for who you are!

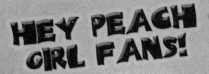

HEY PEACH GIRL FANS!

Keep those fan art and letters coming 'cause we might just publish 'em! We love hearing from you so write me, okay?

By: gabby the peachgirl freak
12/1/03
Old NAVY
WET SEAL
GAP
MACY'S
Momo as an Angel

Nora Wong, Editor
Peach Girl
TOKYOPOP
5900 Wilshire Blvd., Suite 2000
Los Angeles, CA 90036

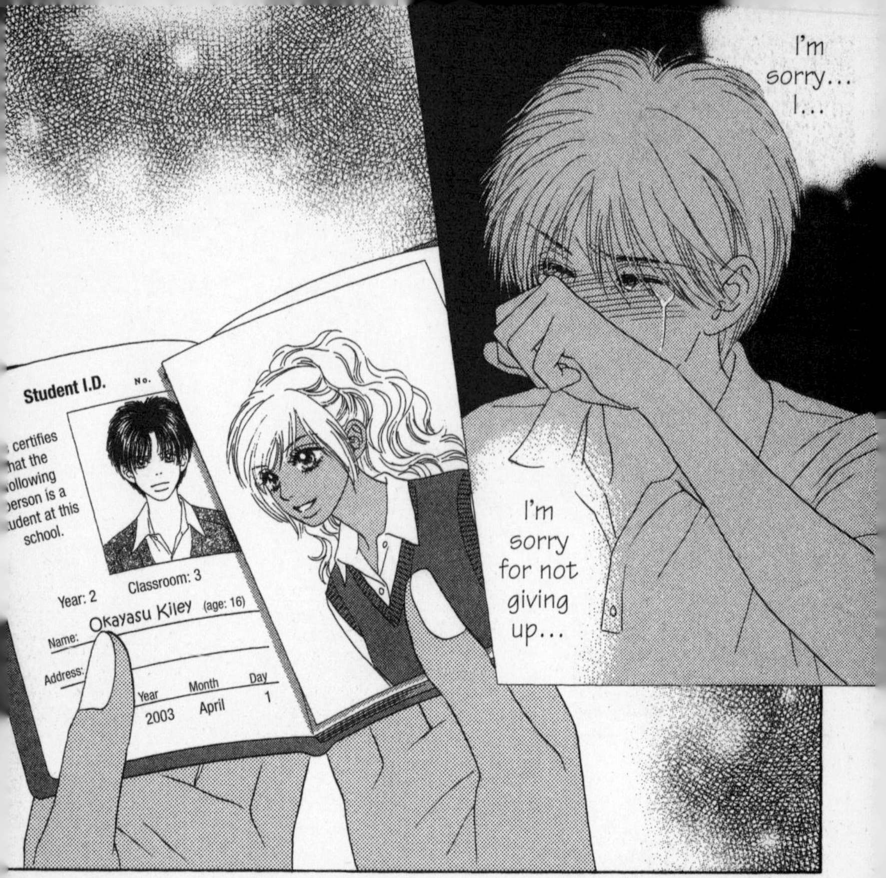
I'm sorry... I...
I'm sorry for not giving up...
Student I.D. No.
certifies hat the ollowing person is a udent at this school.
Year: 2 Classroom: 3
Name: Okayasu Kiley (age: 16)
Address:
Year 2003 Month April Day 1

WHY IS MOMO'S LOVE ALWAYS STORMY?!

Momo and Toji were happily in love. But Sae engineered their breakup. Momo eventually bounced back when she fell in love with Kiley, but she was totally shocked to find out that Kiley's true love is Misao!! He then tried to settle the issue by admitting his feelings to Misao but was rebuffed, so he took a road trip to do some soul searching. Before he left, Kiley made a promise to Momo that if he decides to get back together with her, they will meet up at Shiranami beach, where they first met. When he doesn't show up, Momo is completely devastated! Out of the blue, Toji shows up at the beach and Momo runs into his arms, and that night, loses her virginity to him. When Kiley realizes what a fool he's been, he shows up at Momo's house and tearfully admits that he can't give up on her. Seeing his tears, Momo's feelings begin to fluctuate...again! As if that's not enough, Sae declares that she's pregnant, and demands that Ryo take responsibility!

Everything you need to know.

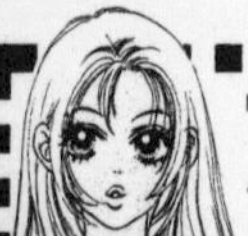

MOMO ADACHI: Her romance with Kiley is apparently over. Will she start over with Toji?!

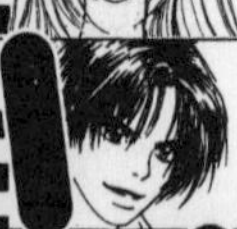

KILEY OKAYASU: Momo's ex-boyfriend. He broke his promise with Momo, and now regrets it.

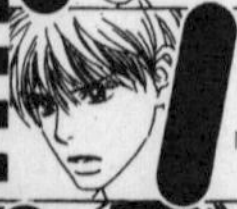

TOJI TOJIKAMORI: He's still in love with Momo. She loses her virginity to him.

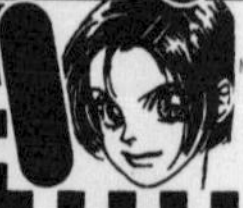

SAE KASHIWAGI: Momo's sworn enemy. Pregnant with Ryo's child. Hates Misao, who also admits to being in love with Ryo.

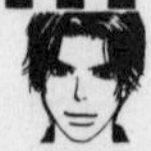

RYO: Kiley's older brother. Previously pimped Sae. He's in love with Misao.

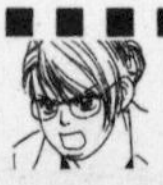

MISAO: The school nurse. Kiley was in love with her, but she's in love with Ryo.

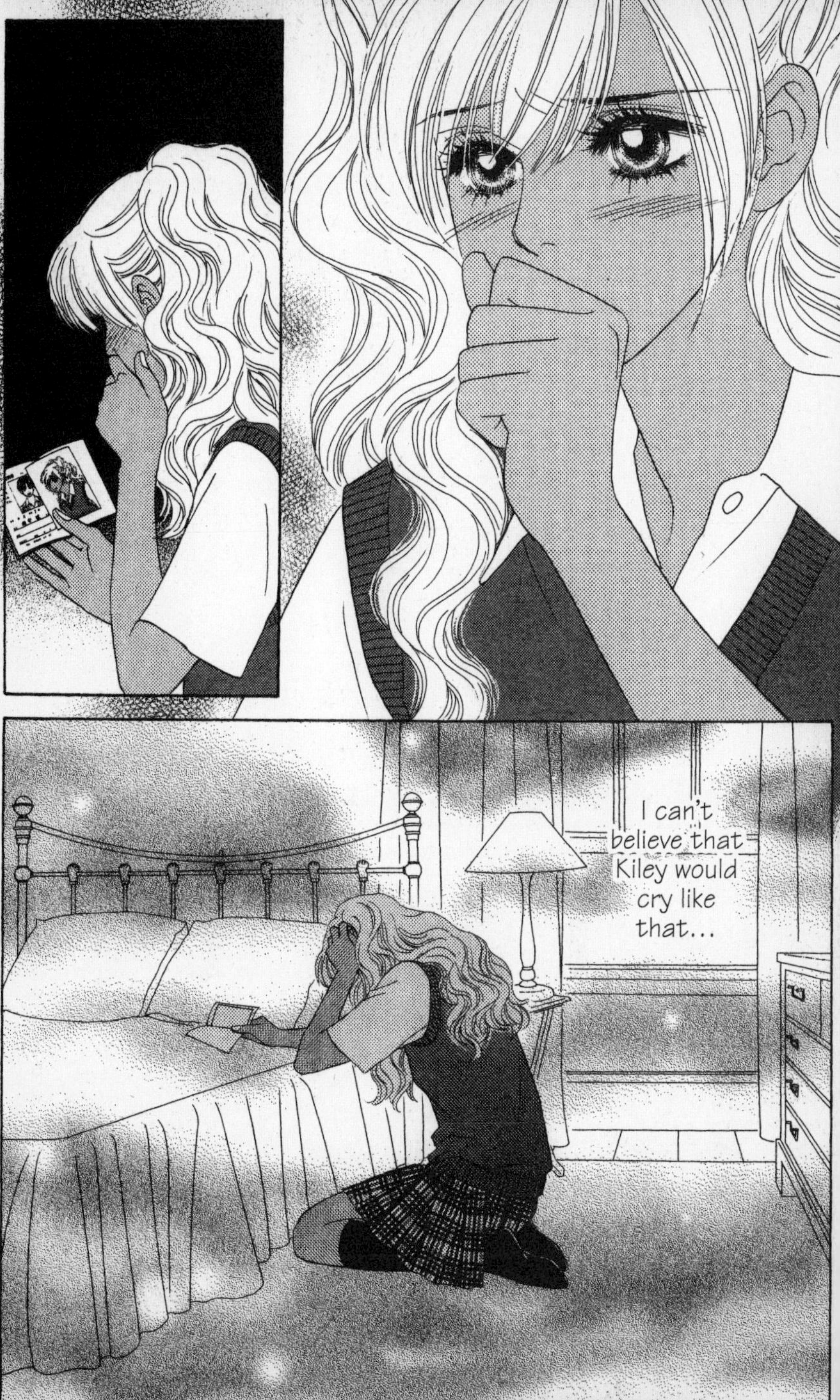
I can't believe that Kiley would cry like that...

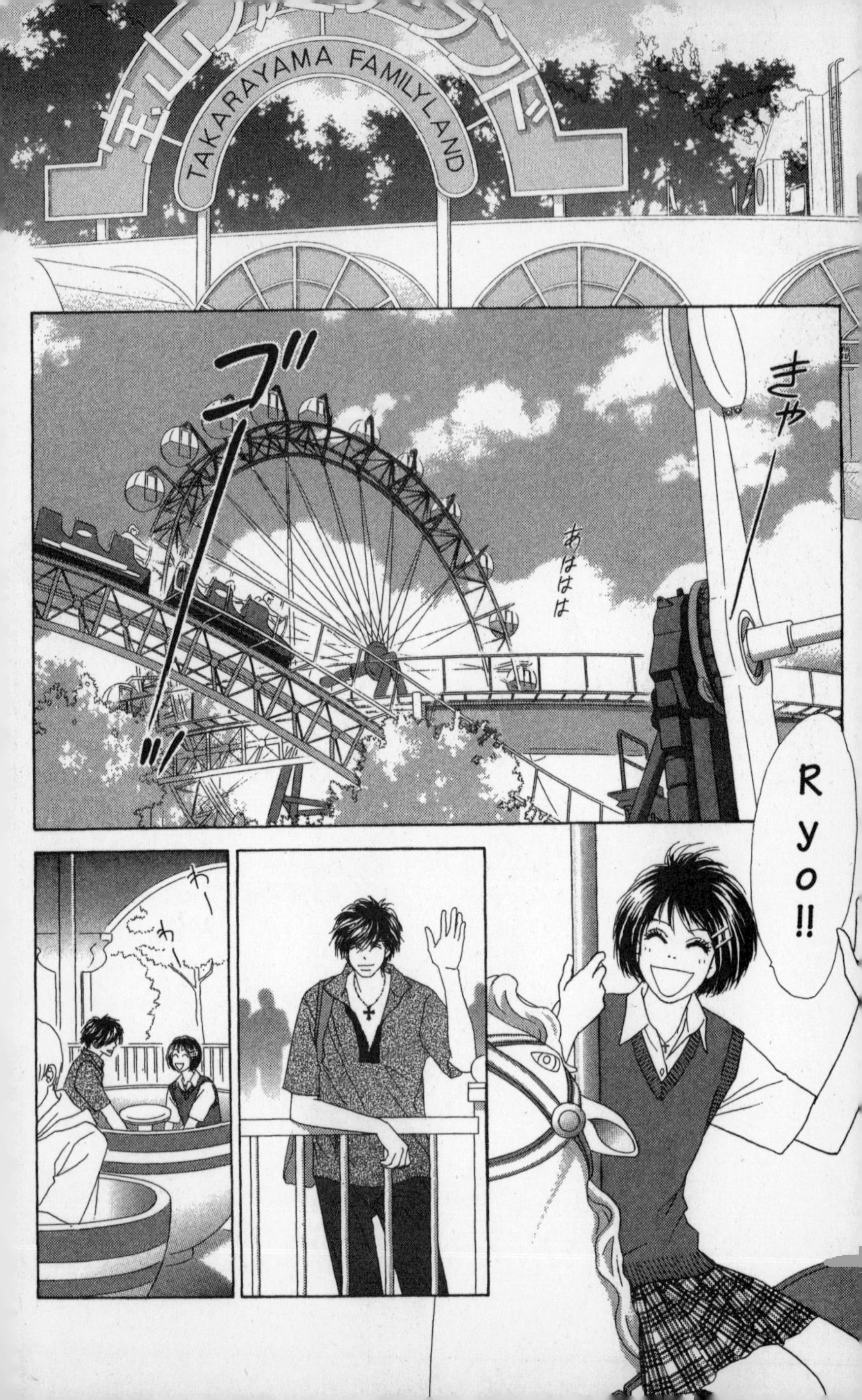
TAKARAYAMA FAMILYLAND
きゃー
あははは
ゴ
Ryo!!
わー
わー

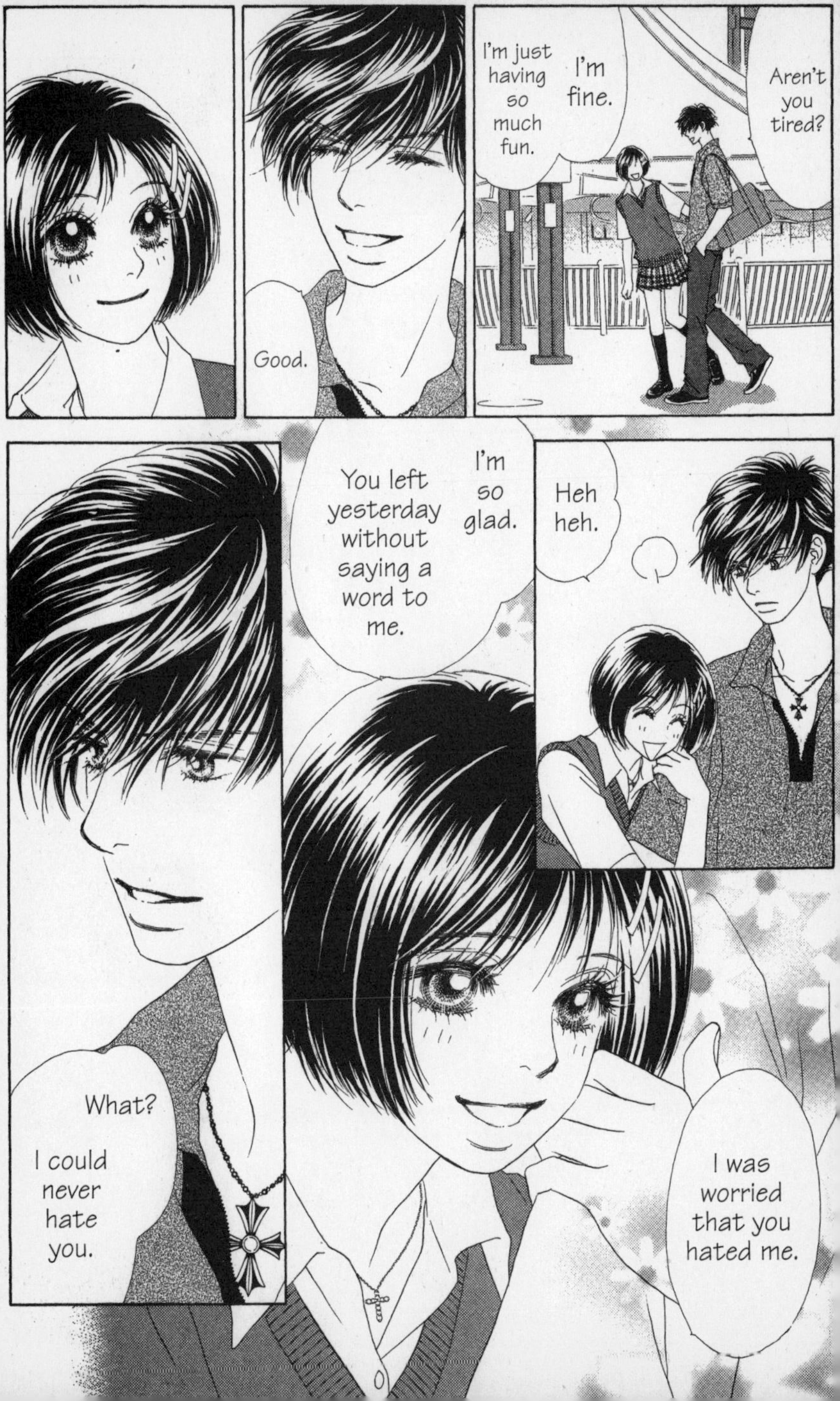
Aren't you tired?
I'm fine.
I'm just having so much fun.
Good.
Heh heh.
I'm so glad.
You left yesterday without saying a word to me.
I was worried that you hated me.
What?
I could never hate you.

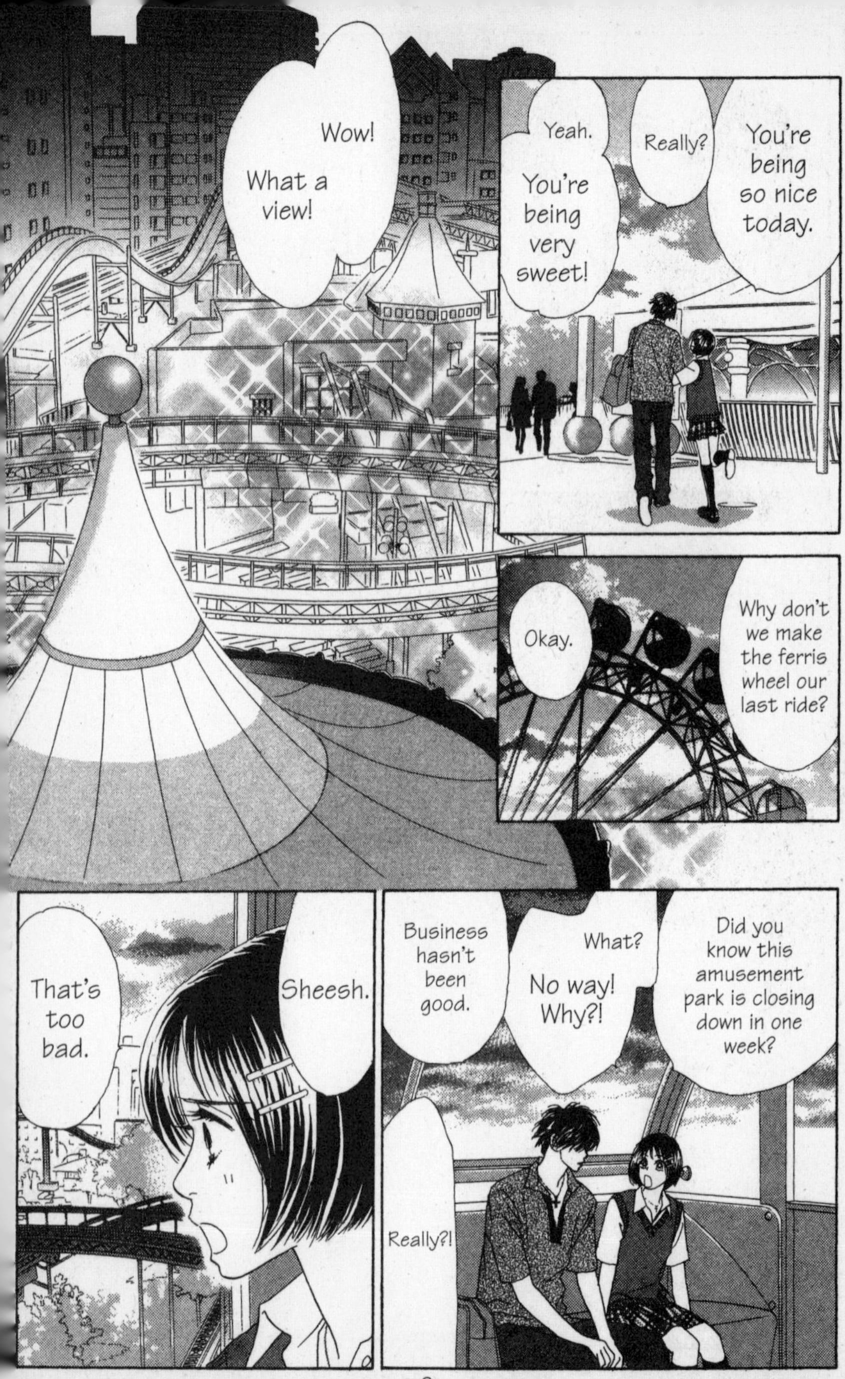
You're being so nice today.
Really?
Yeah.
You're being very sweet!
Why don't we make the ferris wheel our last ride?
Okay.
Wow!
What a view!
Did you know this amusement park is closing down in one week?
What?
No way! Why?!
Business hasn't been good.
Really?!
Sheesh.
That's too bad.

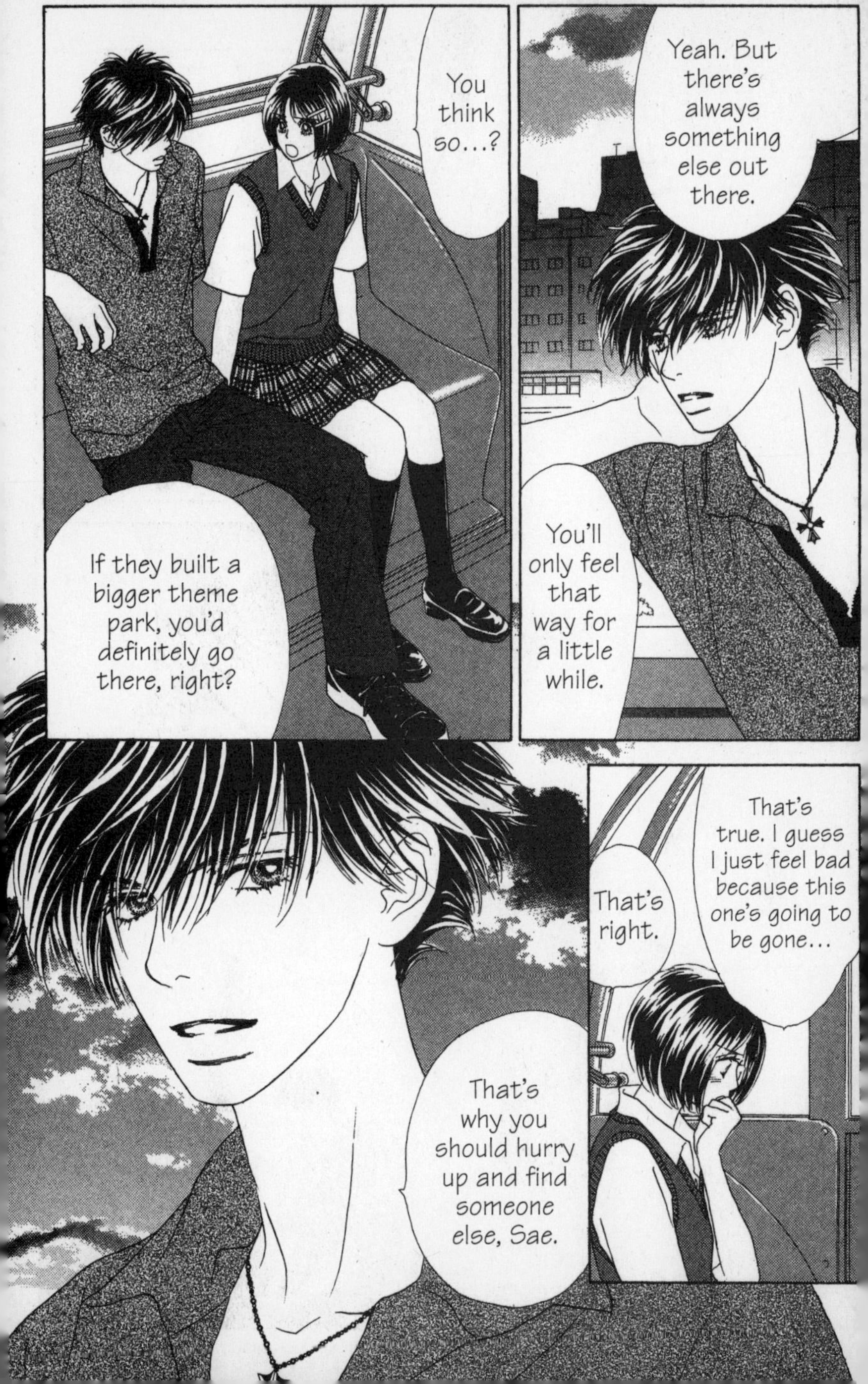
Yeah. But there's always something else out there.
You'll only feel that way for a little while.
You think so...?
If they built a bigger theme park, you'd definitely go there, right?
That's true. I guess I just feel bad because this one's going to be gone...
That's right.
That's why you should hurry up and find someone else, Sae.

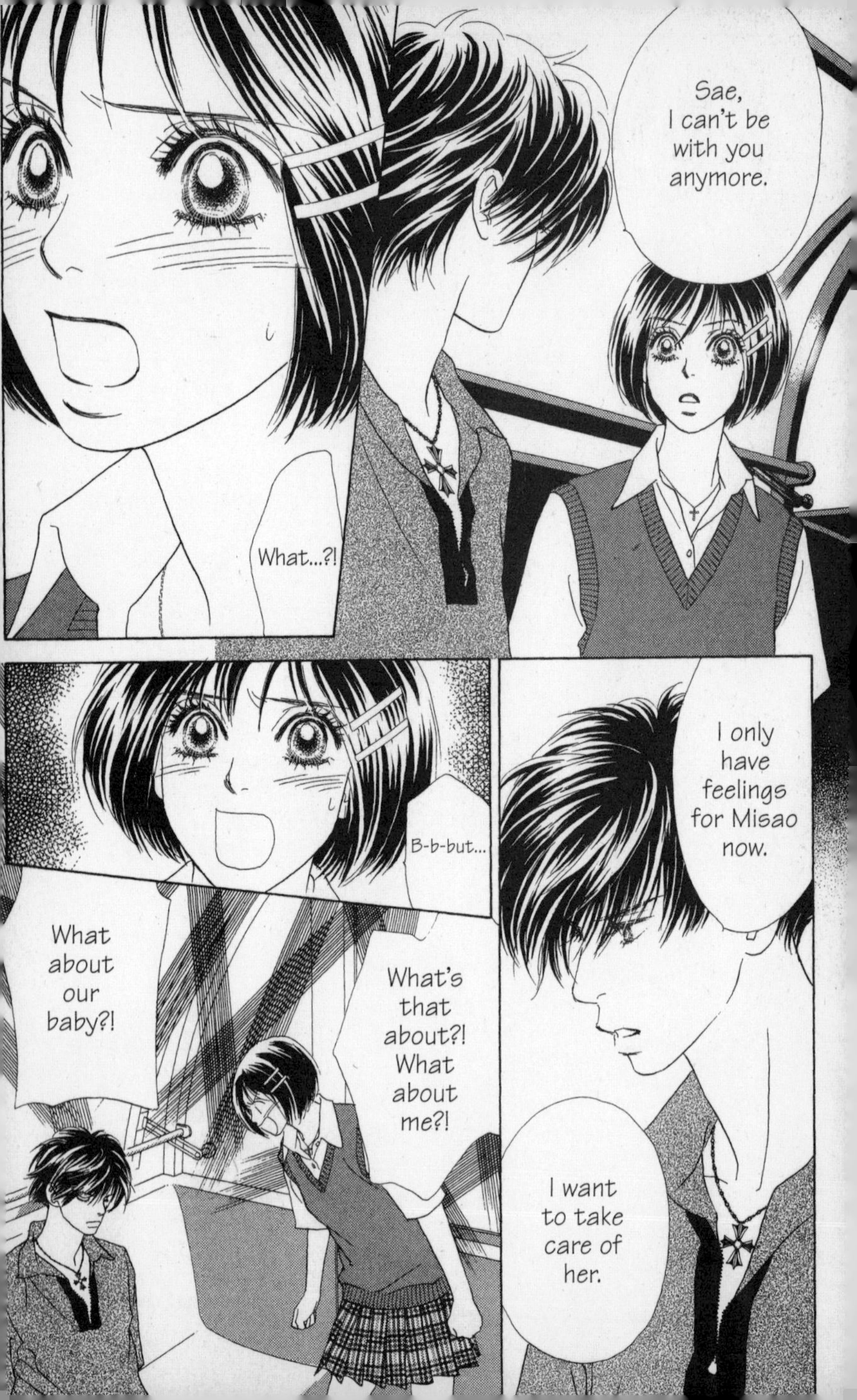
Sae, I can't be with you anymore.
What...?!
I only have feelings for Misao now.
I want to take care of her.
B-b-but...
What's that about?! What about me?!
What about our baby?!

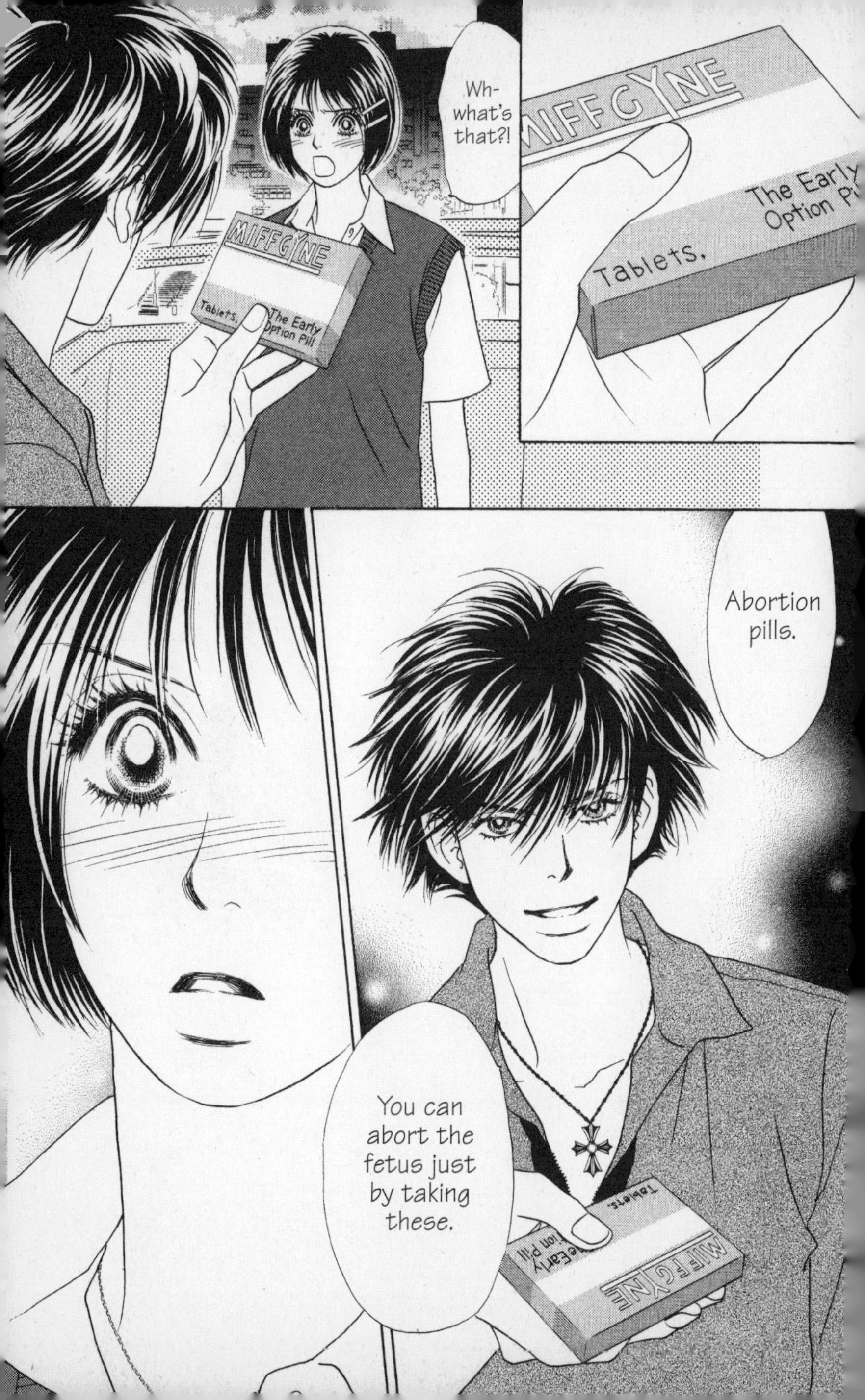
MIFFGYNE
Tablets.
Wh- what's that?!
MIFFGYNE
Tablets.
The Early Option Pill
Abortion pills.
You can abort the fetus just by taking these.

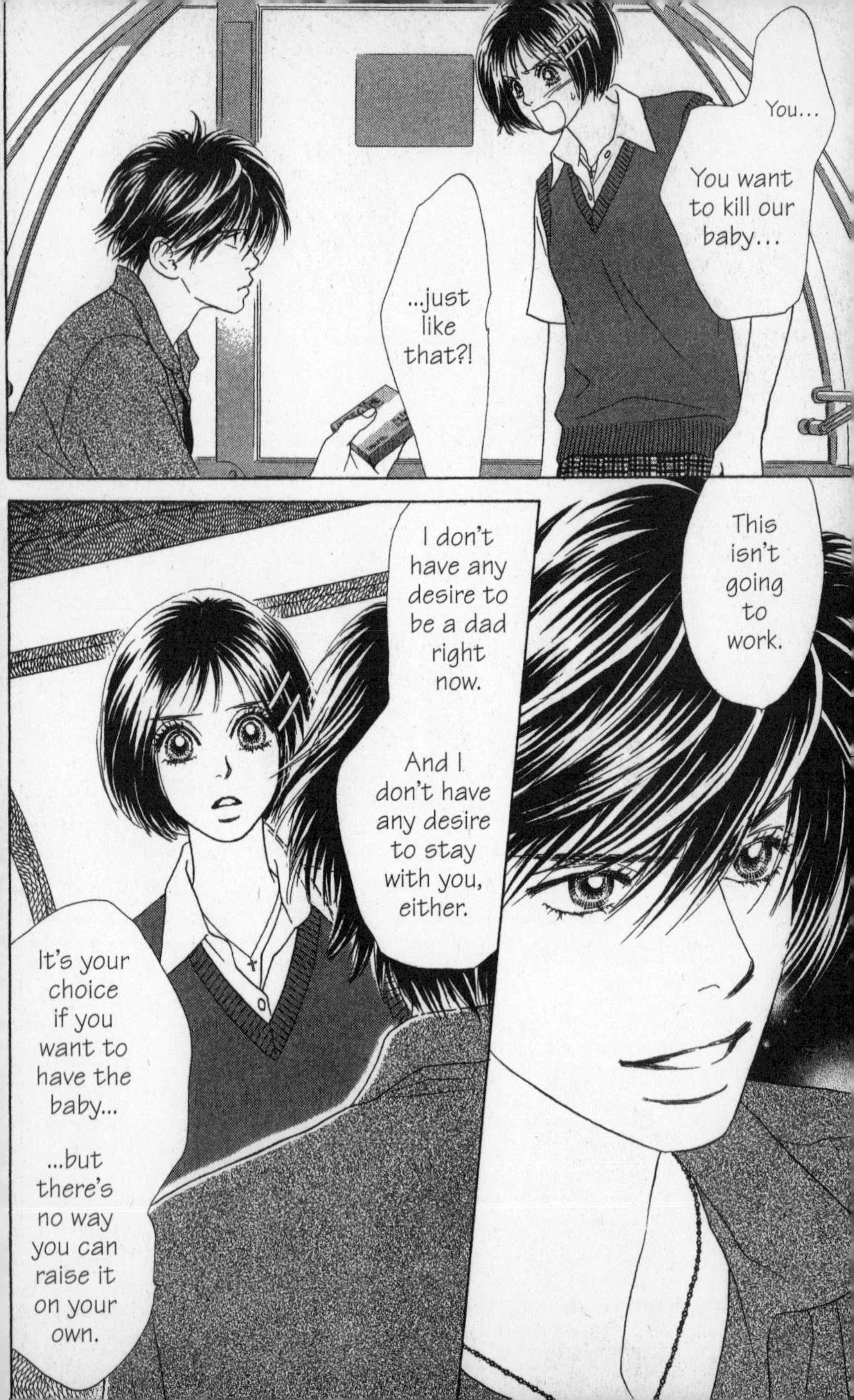
You...
You want to kill our baby...
...just like that?!
This isn't going to work.
I don't have any desire to be a dad right now.
And I don't have any desire to stay with you, either.
It's your choice if you want to have the baby...
...but there's no way you can raise it on your own.

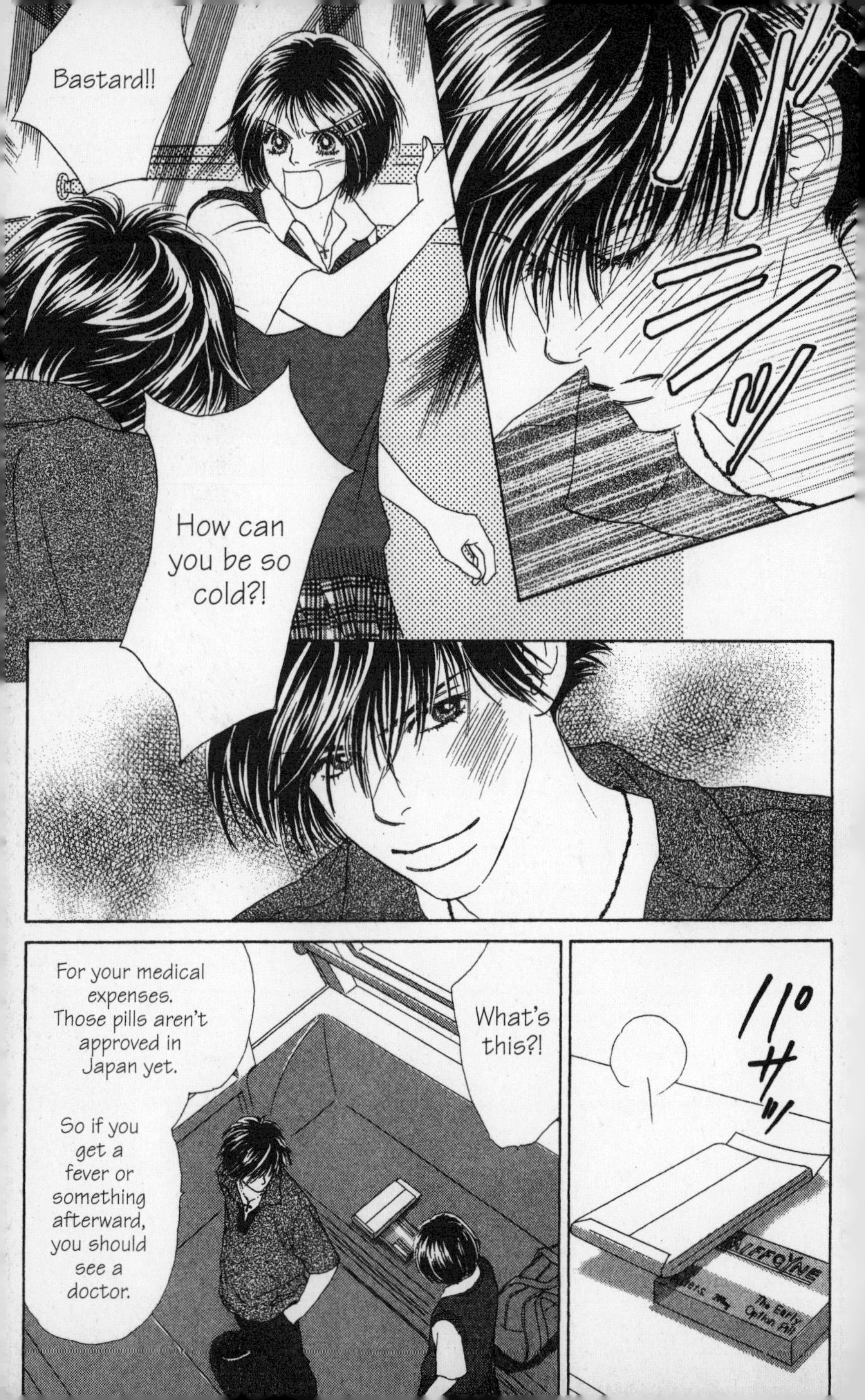
Bastard!!
How can you be so cold?!
What's this?!
For your medical expenses. Those pills aren't approved in Japan yet.
So if you get a fever or something afterward, you should see a doctor.

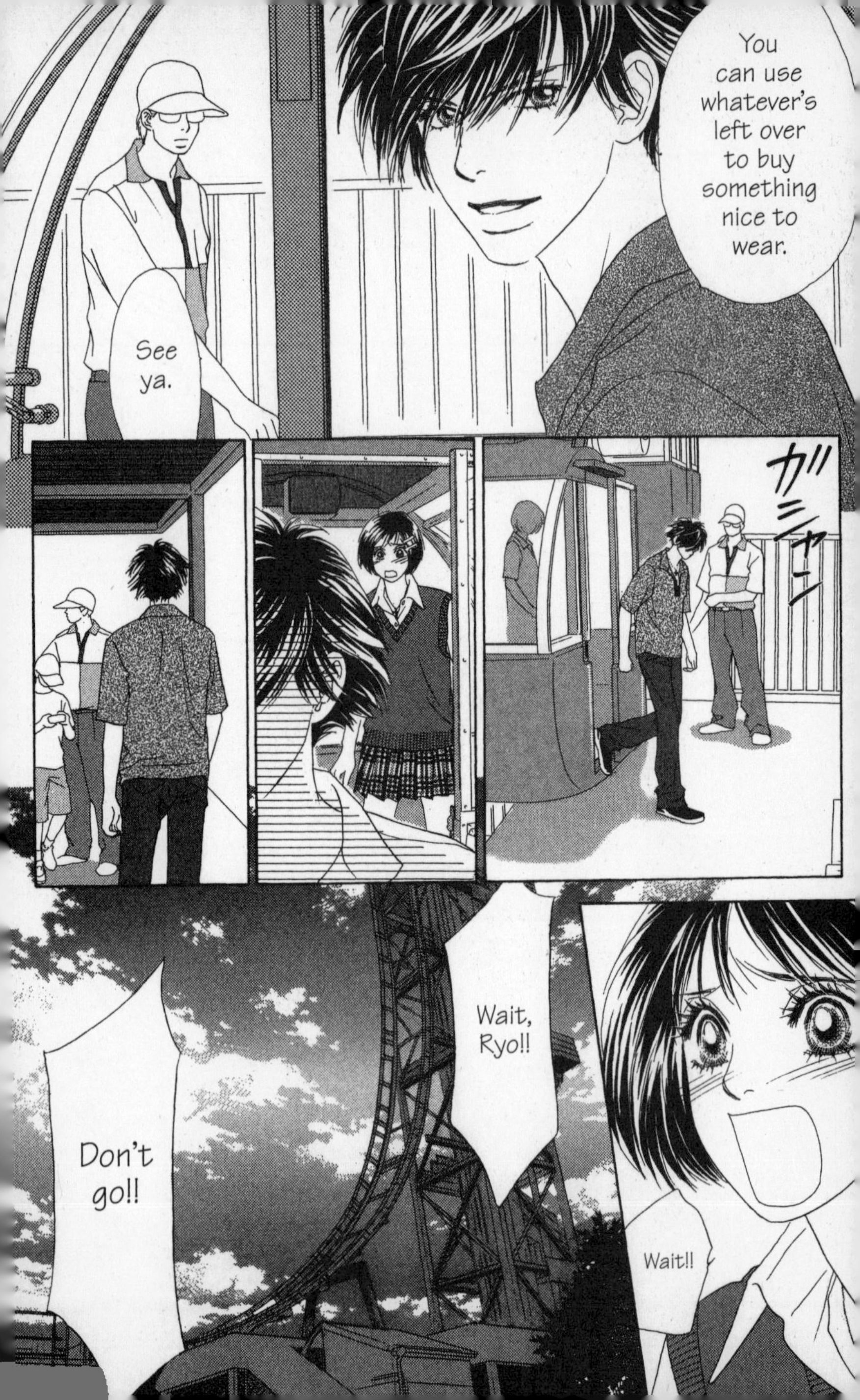
You can use whatever's left over to buy something nice to wear.
See ya.
ガシャン
Wait!!
Wait, Ryo!!
Don't go!!

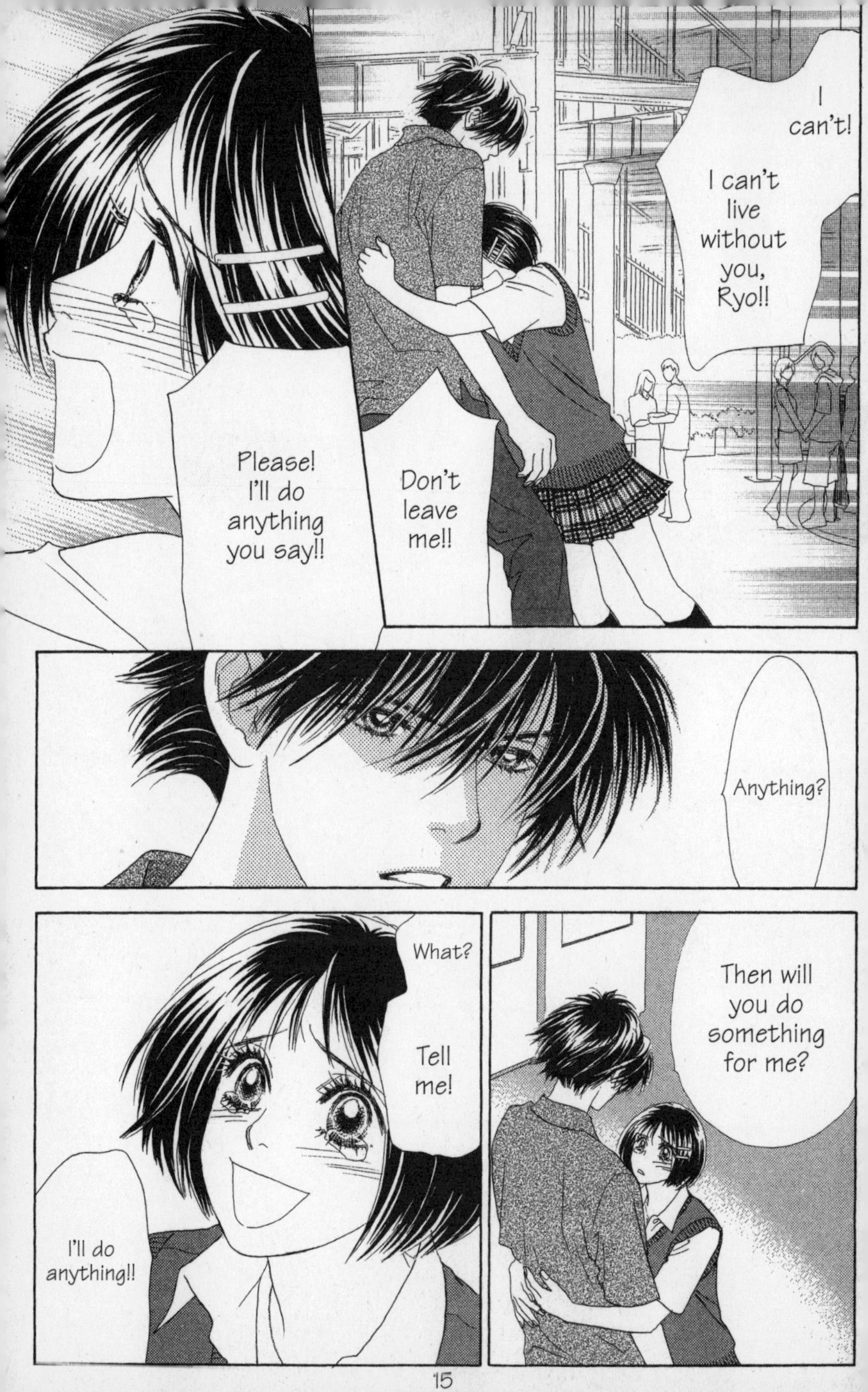
I can't!
I can't live without you, Ryo!!
Don't leave me!!
Please! I'll do anything you say!!
Anything?
Then will you do something for me?
What?
Tell me!
I'll do anything!!

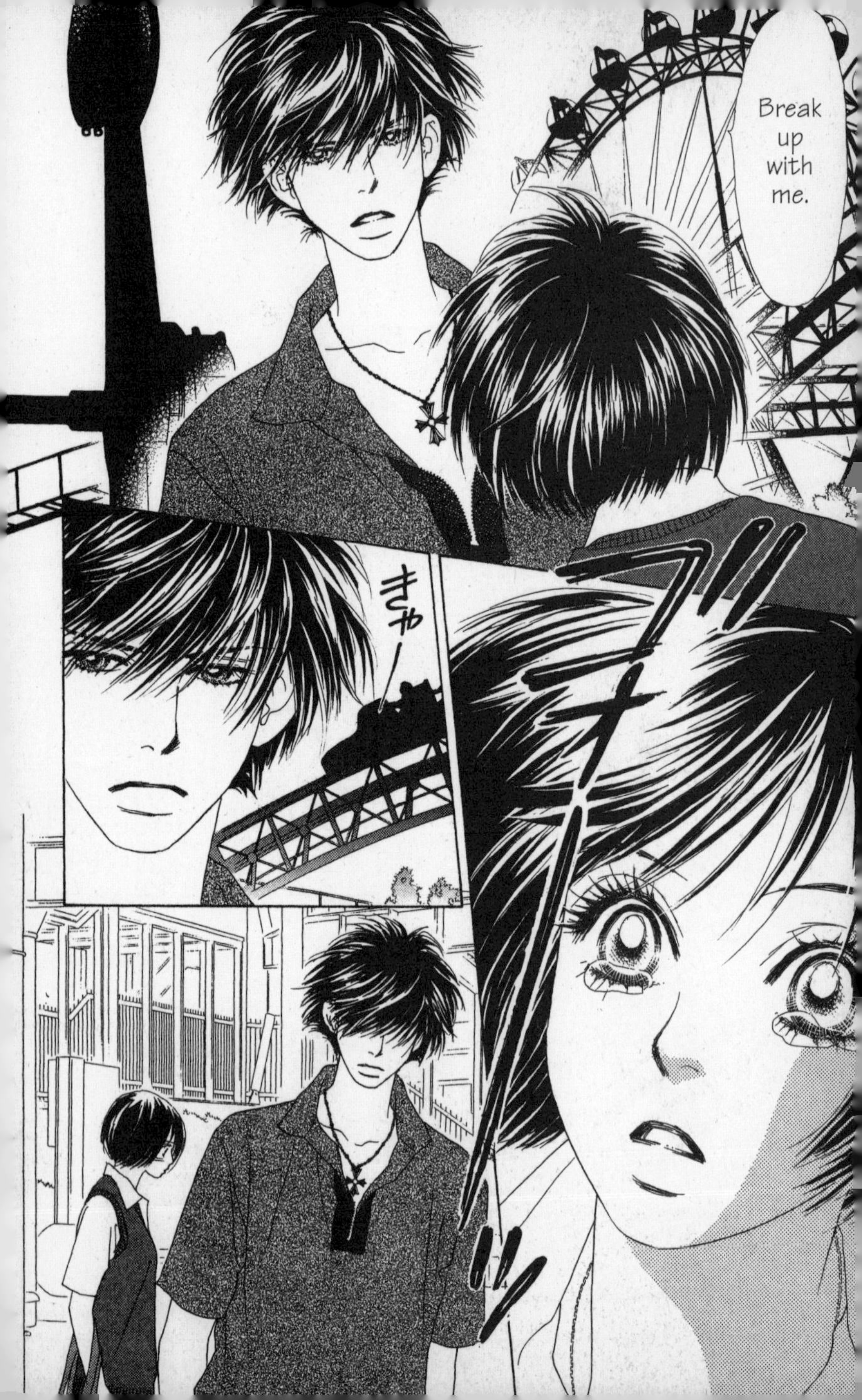
Break up with me.
ブツッ
きゃー

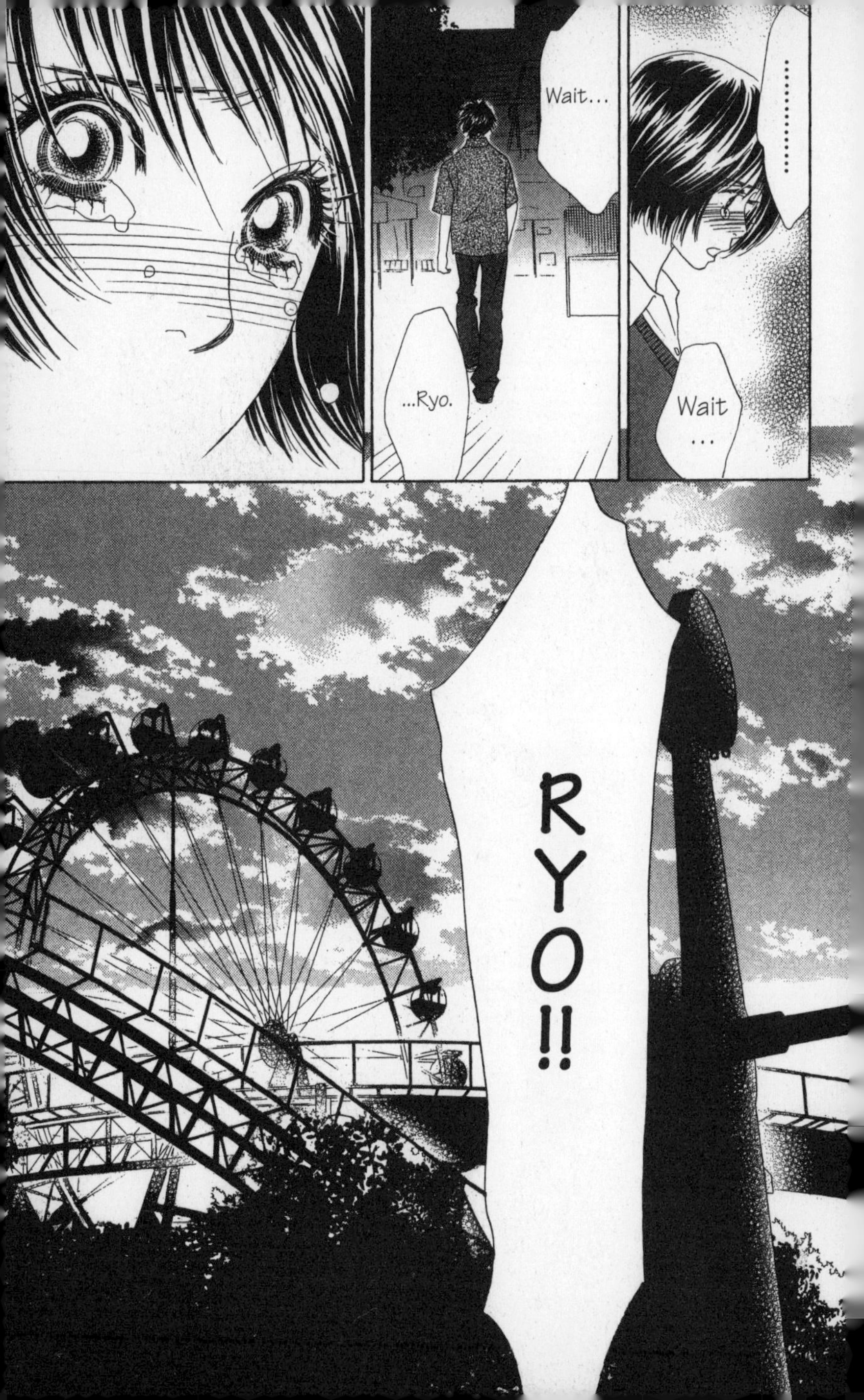
......
Wait ...
Wait...
...Ryo.
RYO!!

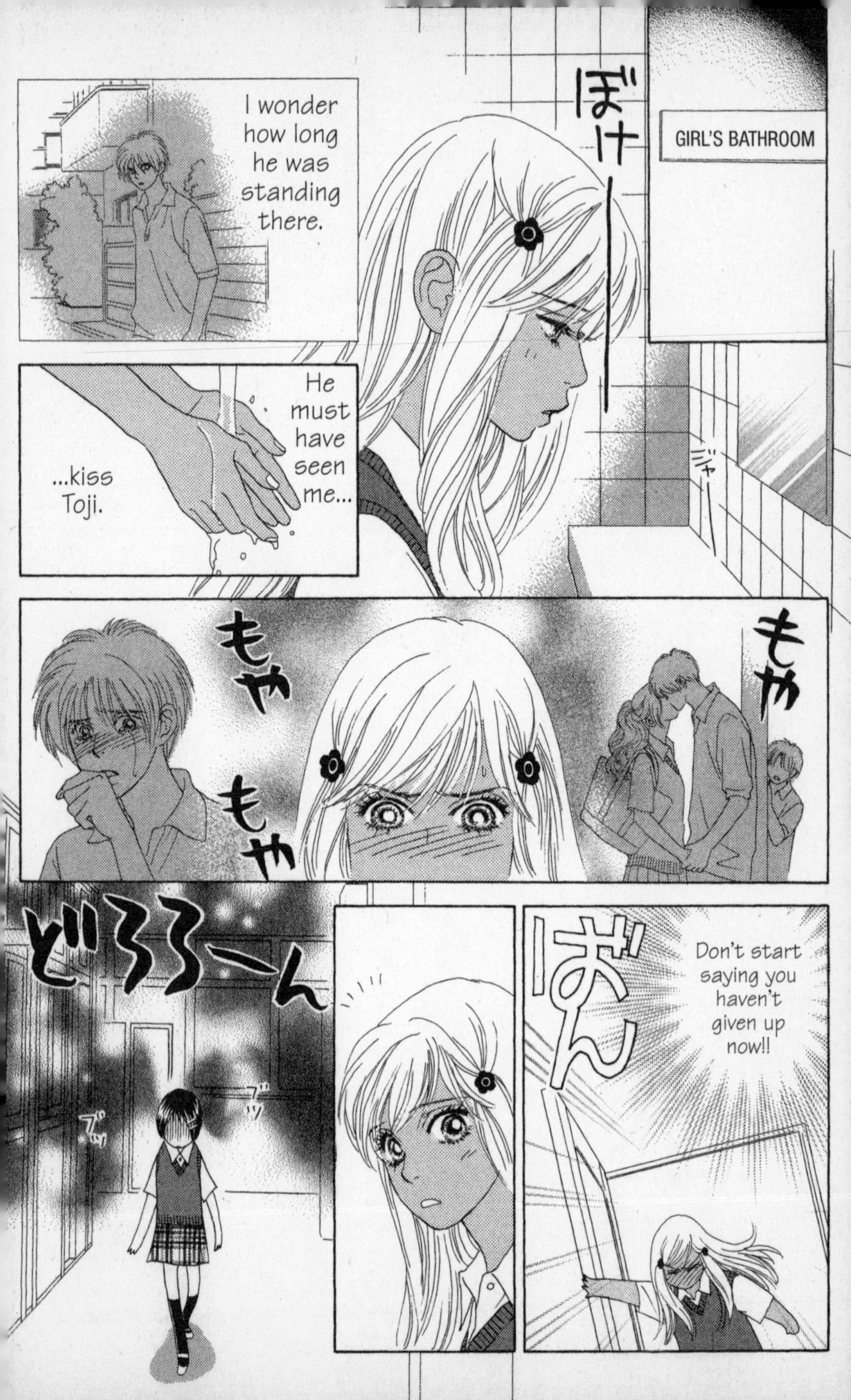
GIRL'S BATHROOM
ぼけー
ジャー
I wonder how long he was standing there.
He must have seen me...
...kiss Toji.
もや
もや
もや
ぼん
Don't start saying you haven't given up now!!
どろろ～ん

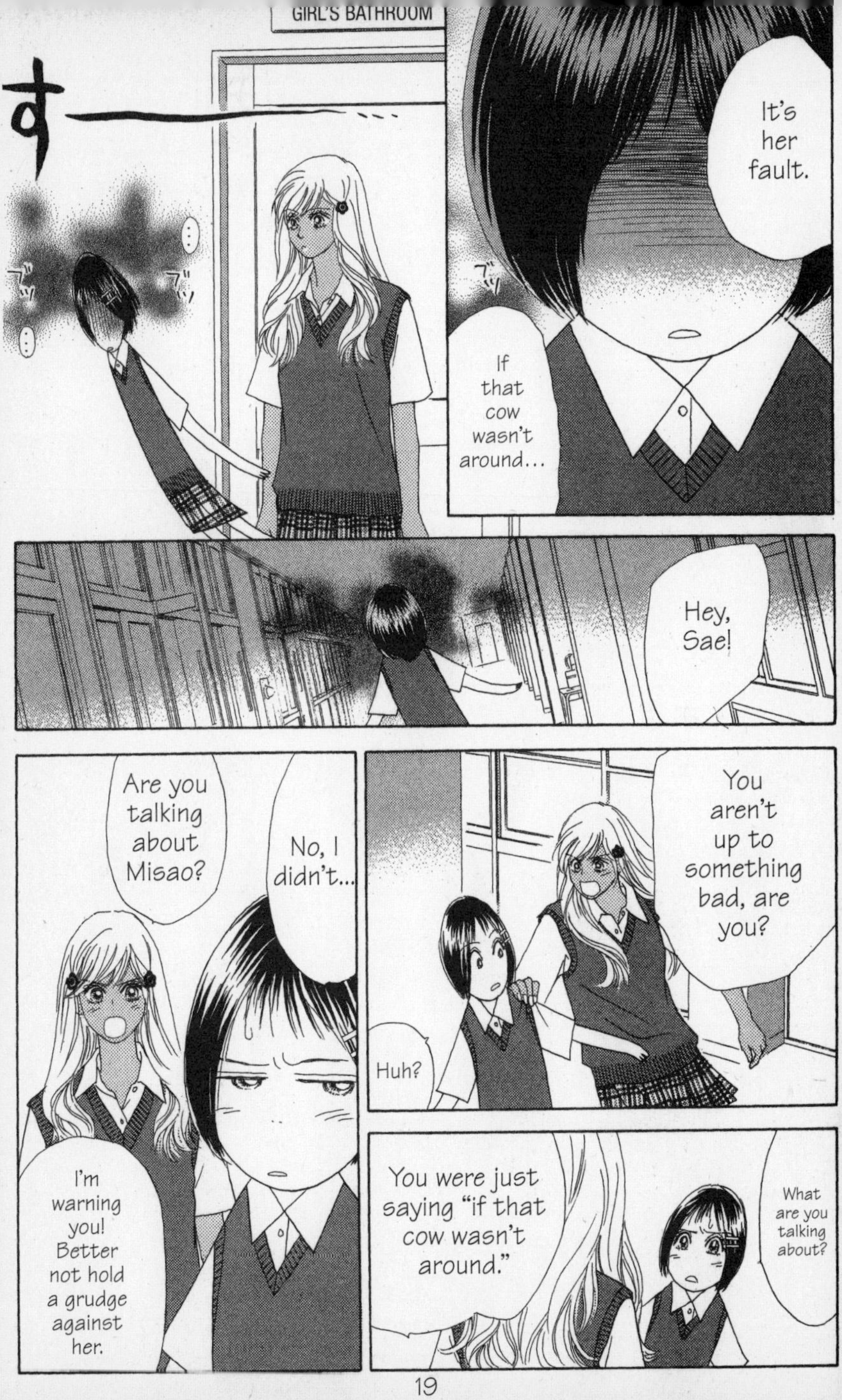

It's her fault.
ブツ
If that cow wasn't around...
GIRL'S BATHROOM
す——...
...
ブツ
ブツ
...
Hey, Sae!
You aren't up to something bad, are you?
Huh?
You were just saying "if that cow wasn't around."
What are you talking about?
No, I didn't...
Are you talking about Misao?
I'm warning you! Better not hold a grudge against her.

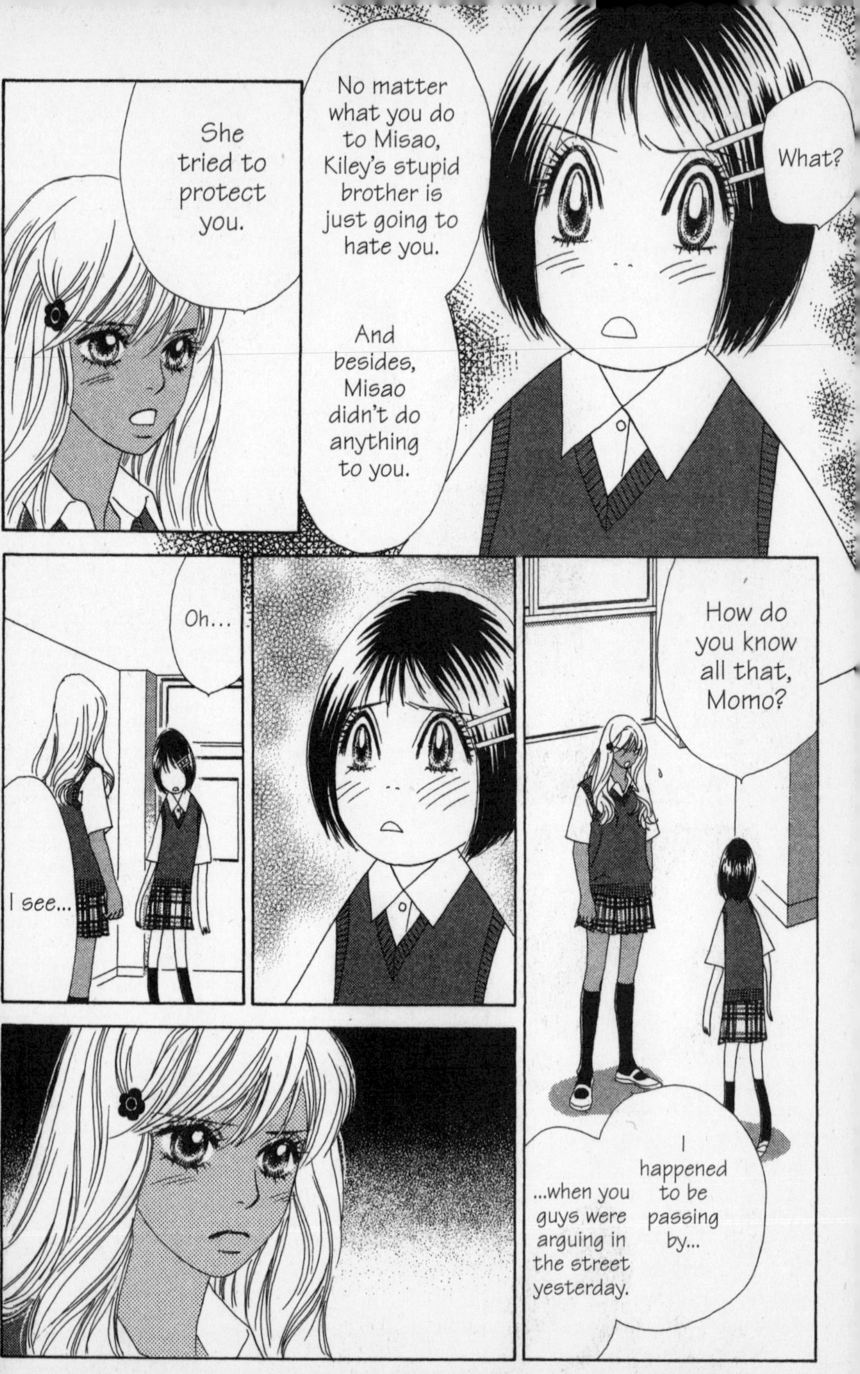
What?
No matter what you do to Misao, Kiley's stupid brother is just going to hate you.
And besides, Misao didn't do anything to you.
She tried to protect you.
How do you know all that, Momo?
I happened to be passing by...
...when you guys were arguing in the street yesterday.
Oh...
I see...

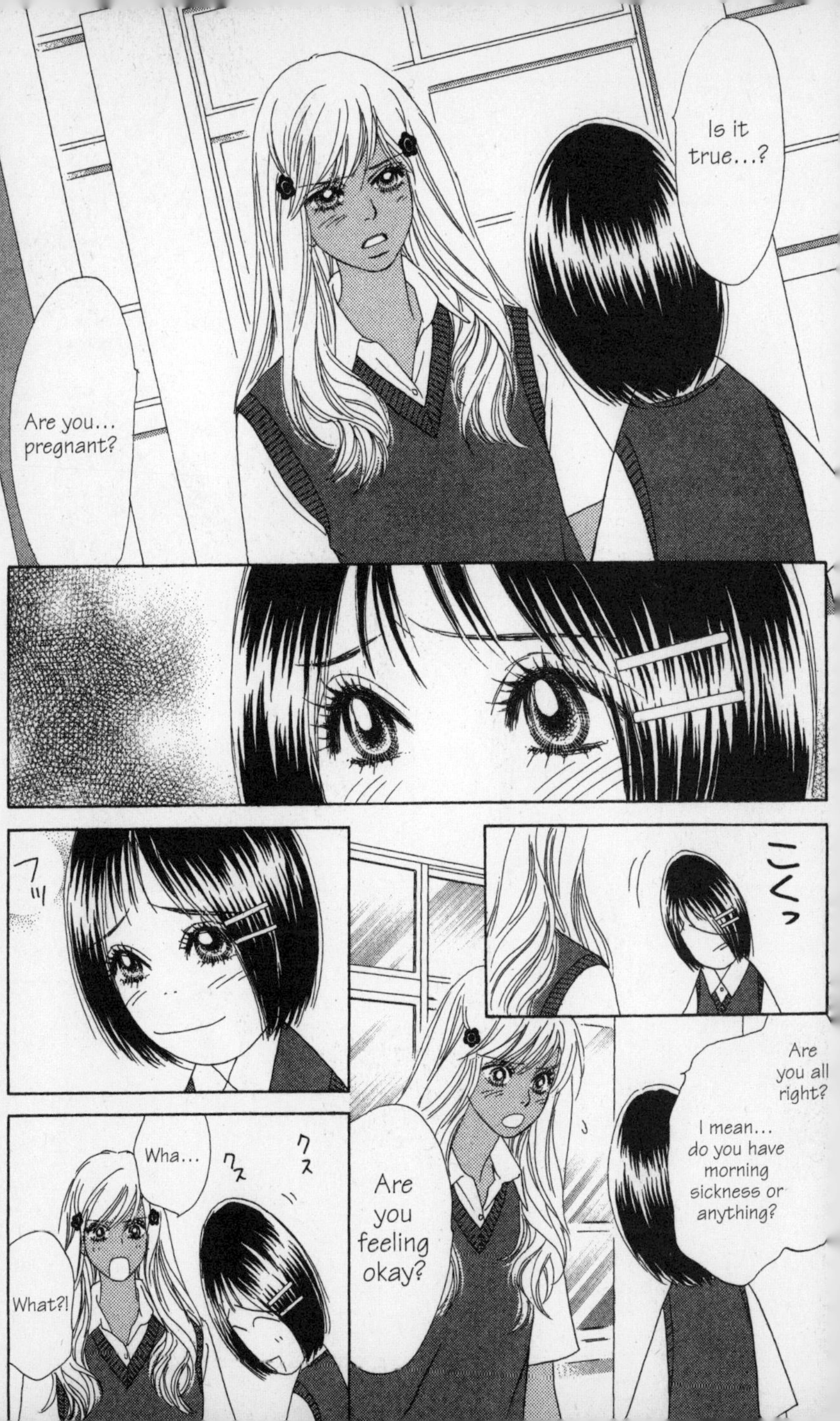

Is it true...?
Are you... pregnant?
こくっ
Are you all right?
I mean... do you have morning sickness or anything?
Are you feeling okay?
フッ
クス
クス
Wha...
What?!

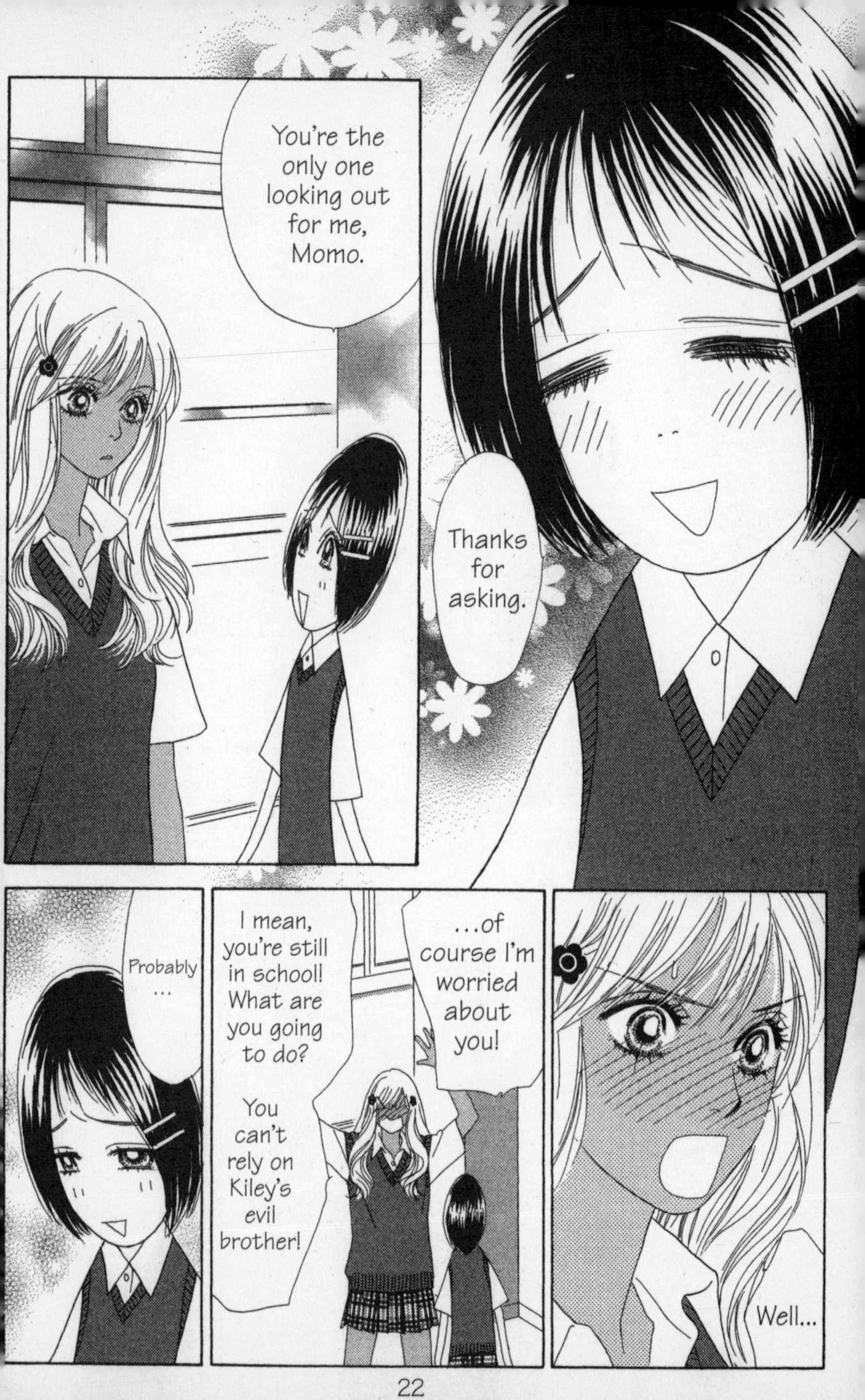
Thanks for asking.
You're the only one looking out for me, Momo.
Well...
...of course I'm worried about you!
I mean, you're still in school! What are you going to do?
You can't rely on Kiley's evil brother!
Probably...

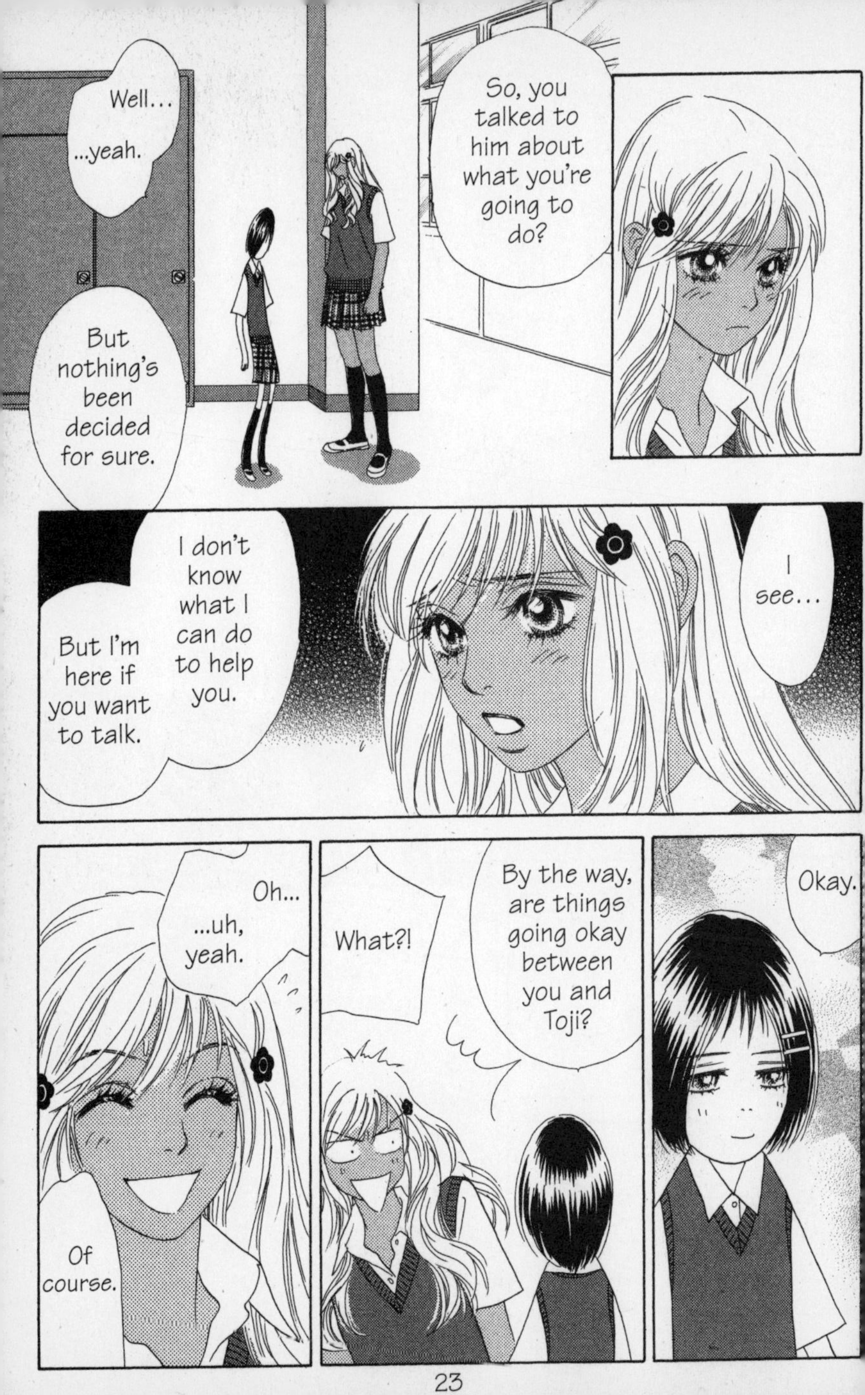
So, you talked to him about what you're going to do?
Well... ...yeah.
But nothing's been decided for sure.
I see...
I don't know what I can do to help you.
But I'm here if you want to talk.
Okay.
By the way, are things going okay between you and Toji?
What?!
Oh... ...uh, yeah.
Of course.

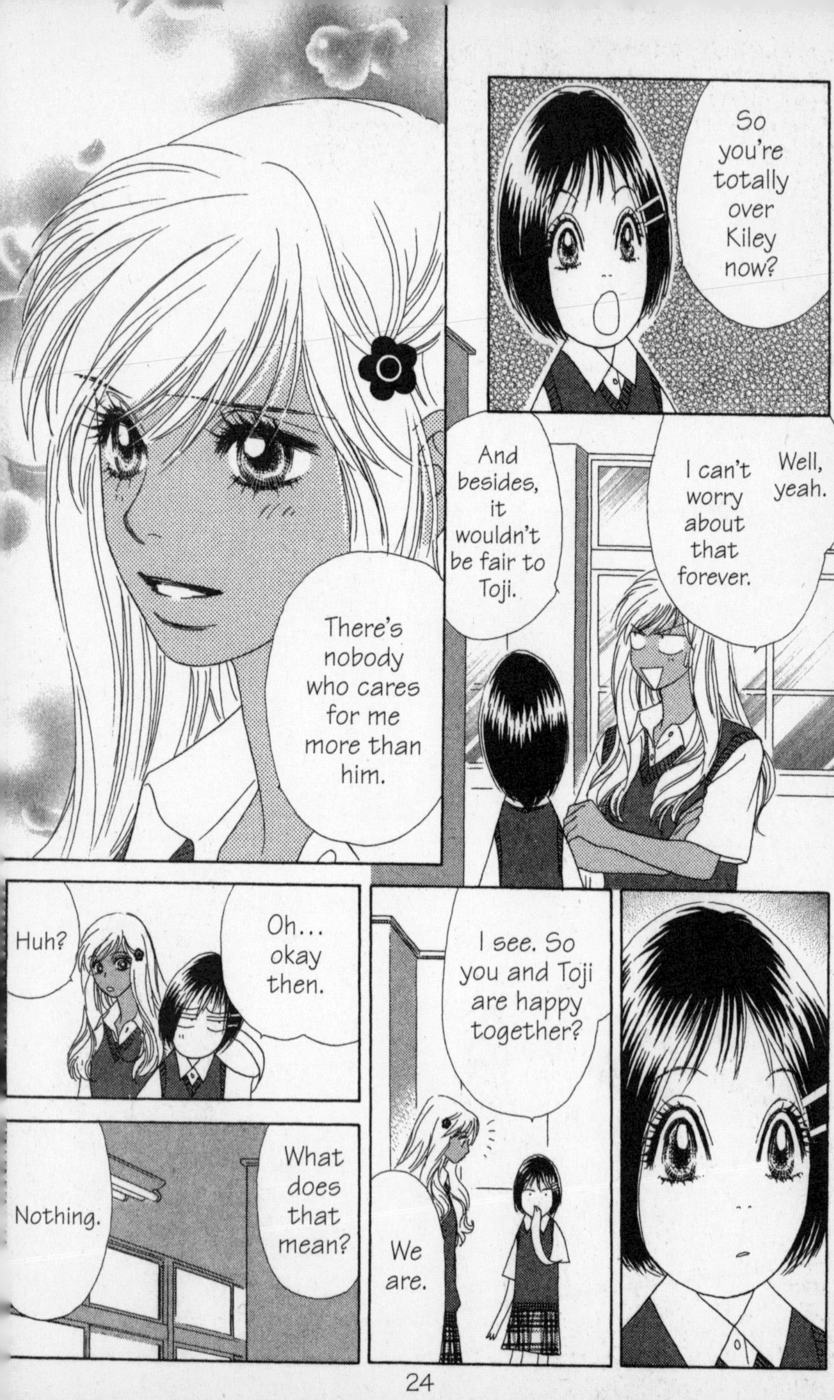

So you're totally over Kiley now?
Well, yeah.
I can't worry about that forever.
And besides, it wouldn't be fair to Toji.
There's nobody who cares for me more than him.
...
I see. So you and Toji are happy together?
We are.
Oh... okay then.
Huh?
What does that mean?
Nothing.

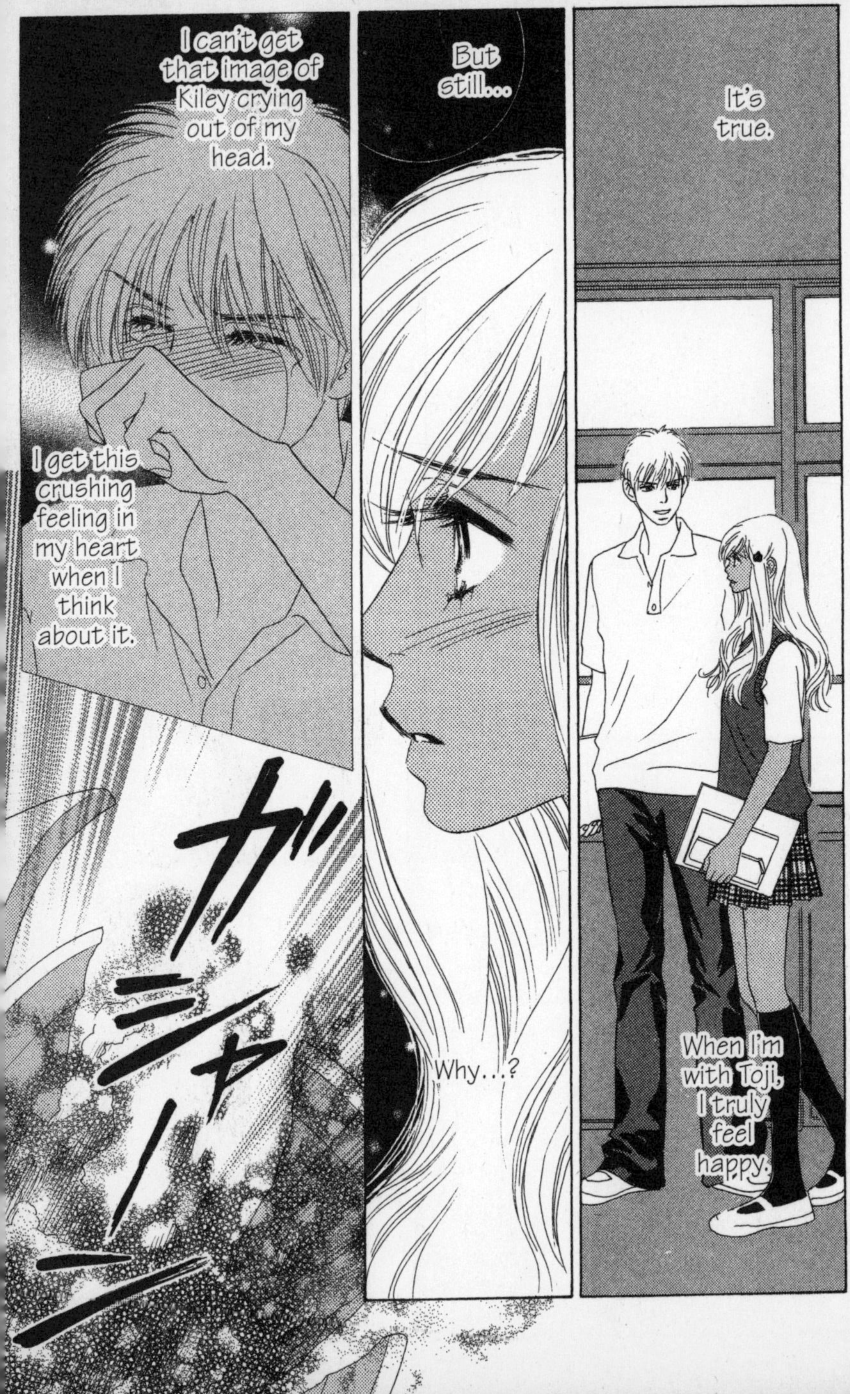
It's true.
When I'm with Toji, I truly feel happy.
But still...
Why...?
I can't get that image of Kiley crying out of my head.
I get this crushing feeling in my heart when I think about it.
ガシャーン

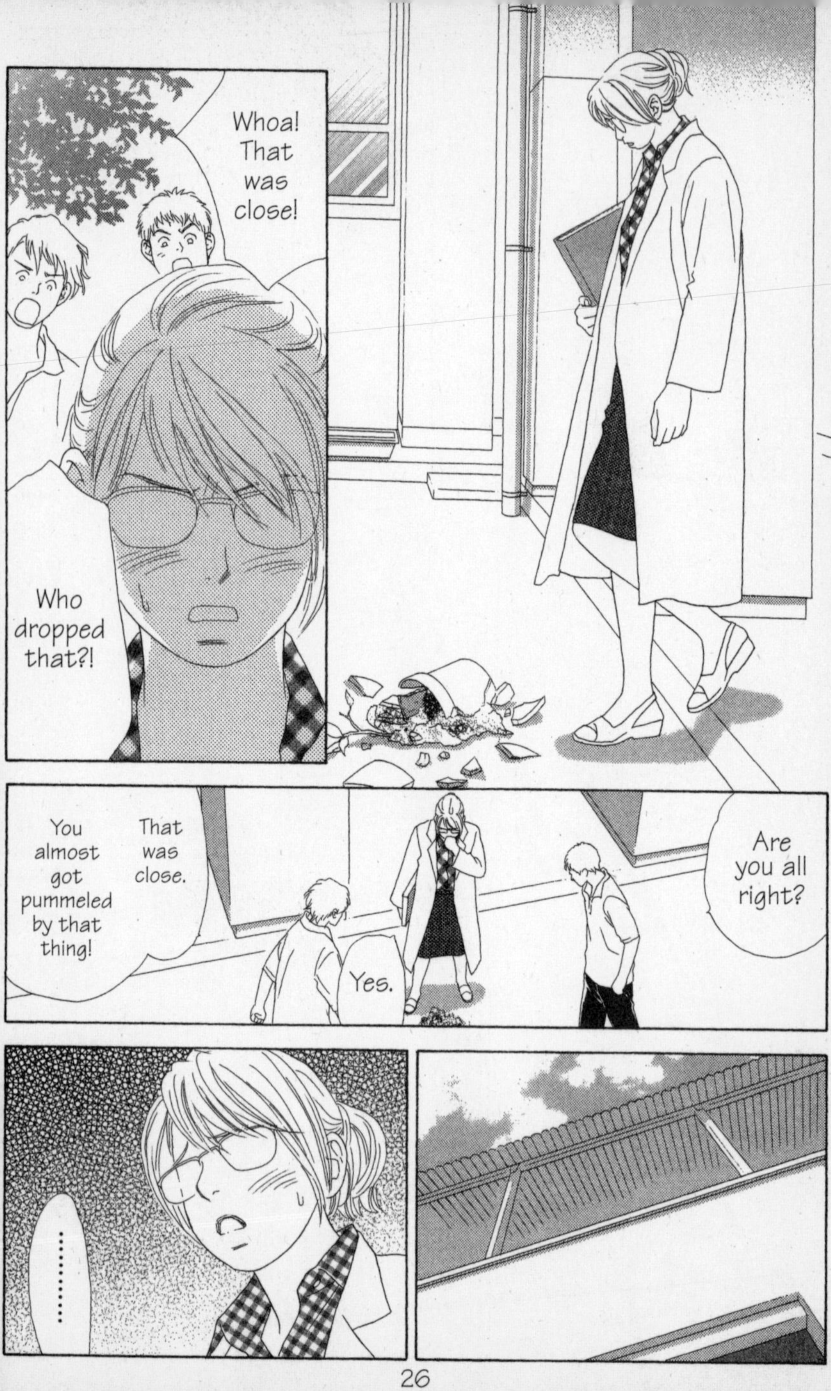
Whoa! That was close!
Who dropped that?!
Are you all right?
Yes.
That was close.
You almost got pummeled by that thing!
......

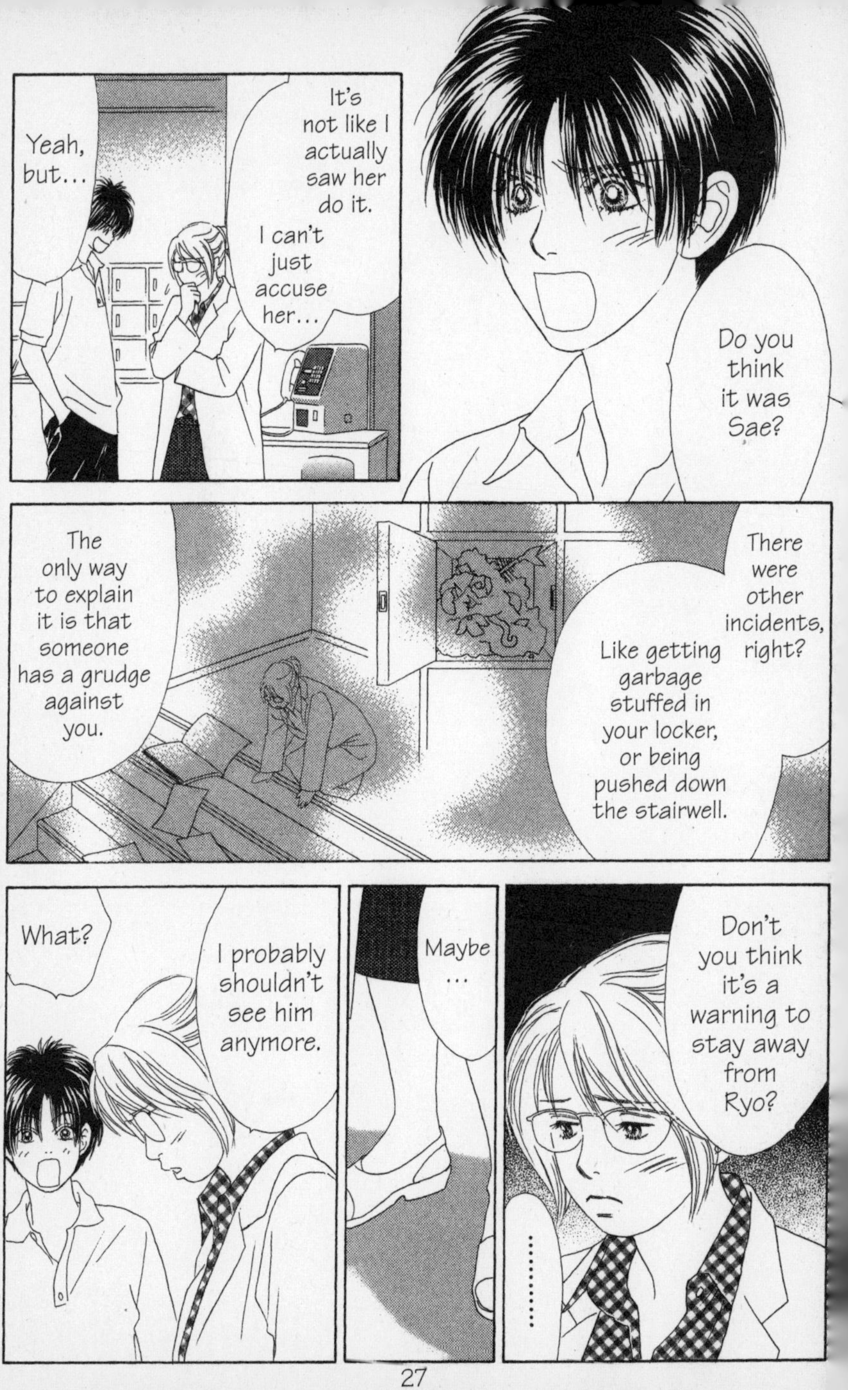
Do you think it was Sae?
It's not like I actually saw her do it.
I can't just accuse her…
Yeah, but…
There were other incidents, right?
Like getting garbage stuffed in your locker, or being pushed down the stairwell.
The only way to explain it is that someone has a grudge against you.
Don't you think it's a warning to stay away from Ryo?
……
Maybe…
I probably shouldn't see him anymore.
What?

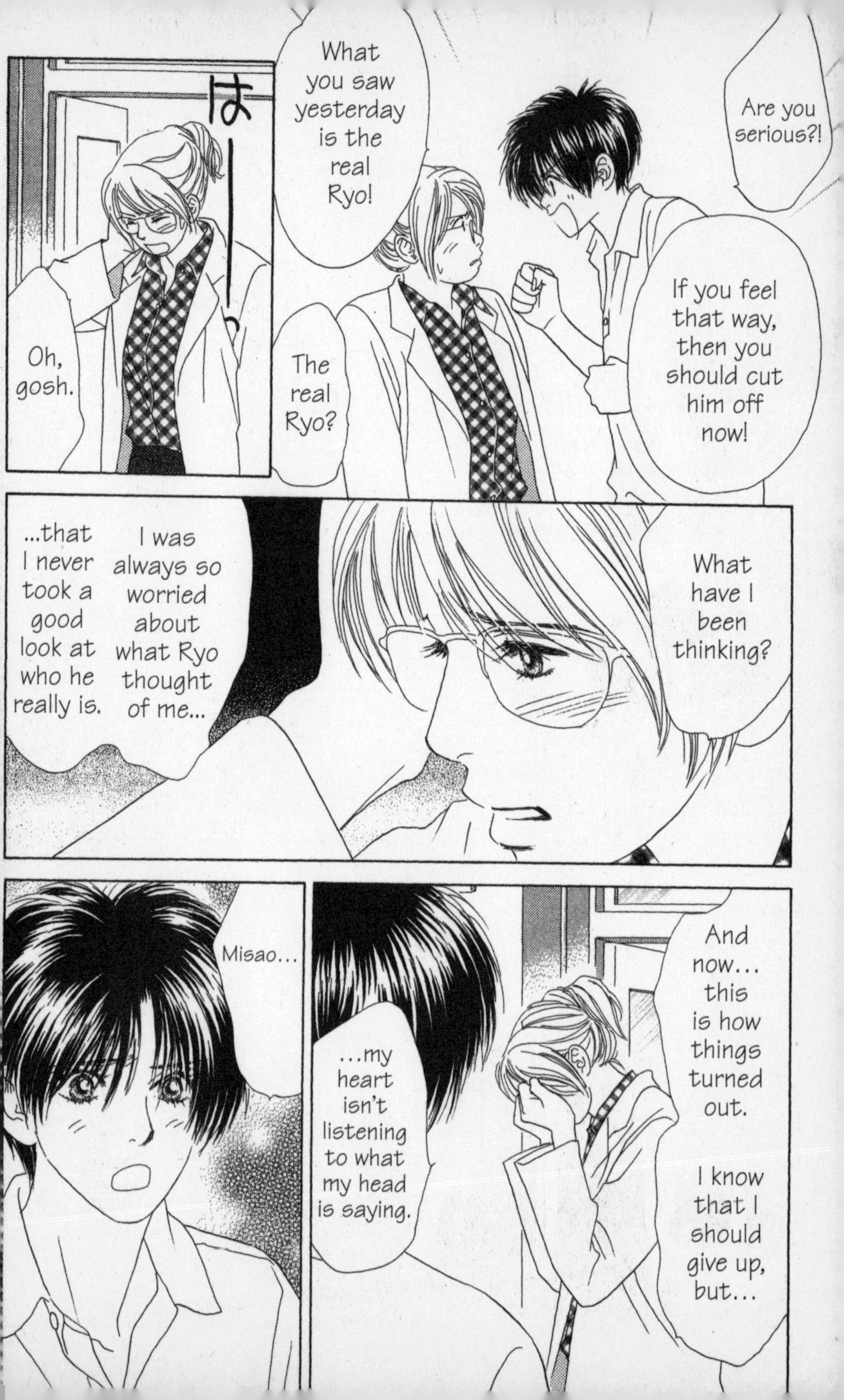
Are you serious?!
If you feel that way, then you should cut him off now!
What you saw yesterday is the real Ryo!
The real Ryo?
は—っ
Oh, gosh.
What have I been thinking?
I was always so worried about what Ryo thought of me...
...that I never took a good look at who he really is.
And now… this is how things turned out.
I know that I should give up, but…
…my heart isn't listening to what my head is saying.
Misao…

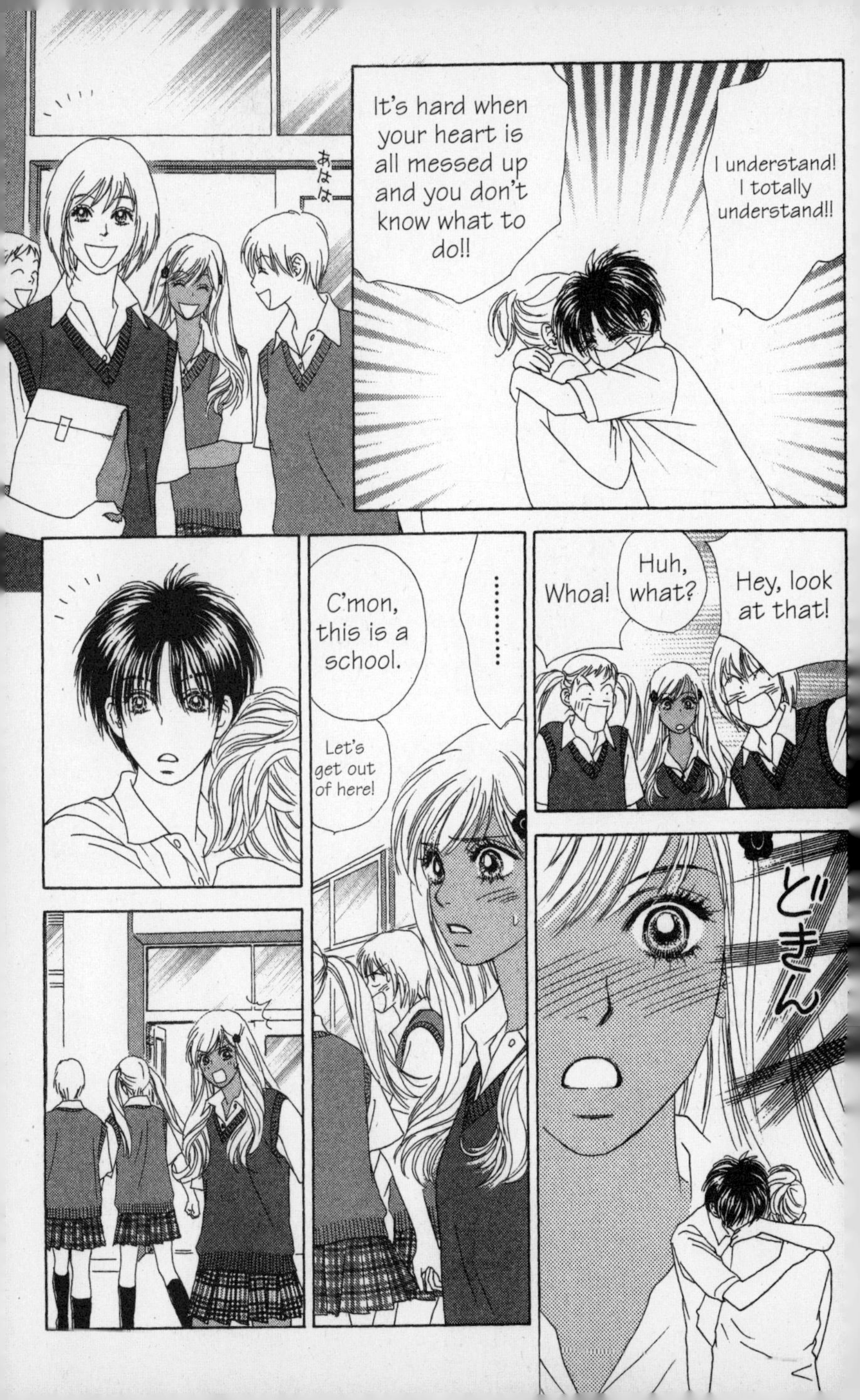
I understand! I totally understand!!
It's hard when your heart is all messed up and you don't know what to do!!
あはは
Hey, look at that!
Huh, what?
Whoa!
....
C'mon, this is a school.
Let's get out of here!
どきん

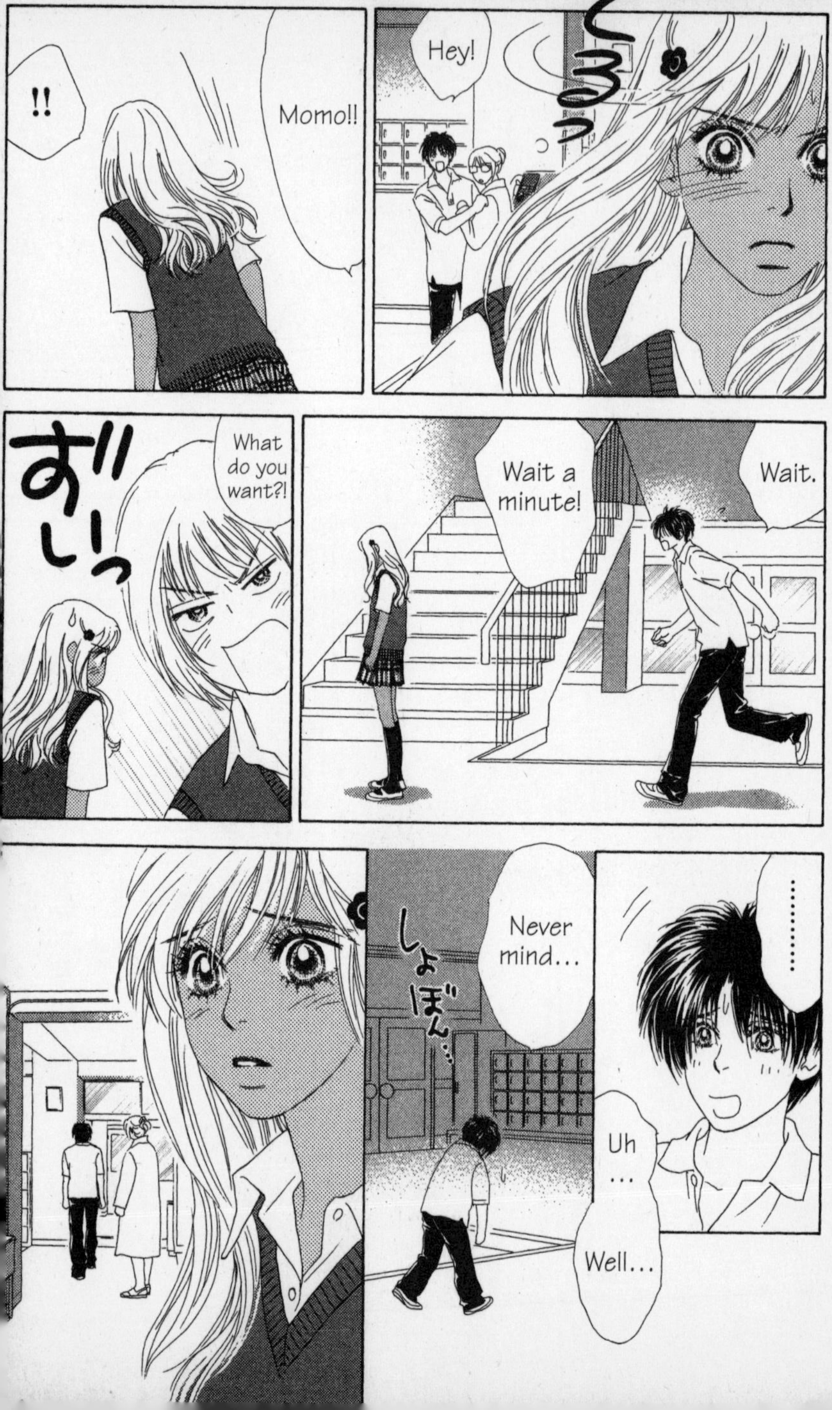

くるっ
Hey!
Momo!!
!!
Wait.
Wait a minute!
What do you want?!
ずいっ
……
Uh…
Well…
Never mind…
しょぼん…

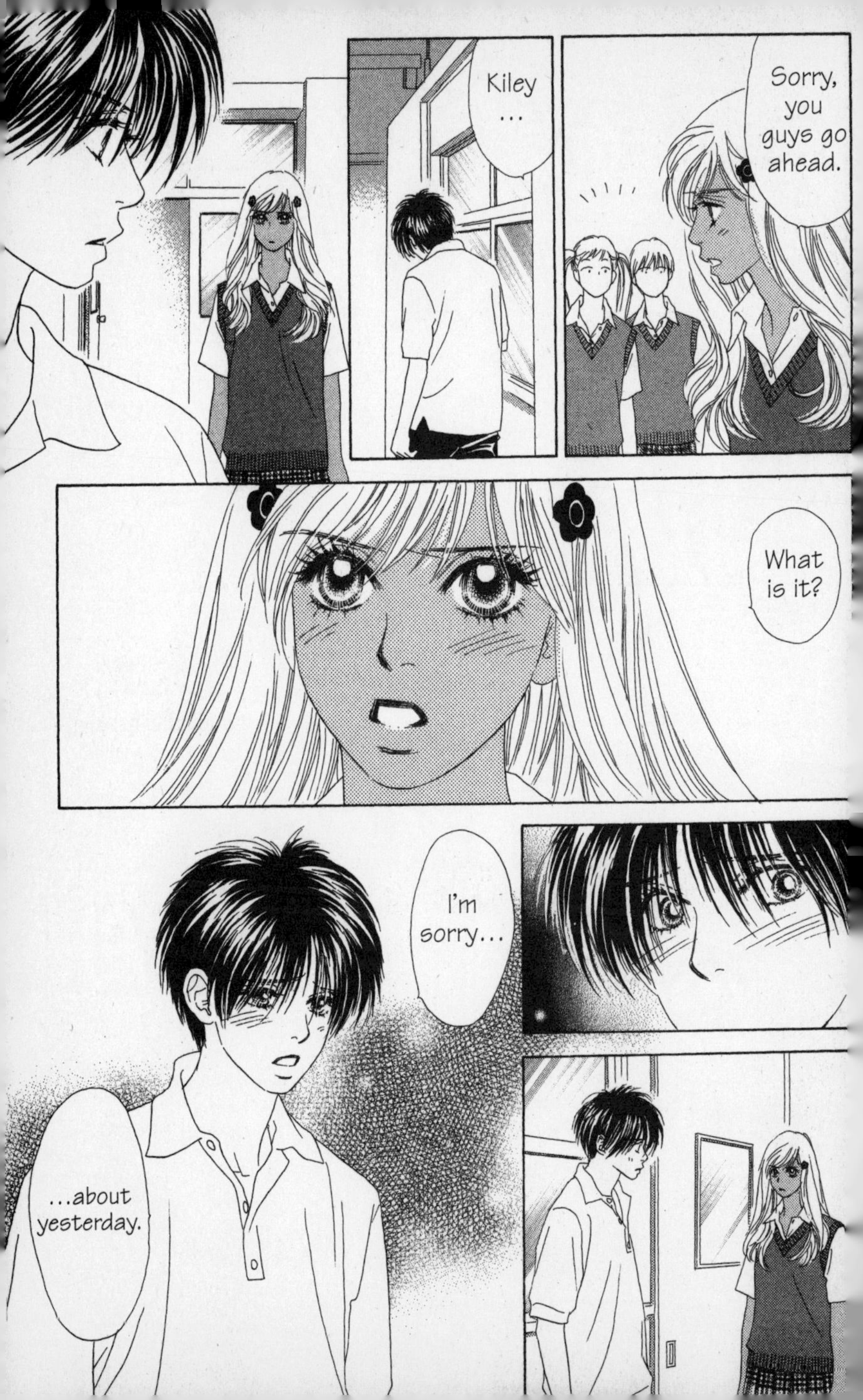
Sorry, you guys go ahead.
Kiley ...
What is it?
I'm sorry...
...about yesterday.

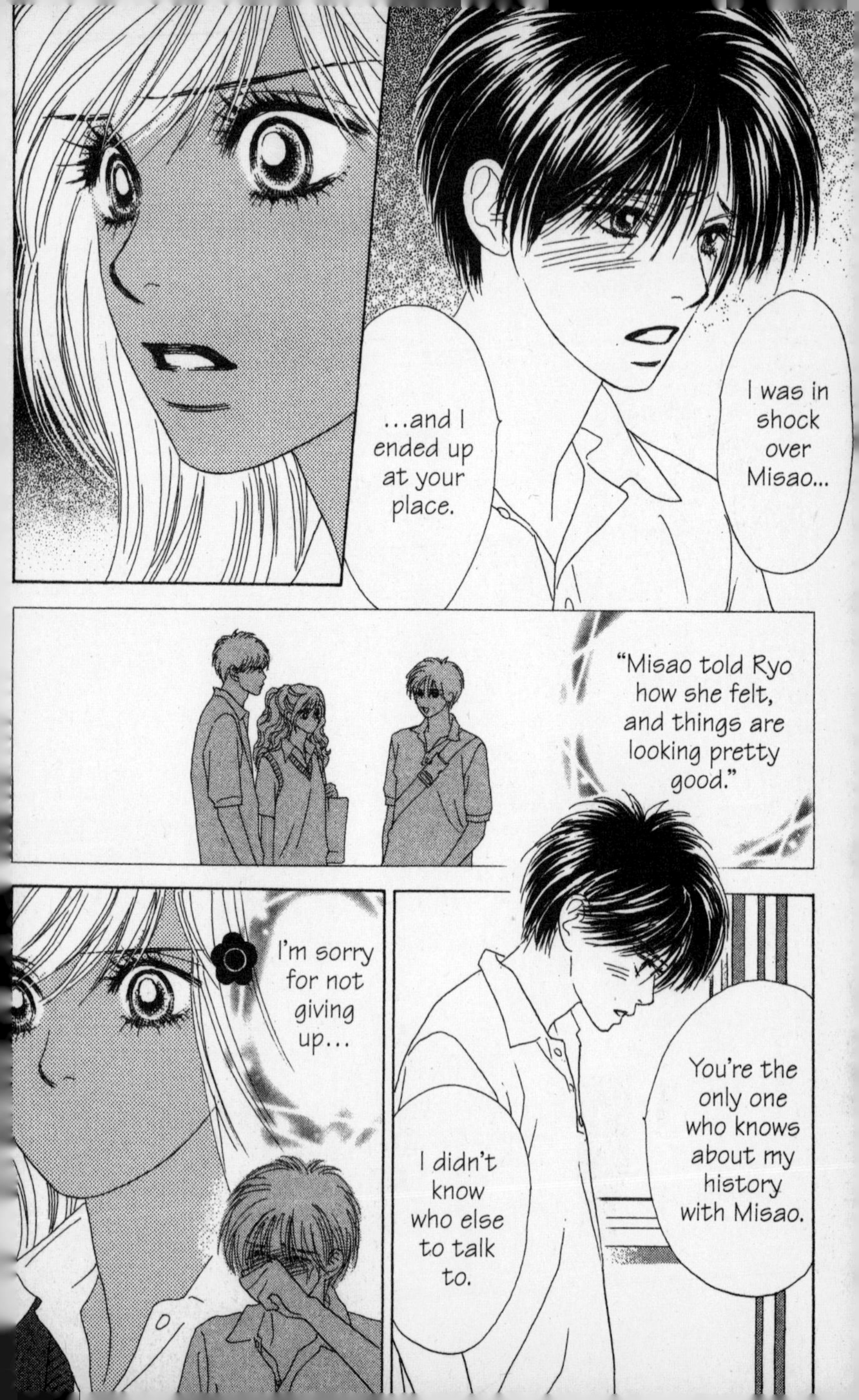
I was in shock over Misao...
...and I ended up at your place.
"Misao told Ryo how she felt, and things are looking pretty good."
You're the only one who knows about my history with Misao.
I didn't know who else to talk to.
I'm sorry for not giving up...

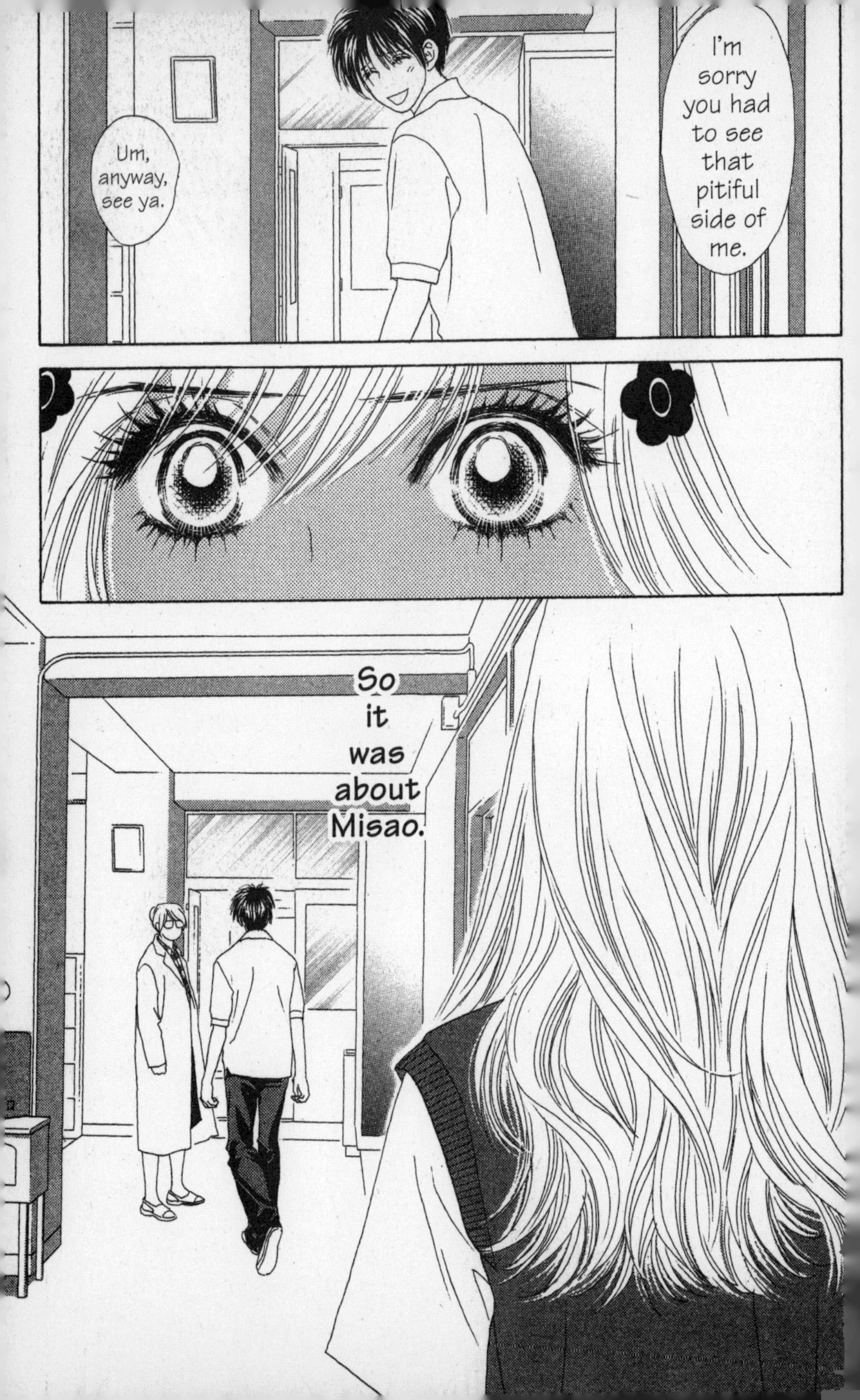
I'm sorry you had to see that pitiful side of me.
Um, anyway, see ya.
So it was about Misao.

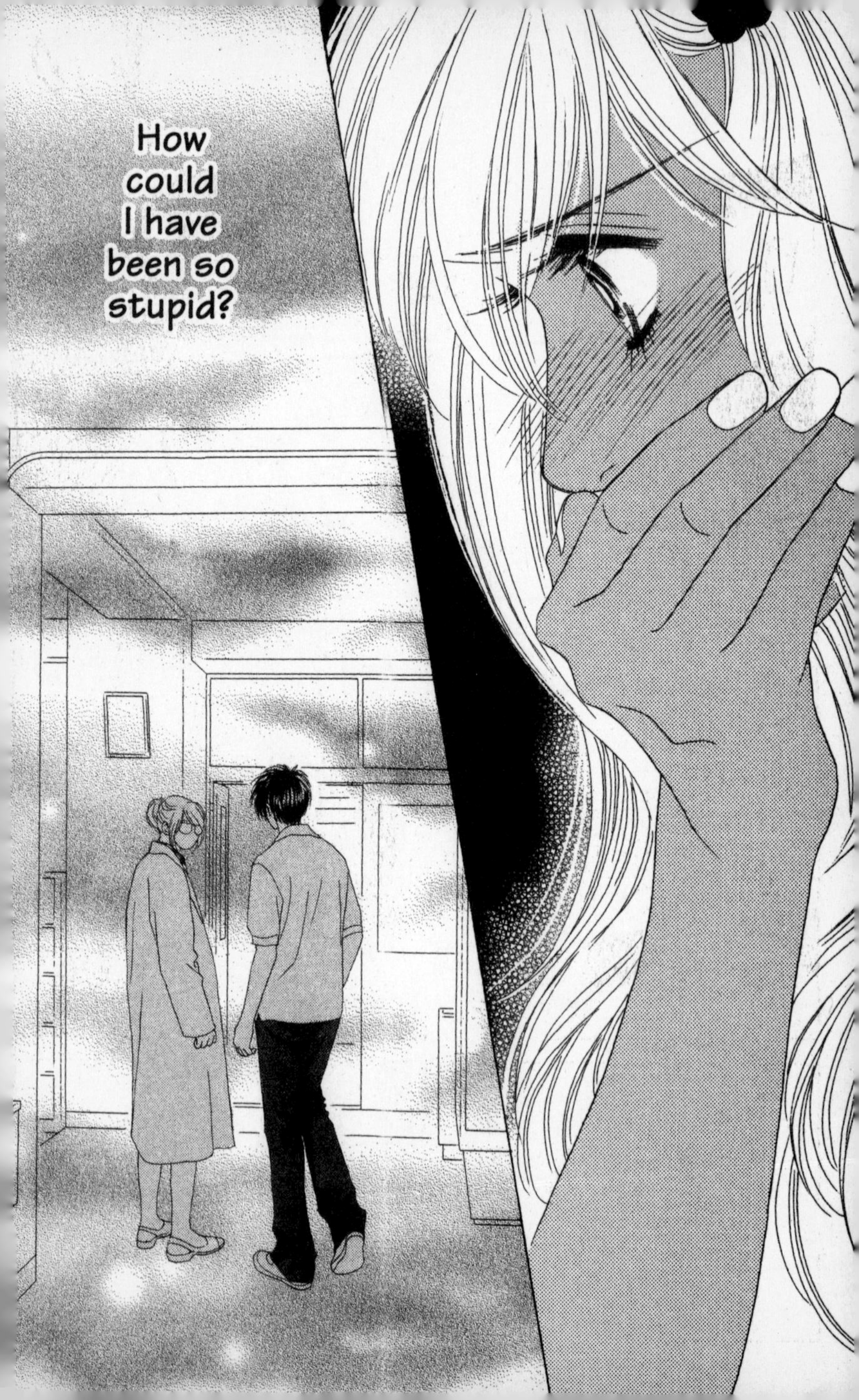
How could I have been so stupid?

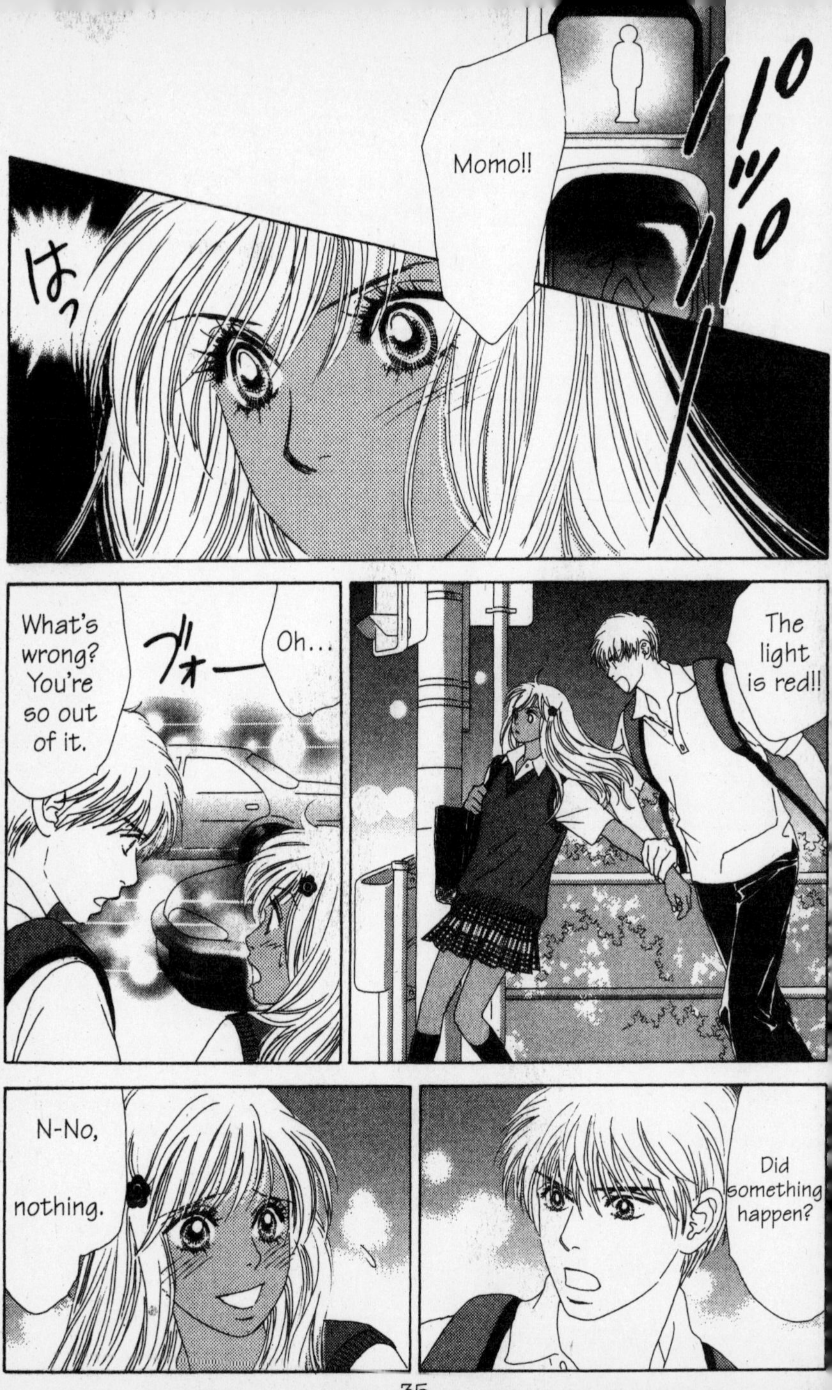
パッパー
Momo!!
はっ
The light is red!!
Oh...
ブォー
What's wrong? You're so out of it.
Did something happen?
N-No,
nothing.

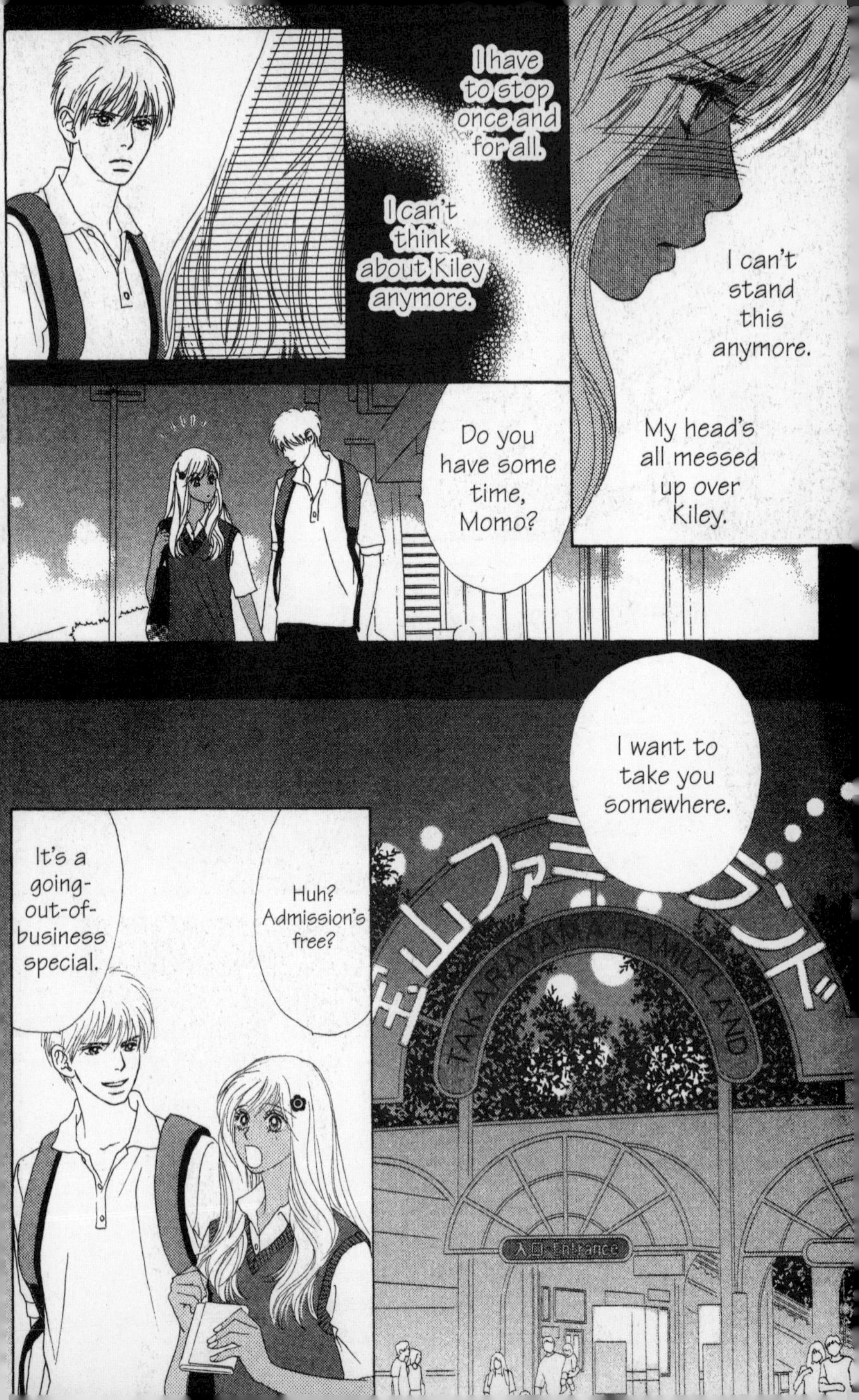
I can't stand this anymore.
My head's all messed up over Kiley.
I have to stop once and for all.
I can't think about Kiley anymore.
Do you have some time, Momo?
I want to take you somewhere.
TAKARAYAMA FAMILYLAND
入口 Entrance
Huh? Admission's free?
It's a going-out-of-business special.

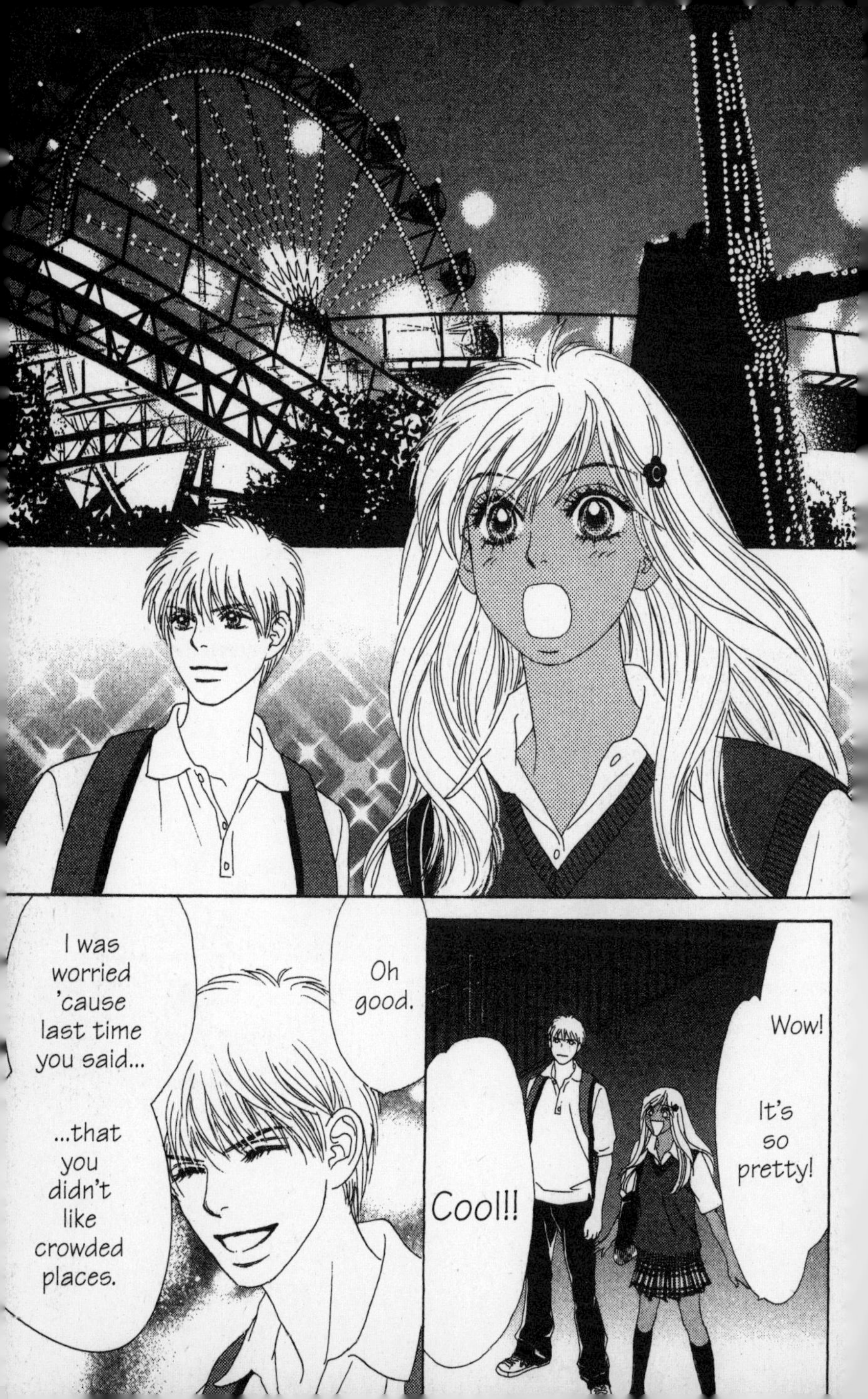
Wow!
It's so pretty!
Cool!!!
Oh good.
I was worried 'cause last time you said...
...that you didn't like crowded places.

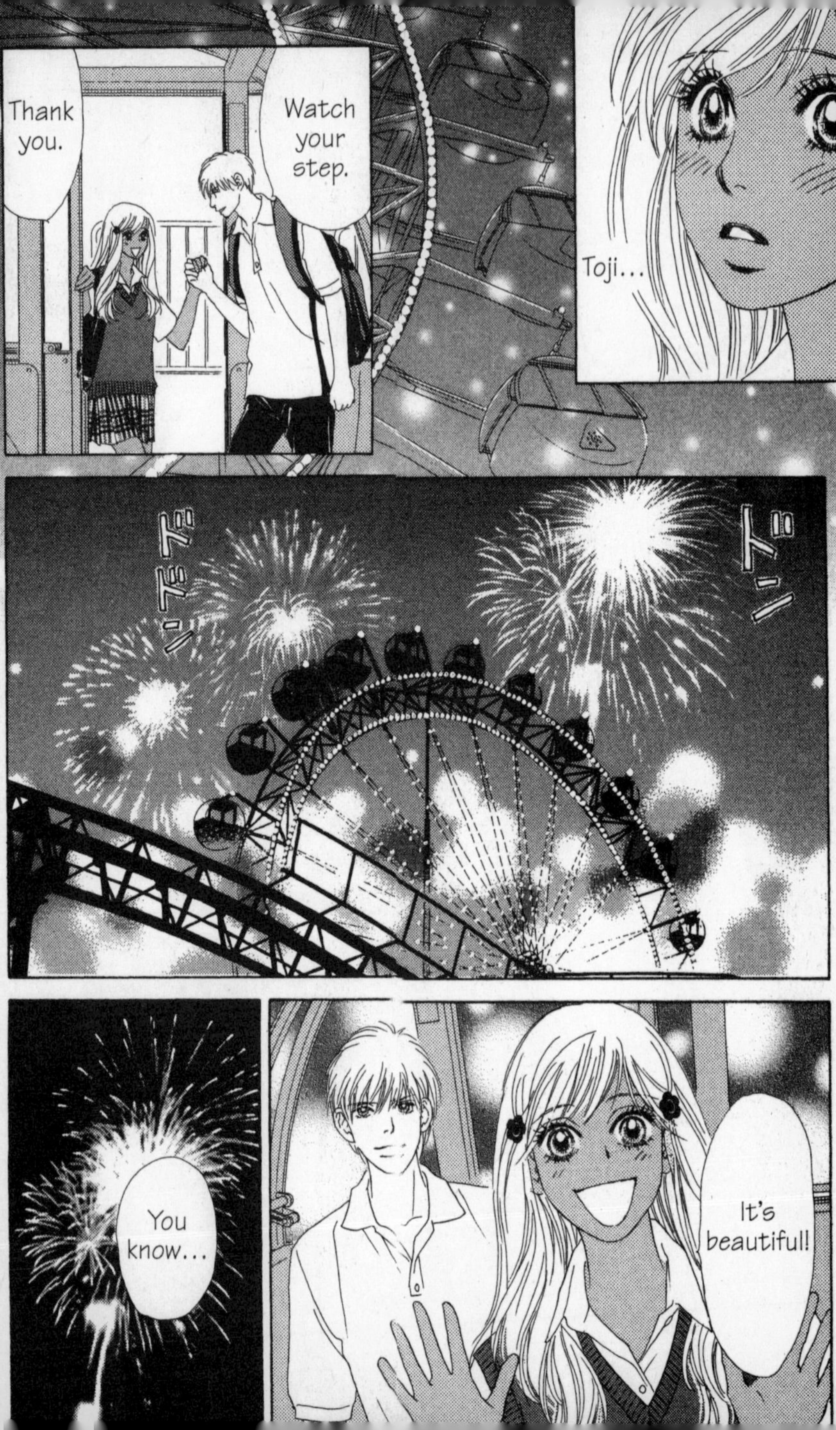
Toji...
Watch your step.
Thank you.
ドーン
ドドーン
It's beautiful!
You know...

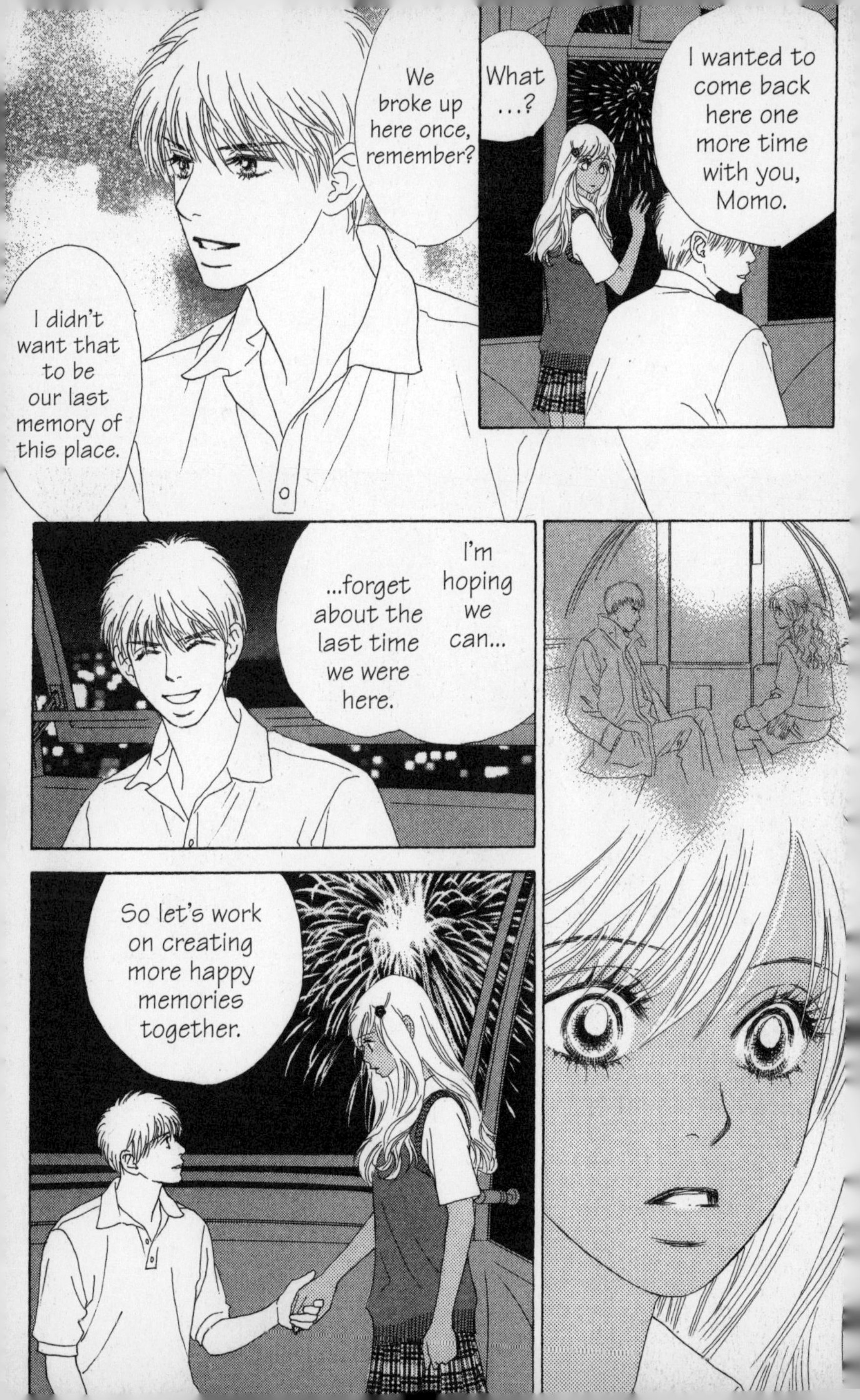
I wanted to come back here one more time with you, Momo.
What ...?
We broke up here once, remember?
I didn't want that to be our last memory of this place.
I'm hoping we can...
...forget about the last time we were here.
So let's work on creating more happy memories together.

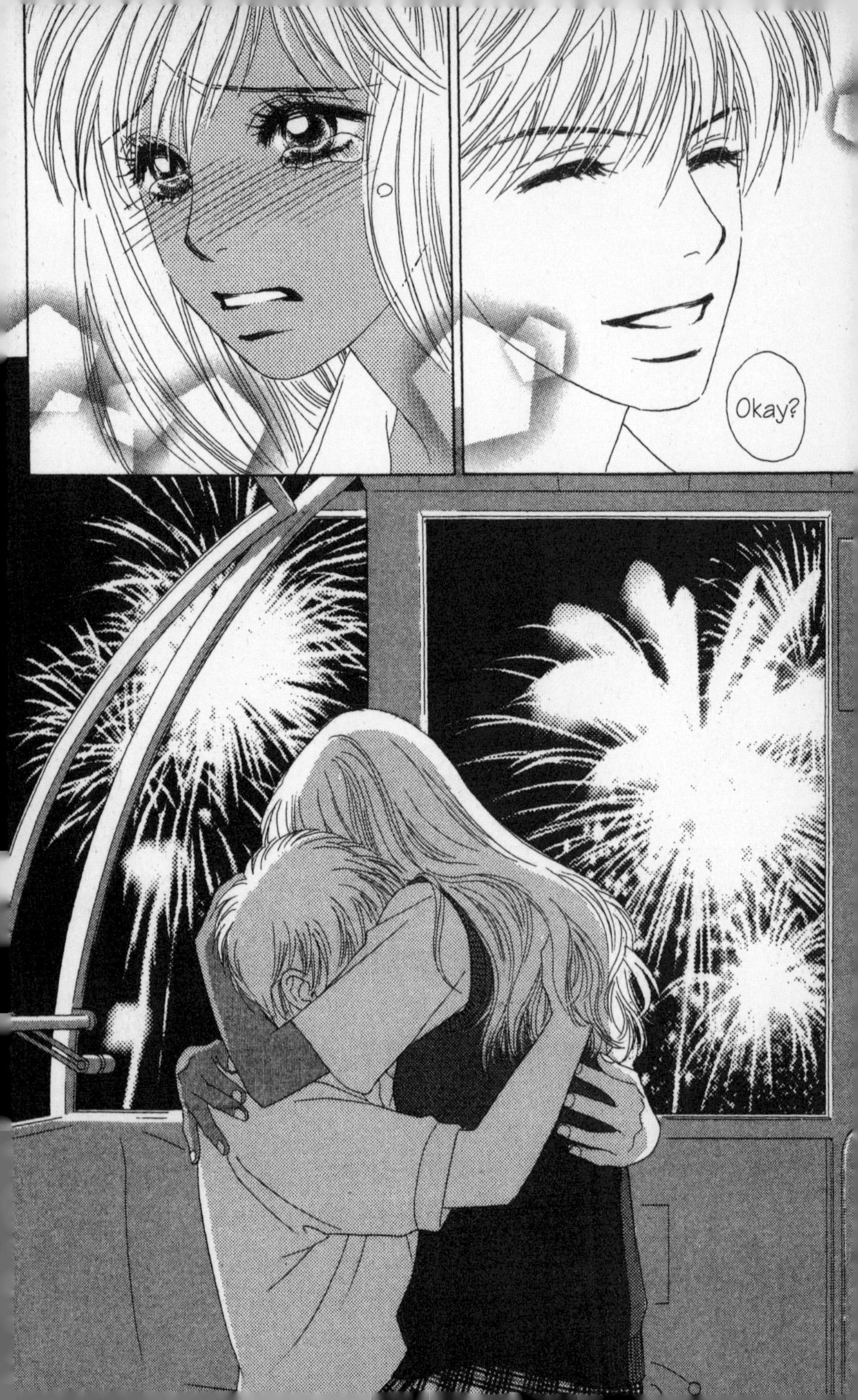
Okay?

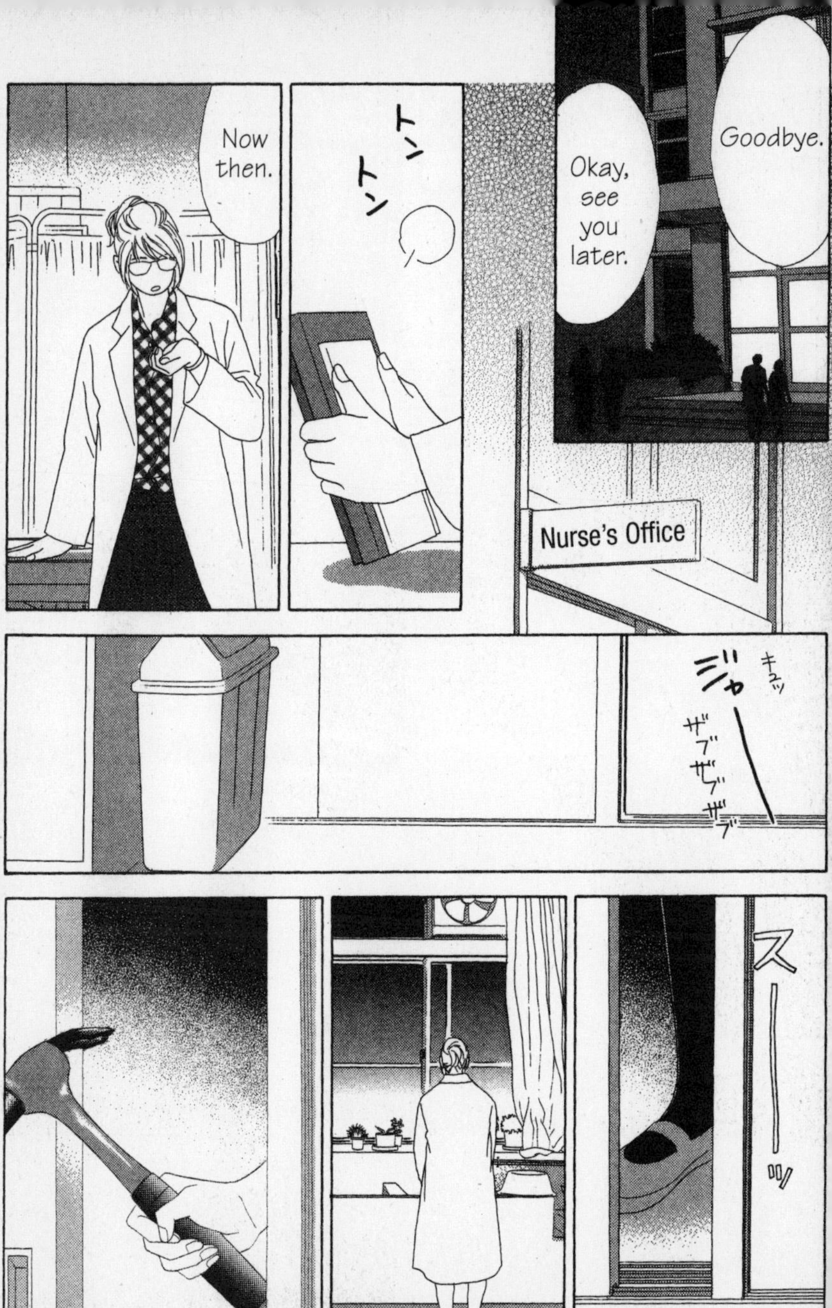

Goodbye.
Okay, see you later.
Nurse's Office
トントン
Now then.
キュッ
ジャー
ザブザブザブ
スーーッ

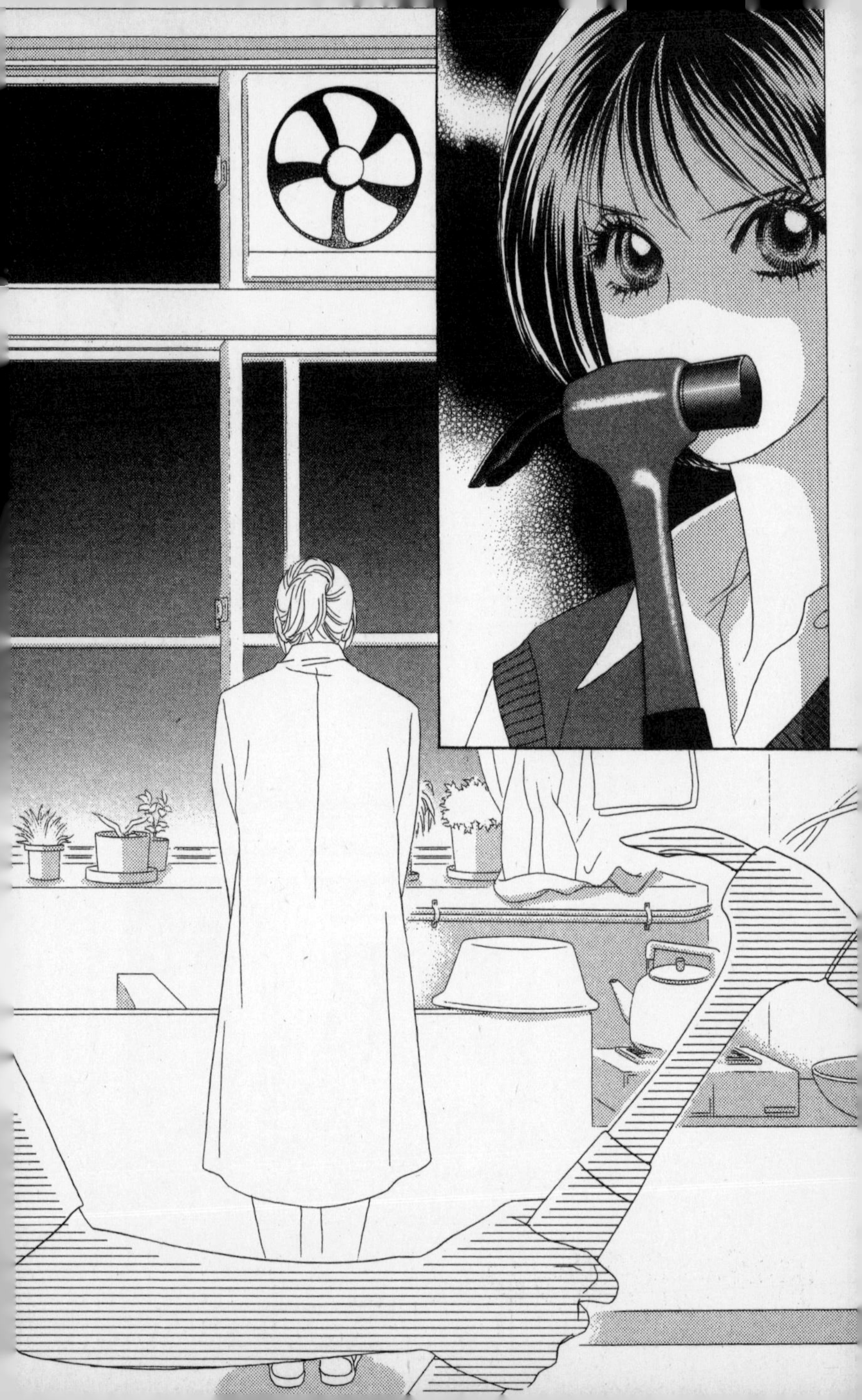

ピーチガール

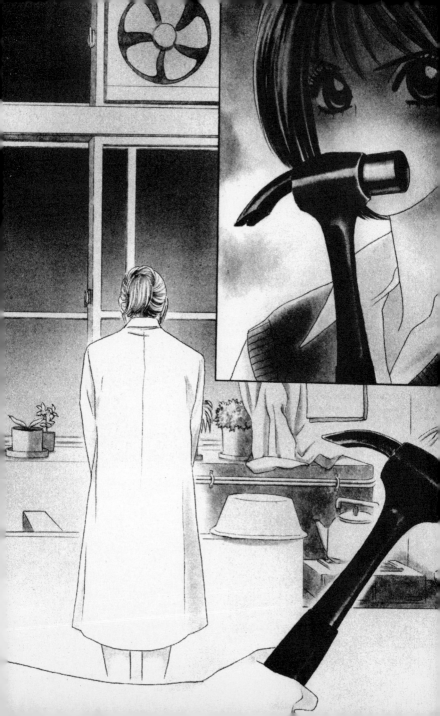

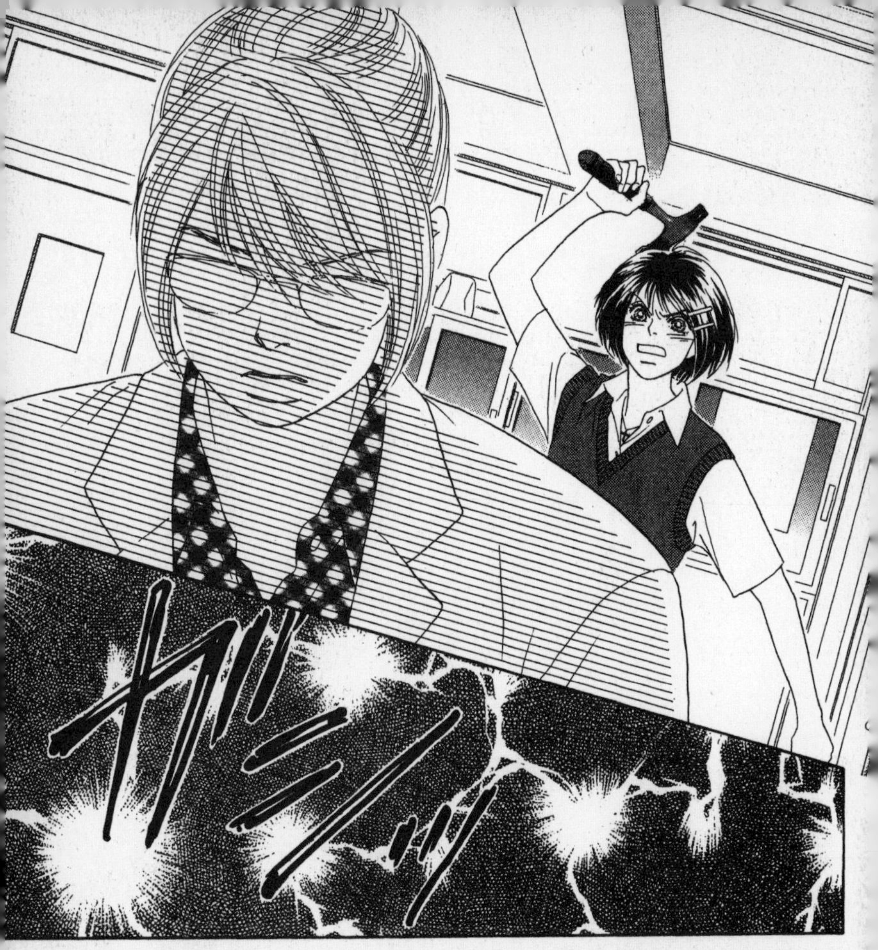

PEACH CLUB

Hello! Thanks to all my readers who picked up *Peach Girl: Change of Heart*, Volume 9. If you don't want to know what happens next, then skip this section! First of all, Morika is back. She first appeared three years ago in *Change of Heart* Volume 1. Even though I'm the one who drew her, I'm not sure I have a clear memory of her character! But in the storyline, only two months have passed since she first appeared. Yup. It's only been one summer between Volumes 1 and 8. I guess Momo and the gang had a pretty busy summer!
--Miwa

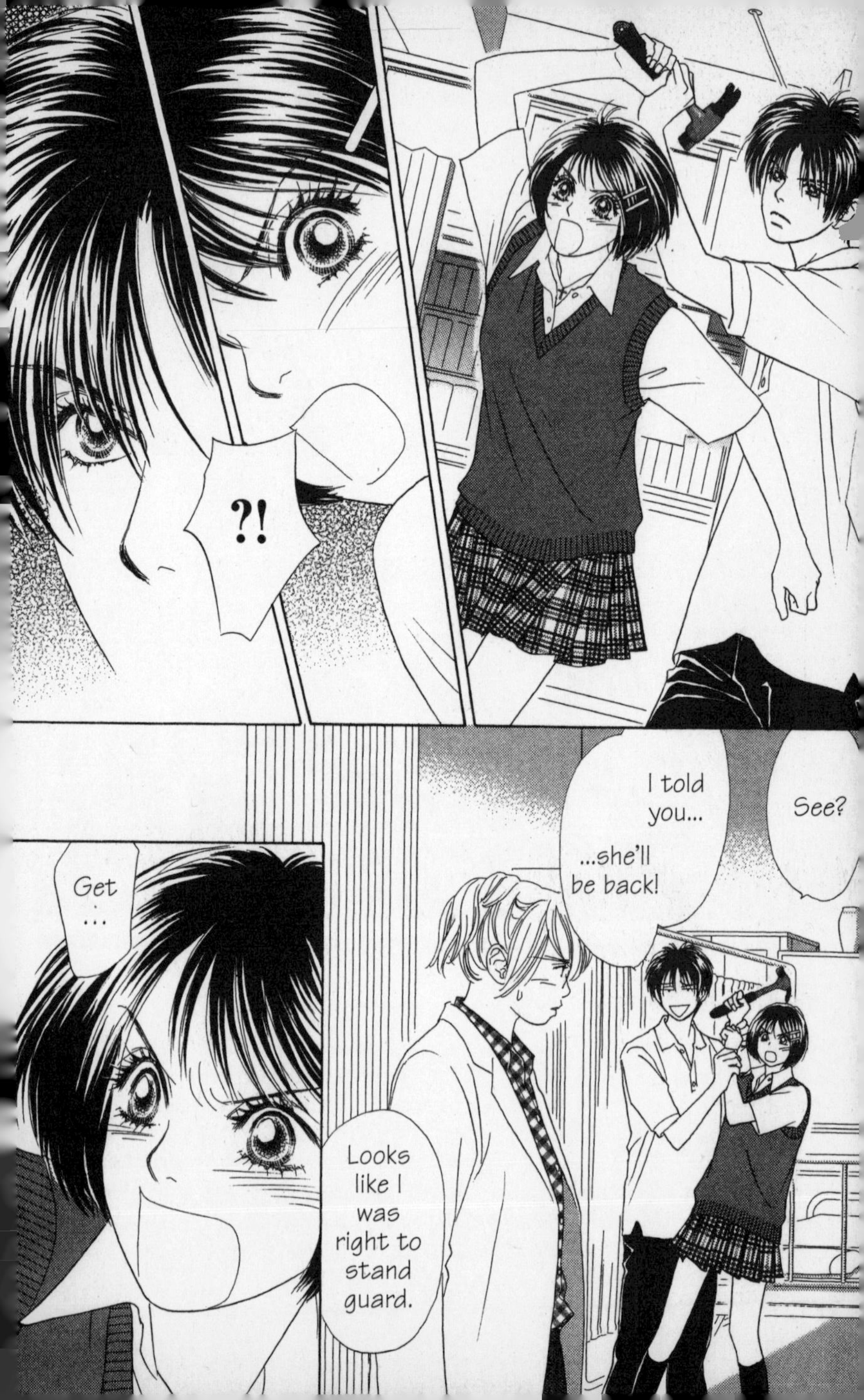
?!
See?
I told you...
...she'll be back!
Looks like I was right to stand guard.
Get...

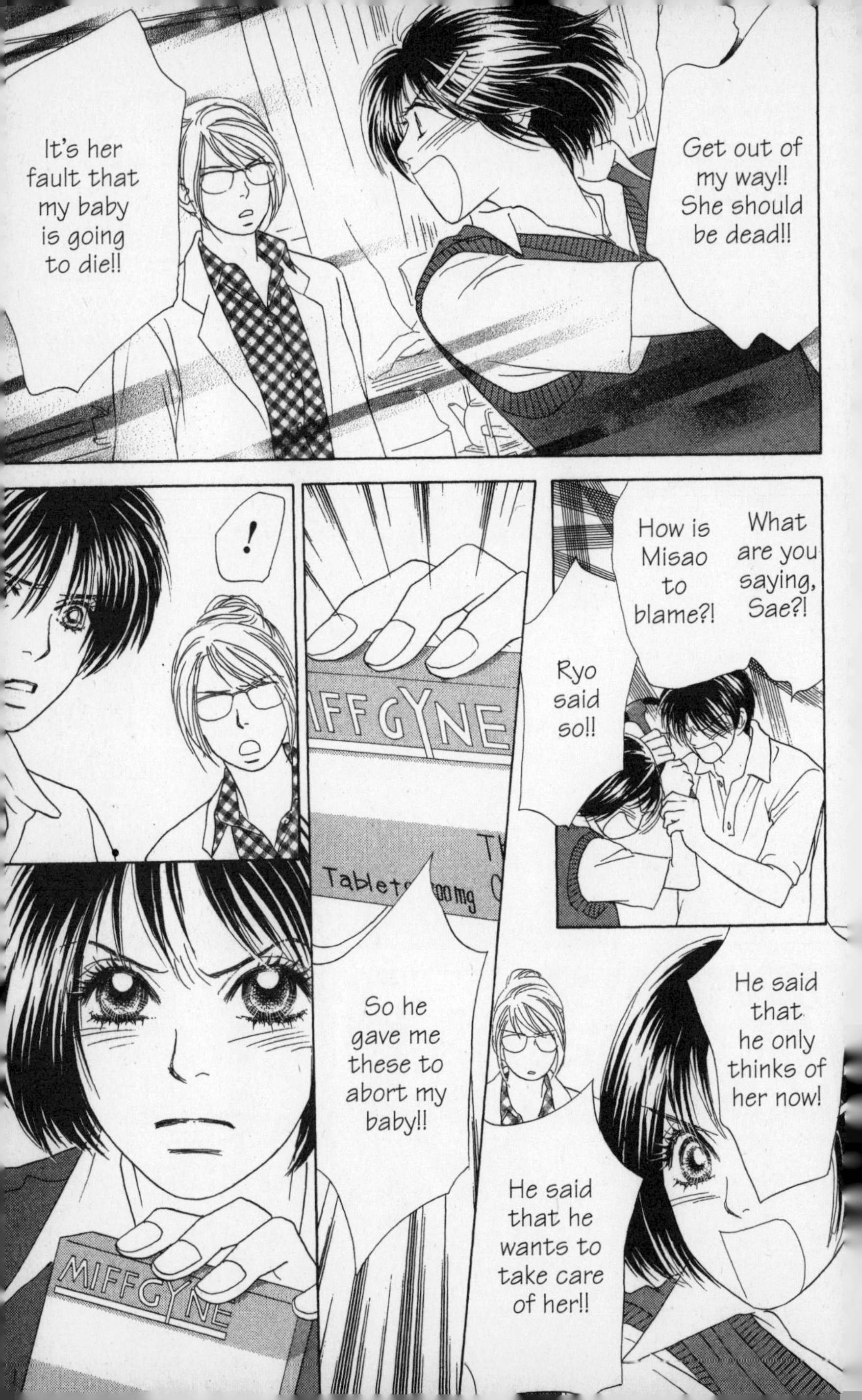
Get out of my way!! She should be dead!!
It's her fault that my baby is going to die!!
What are you saying, Sae?!
How is Misao to blame?!
Ryo said so!!
MIFFGYNE
!
He said that he only thinks of her now!
He said that he wants to take care of her!!
So he gave me these to abort my baby!!
MIFFGYNE

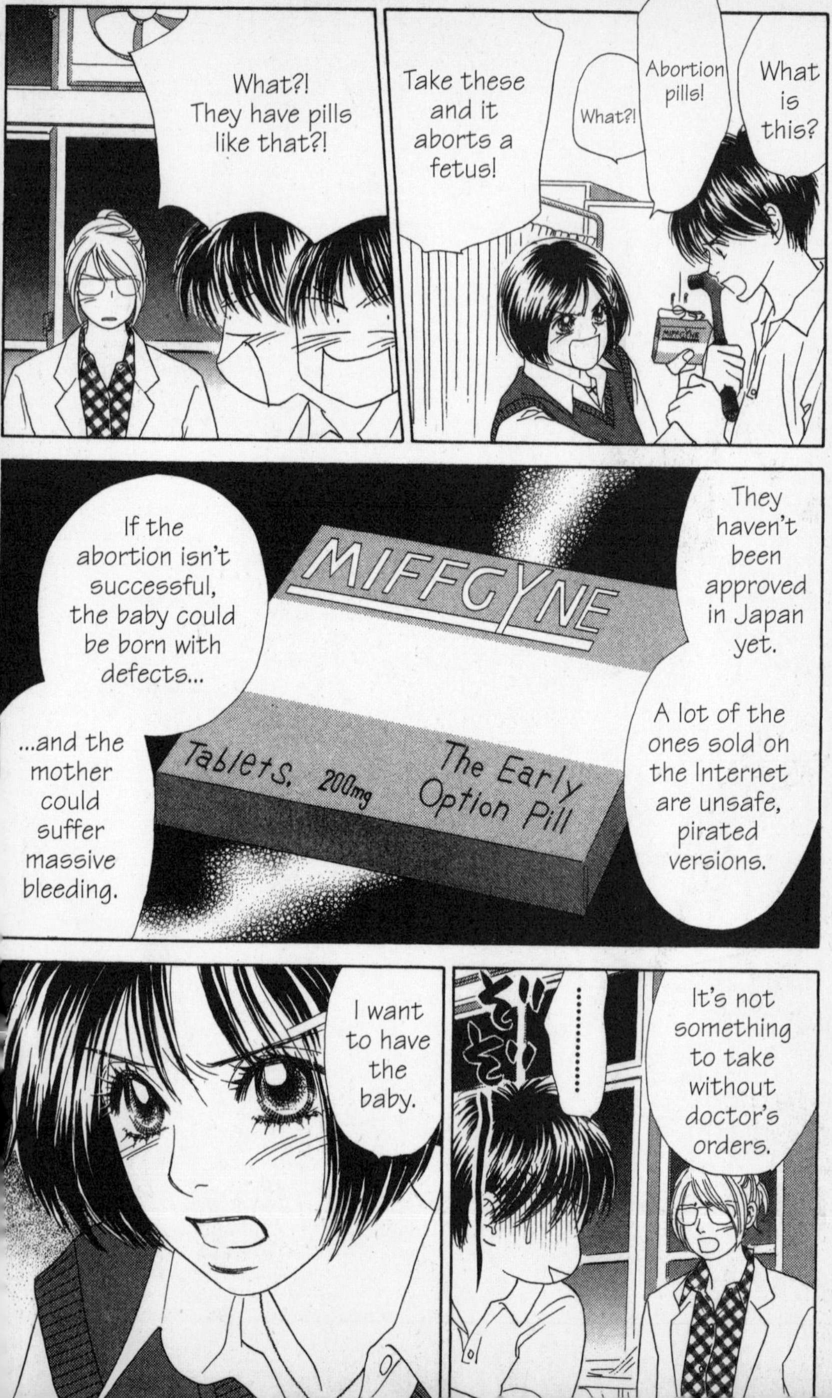
What is this?
Abortion pills!
What?!
Take these and it aborts a fetus!
What?! They have pills like that?!
They haven't been approved in Japan yet.
A lot of the ones sold on the Internet are unsafe, pirated versions.
MIFFGYNE
The Early Option Pill
Tablets. 200mg
If the abortion isn't successful, the baby could be born with defects...
...and the mother could suffer massive bleeding.
It's not something to take without doctor's orders.
......
I want to have the baby.

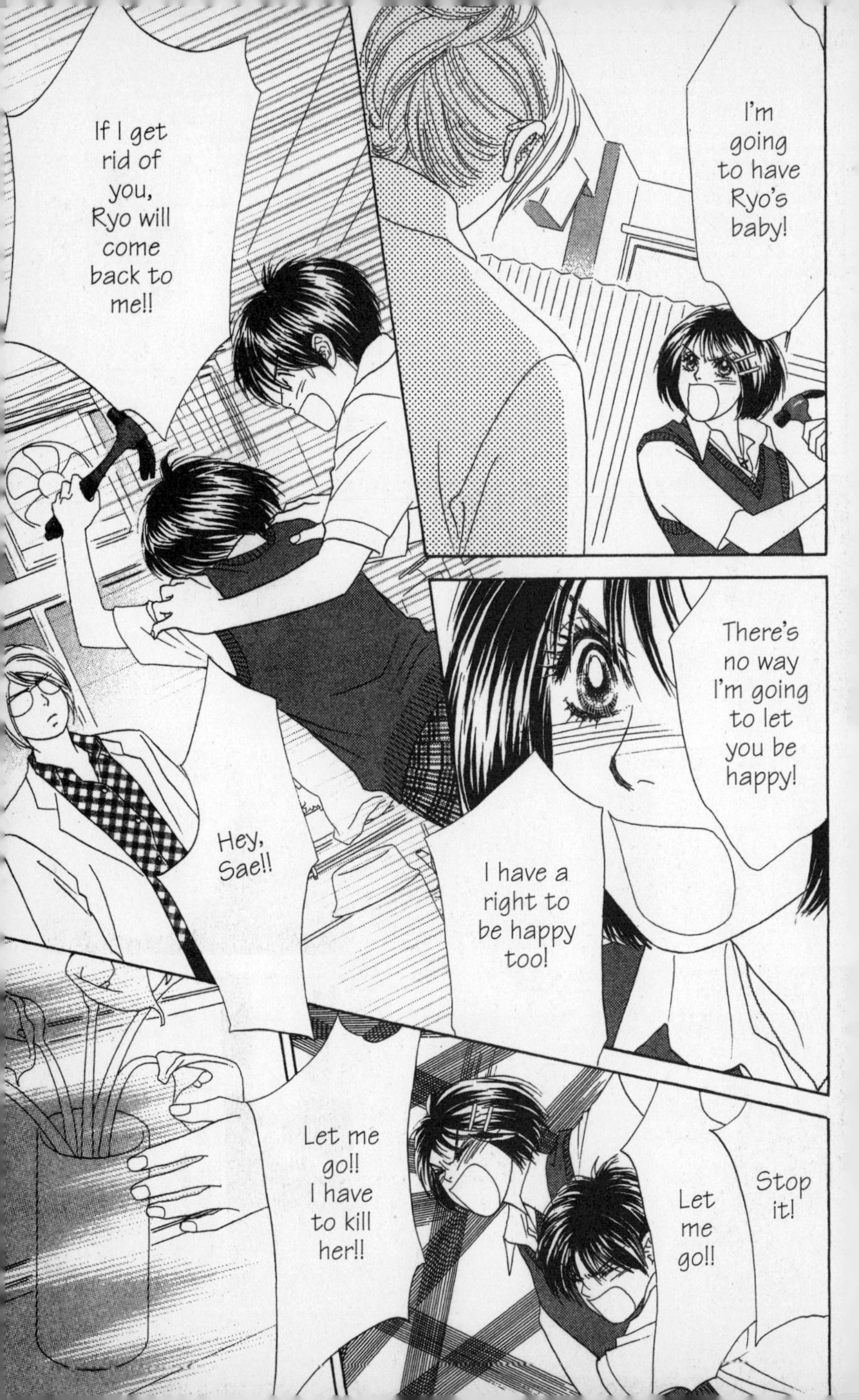
I'm going to have Ryo's baby!
There's no way I'm going to let you be happy!
I have a right to be happy too!
If I get rid of you, Ryo will come back to me!!
Hey, Sae!!
Stop it!
Let me go!!
Let me go!! I have to kill her!!

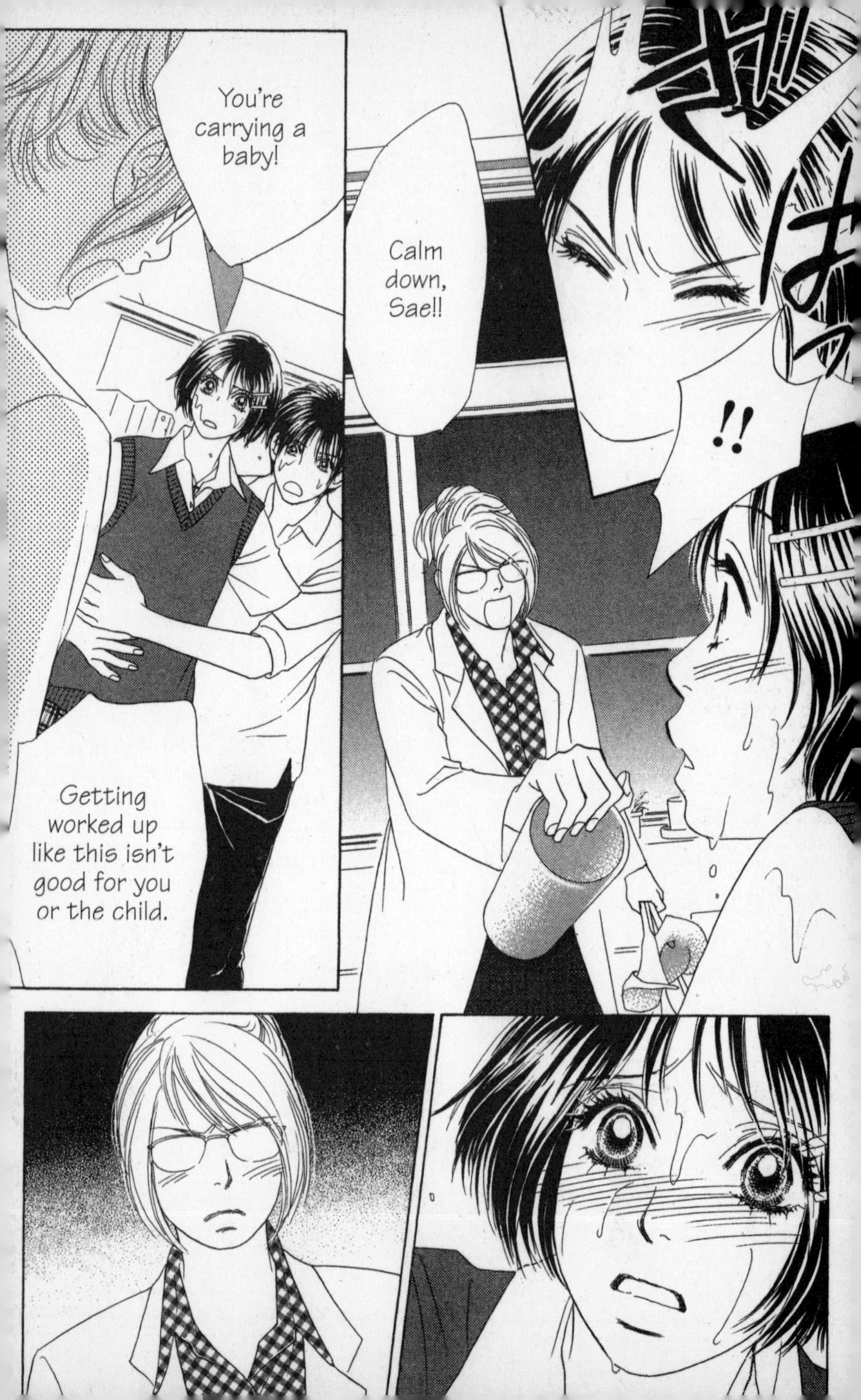
!!
Calm down, Sae!!
You're carrying a baby!
Getting worked up like this isn't good for you or the child.

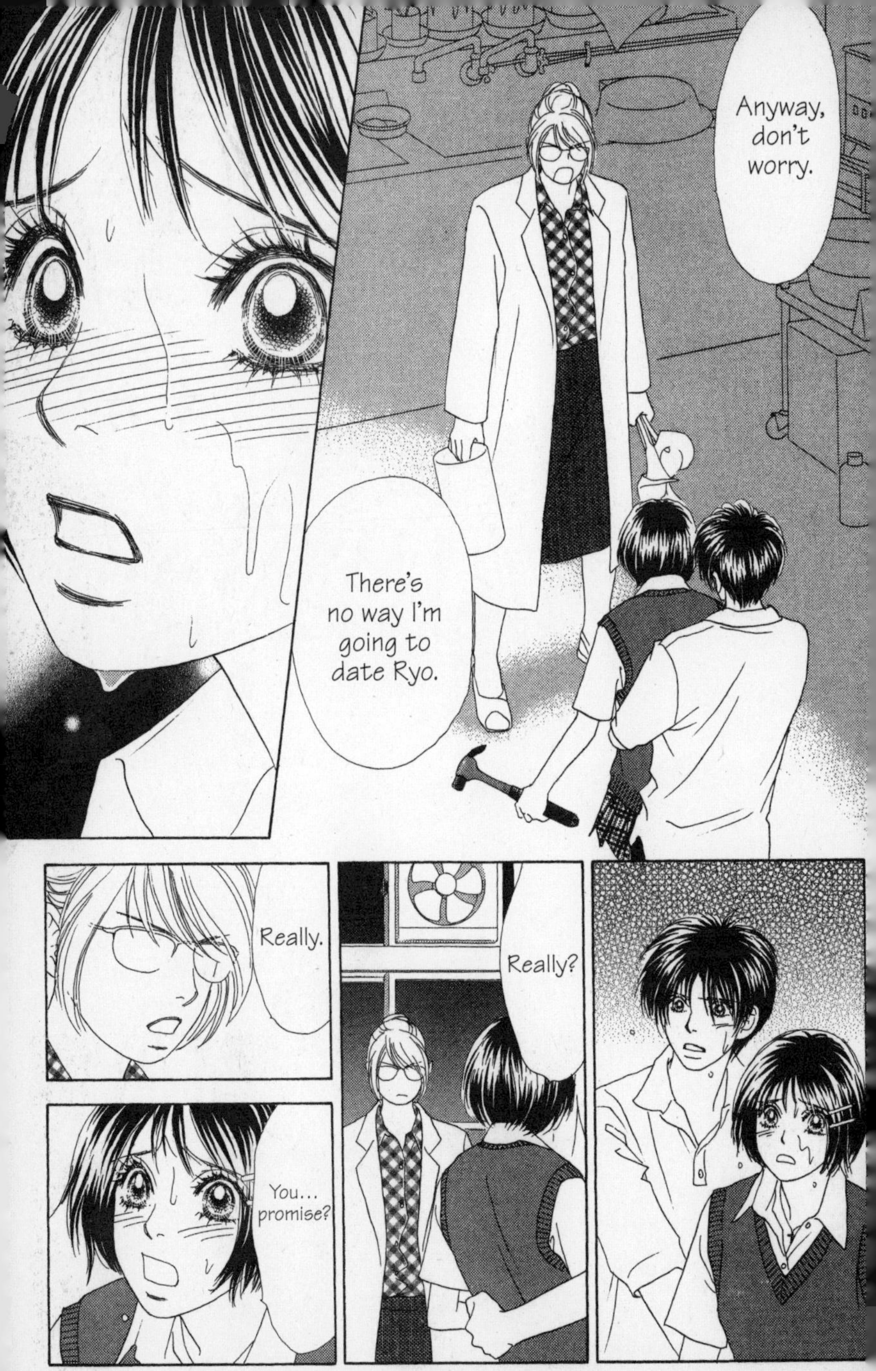
Anyway, don't worry.
There's no way I'm going to date Ryo.
Really?
Really.
You... promise?

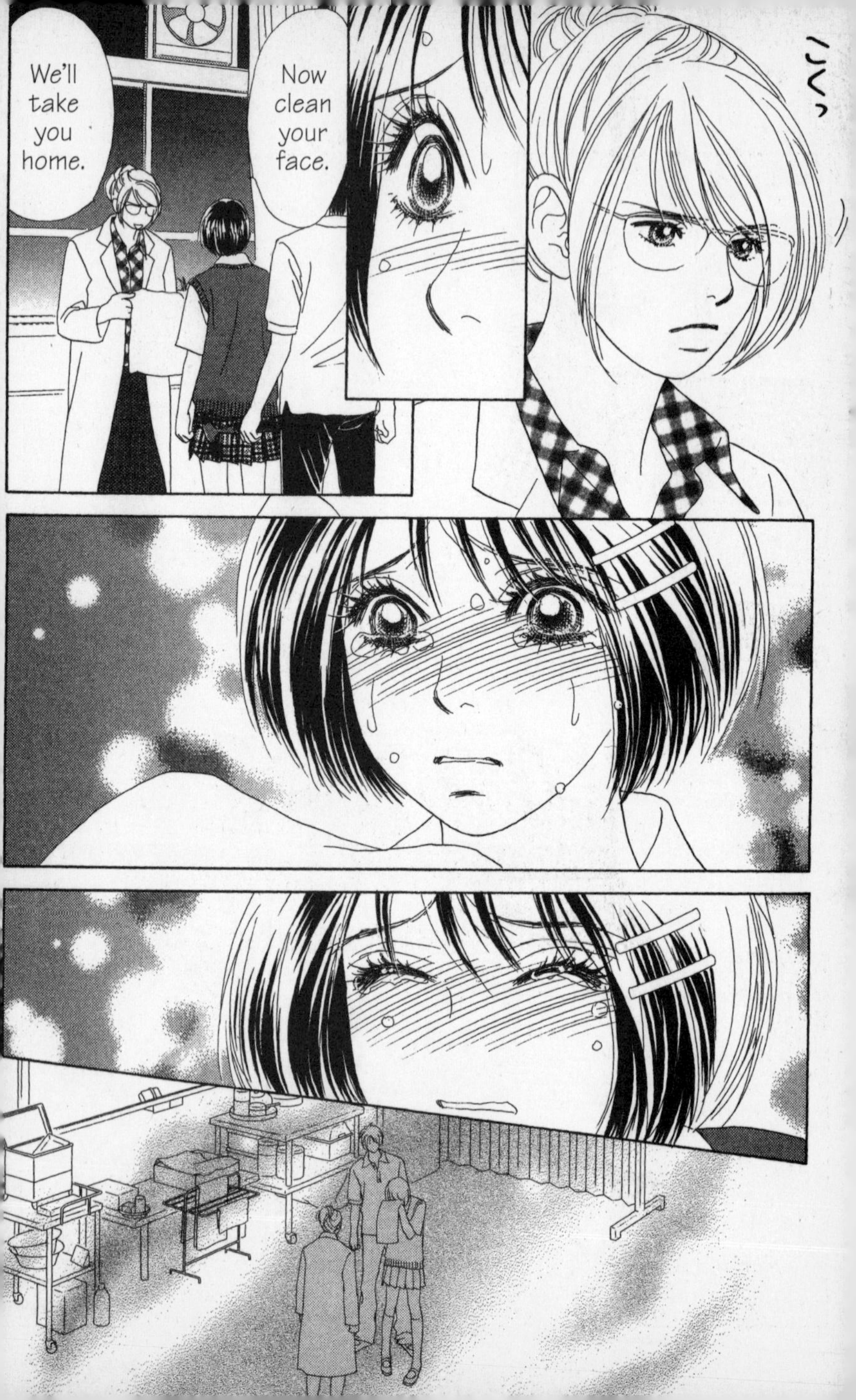
こくっ
Now clean your face.
We'll take you home.

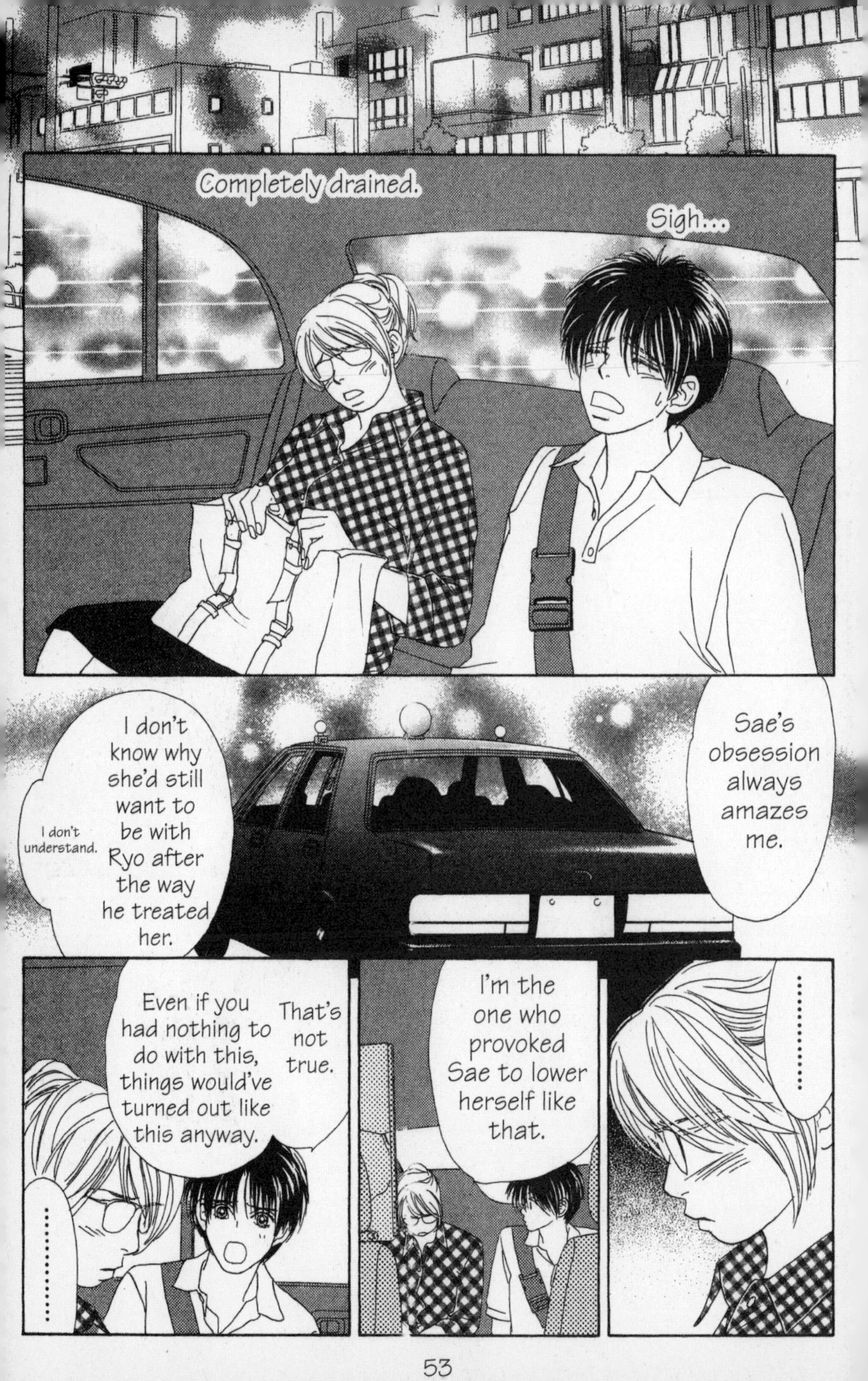
Sigh...
Completely drained.
Sae's obsession always amazes me.
I don't know why she'd still want to be with Ryo after the way he treated her.
I don't understand.
......
I'm the one who provoked Sae to lower herself like that.
That's not true.
Even if you had nothing to do with this, things would've turned out like this anyway.
......

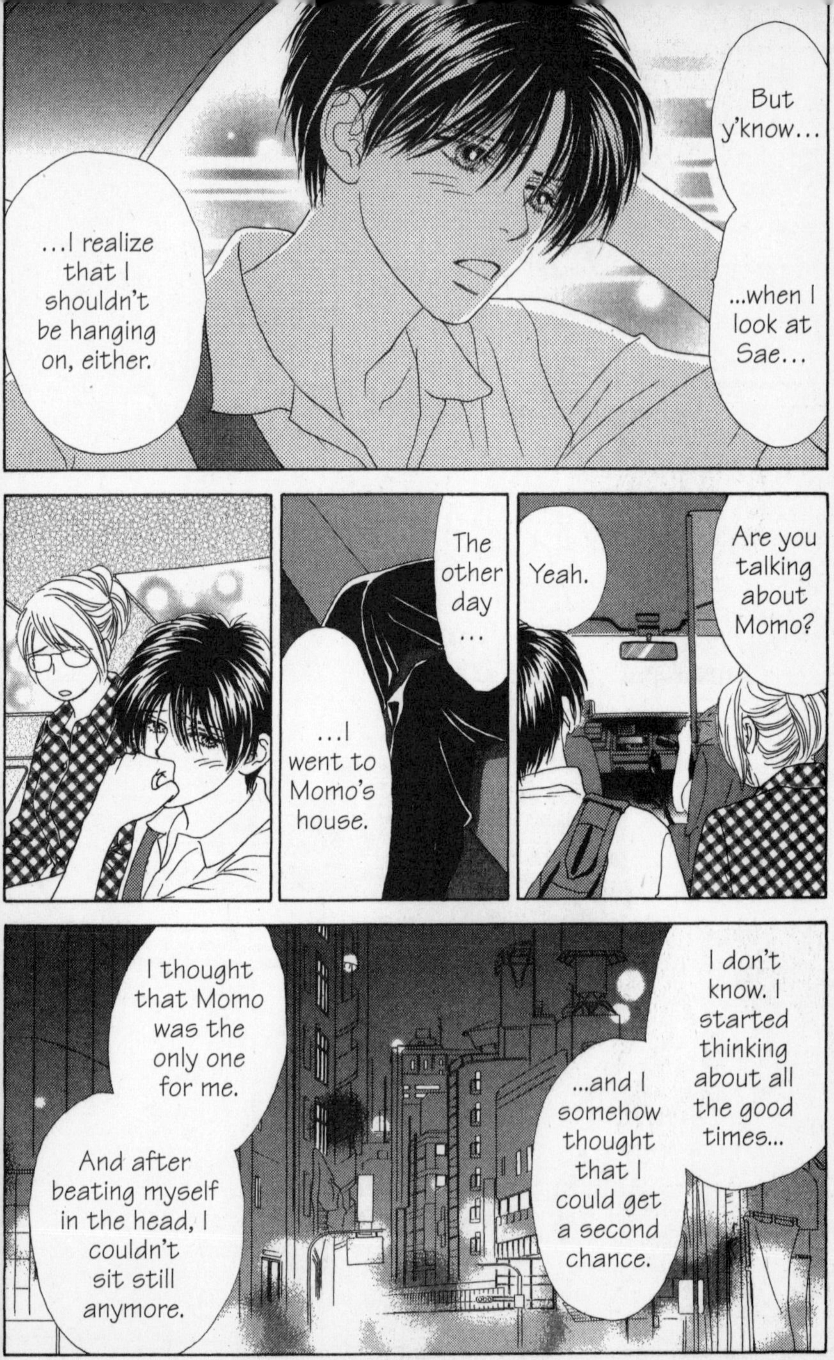
But y'know…
...when I look at Sae…
…I realize that I shouldn't be hanging on, either.
Are you talking about Momo?
Yeah.
The other day …
…I went to Momo's house.
I don't know. I started thinking about all the good times...
...and I somehow thought that I could get a second chance.
I thought that Momo was the only one for me.
And after beating myself in the head, I couldn't sit still anymore.

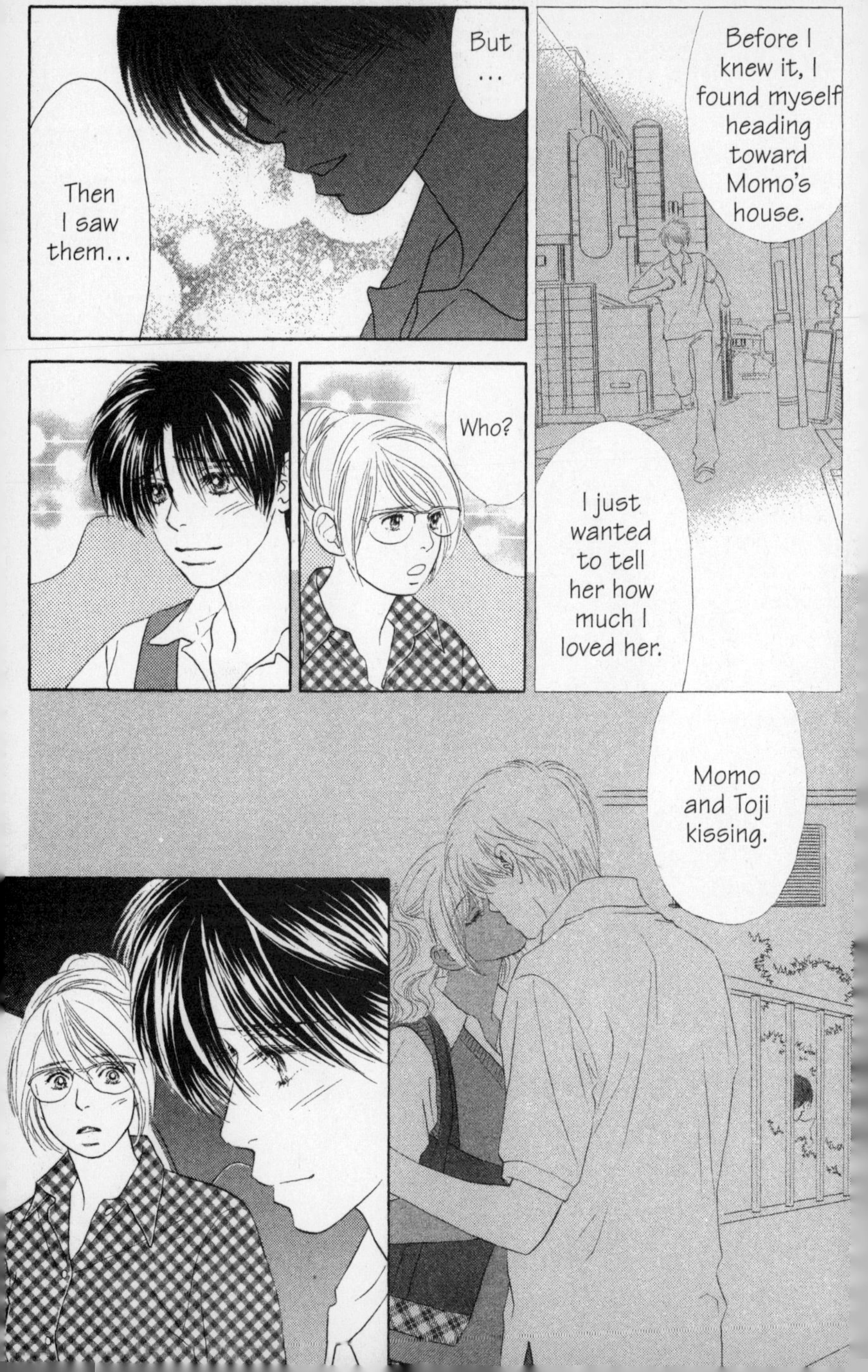
Before I knew it, I found myself heading toward Momo's house.
I just wanted to tell her how much I loved her.
But ...
Then I saw them...
Who?
Momo and Toji kissing.

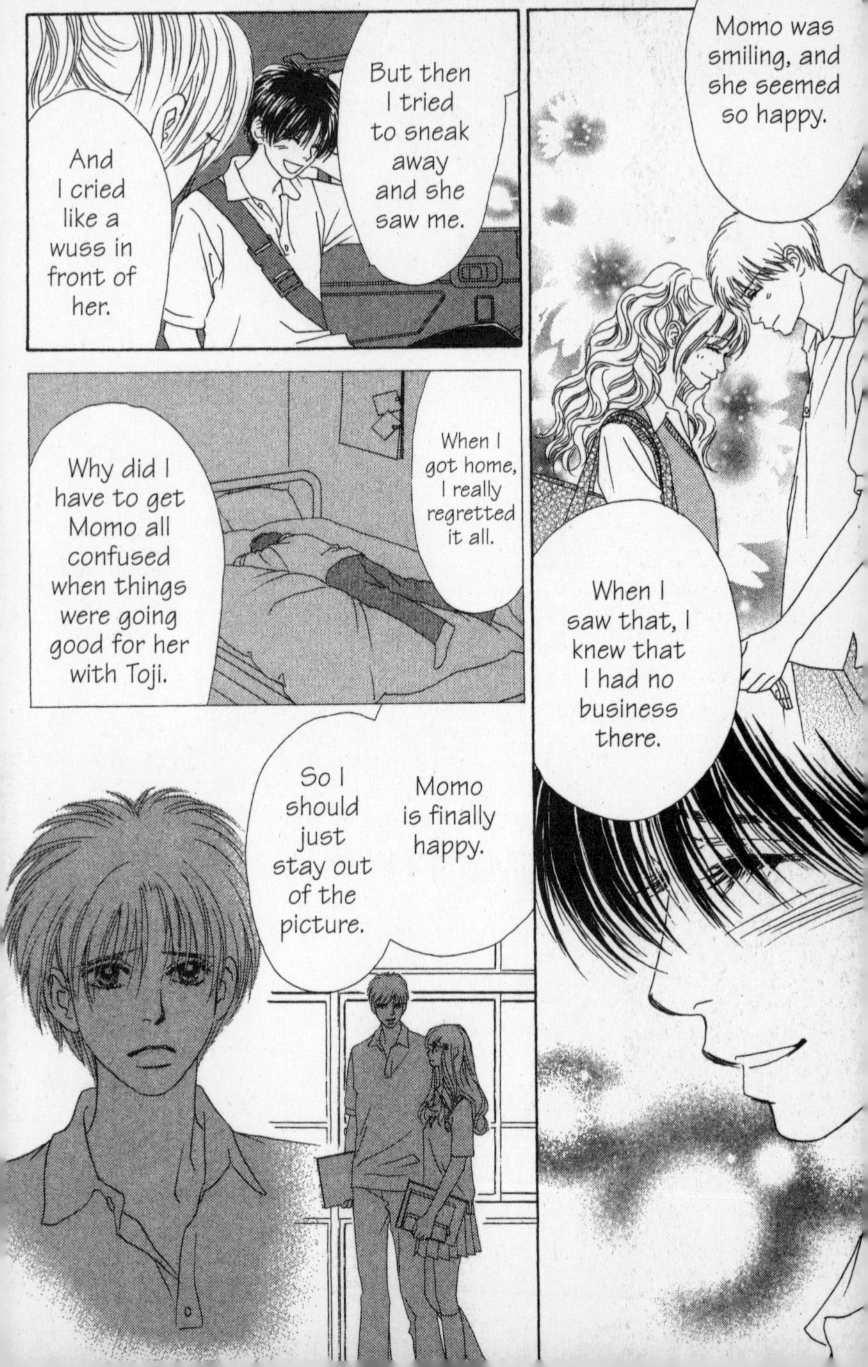
Momo was smiling, and she seemed so happy.
When I saw that, I knew that I had no business there.
But then I tried to sneak away and she saw me.
And I cried like a wuss in front of her.
When I got home, I really regretted it all.
Why did I have to get Momo all confused when things were going good for her with Toji.
Momo is finally happy.
So I should just stay out of the picture.

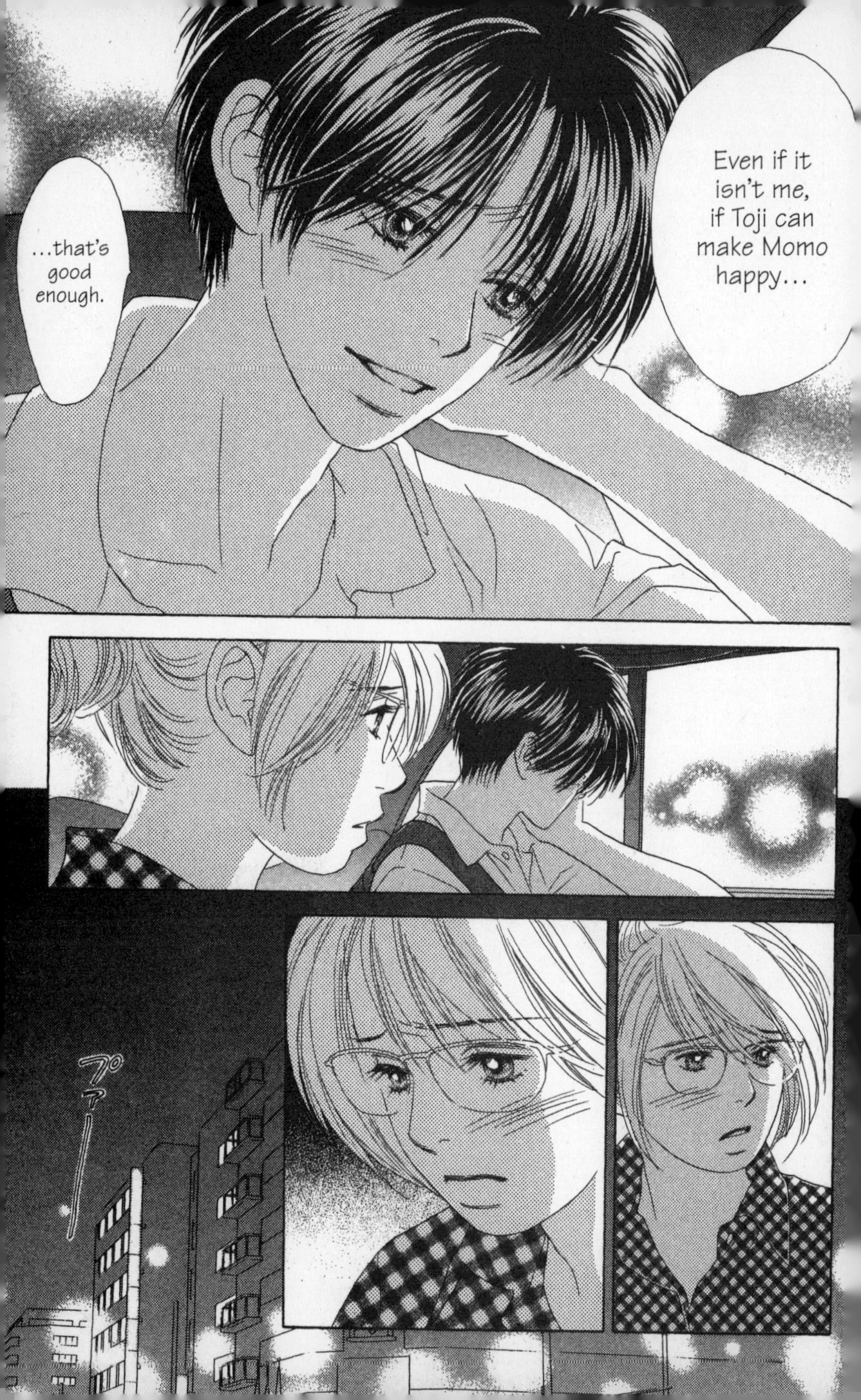
Even if it isn't me, if Toji can make Momo happy...
...that's good enough.
プァー

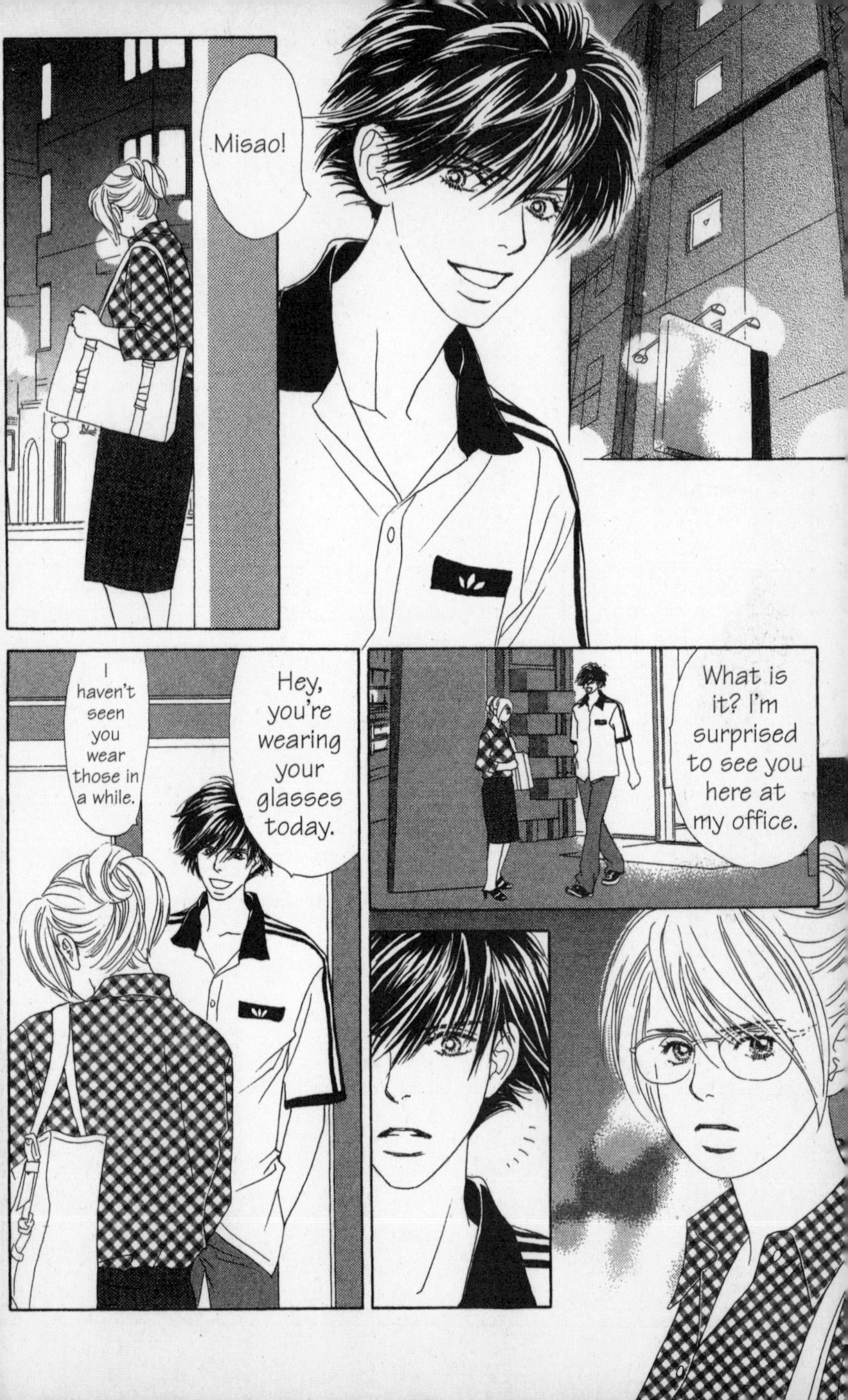
Misao!
What is it? I'm surprised to see you here at my office.
Hey, you're wearing your glasses today.
I haven't seen you wear those in a while.

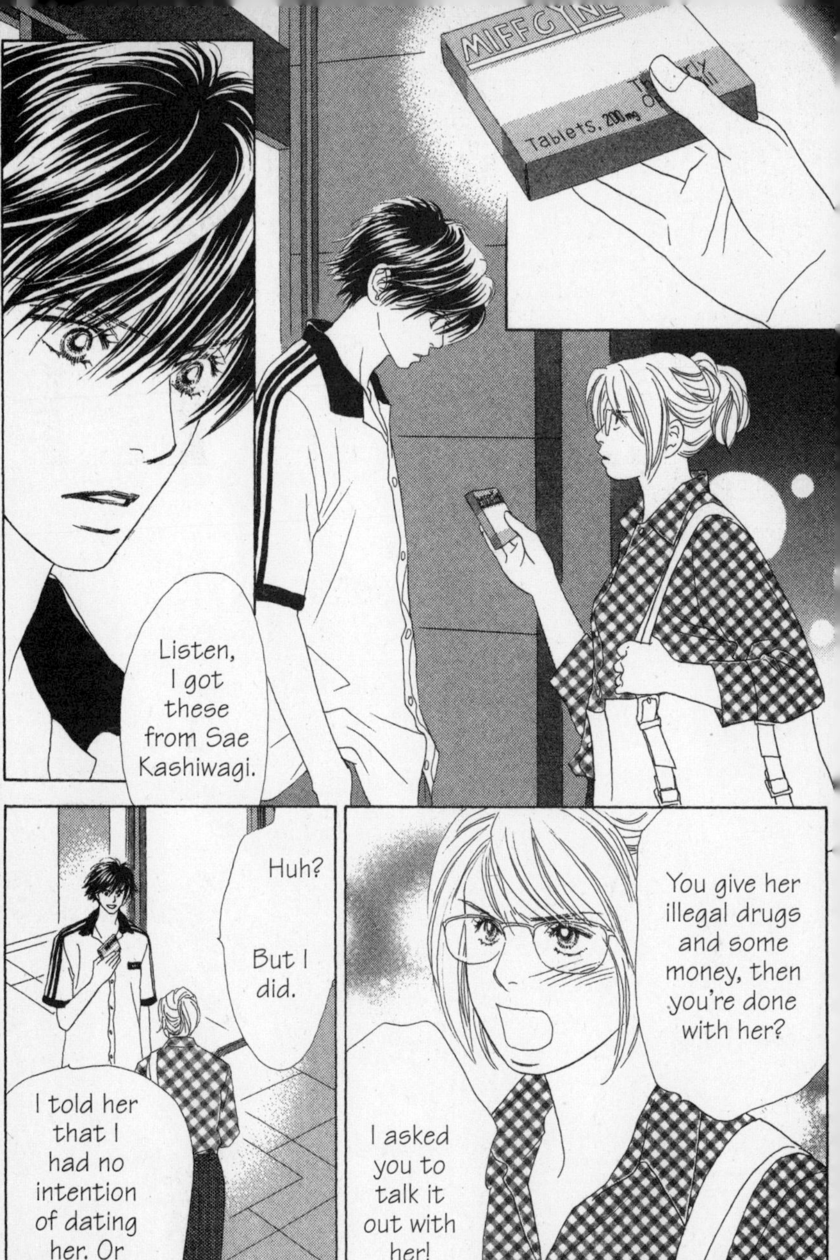
MIFFGYNE
Tablets, 200mg
Listen, I got these from Sae Kashiwagi.
You give her illegal drugs and some money, then you're done with her?
I asked you to talk it out with her!
Huh?
But I did.
I told her that I had no intention of dating her. Or becoming a father.

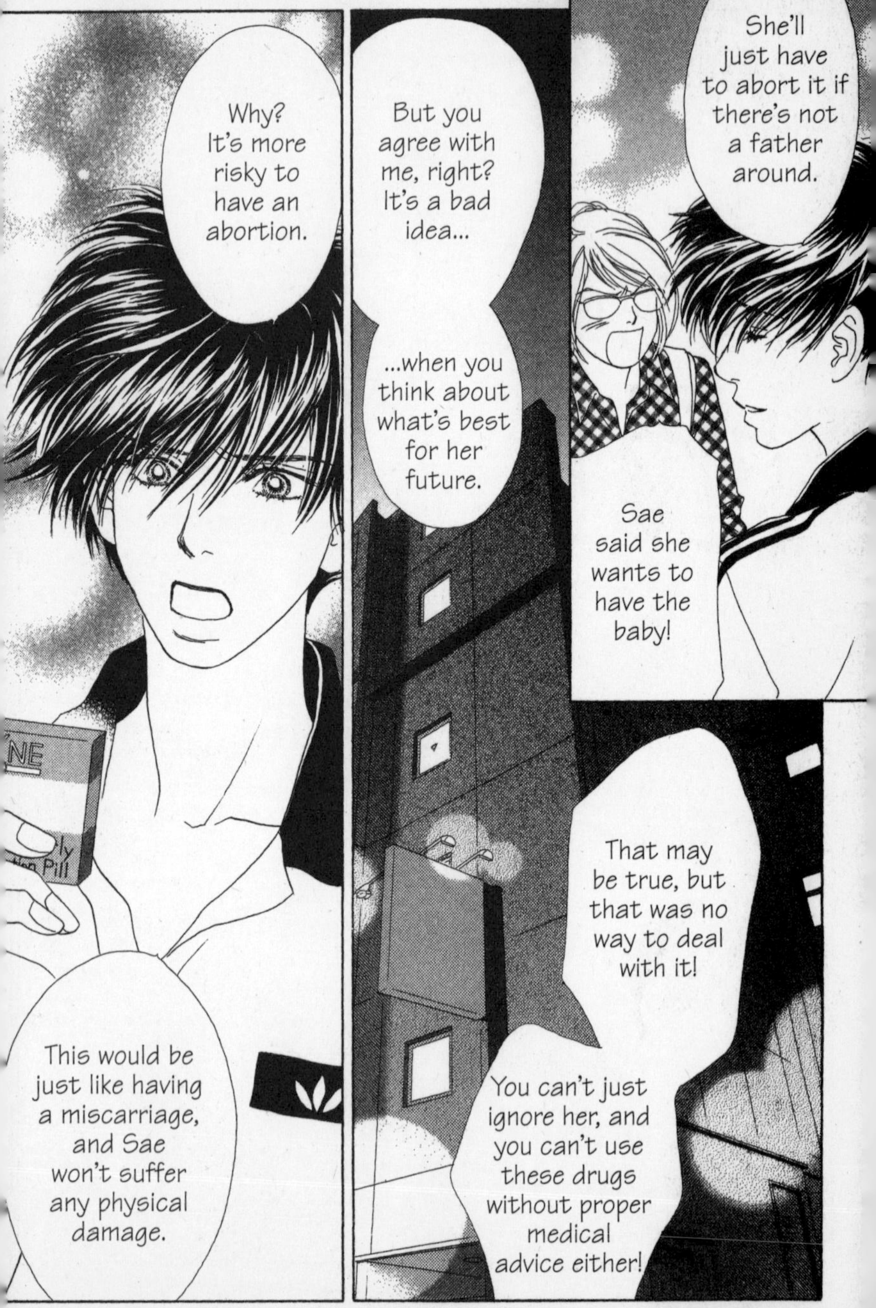
She'll just have to abort it if there's not a father around.
Sae said she wants to have the baby!
That may be true, but that was no way to deal with it!
You can't just ignore her, and you can't use these drugs without proper medical advice either!
But you agree with me, right? It's a bad idea...
...when you think about what's best for her future.
Why? It's more risky to have an abortion.
NE
This would be just like having a miscarriage, and Sae won't suffer any physical damage.

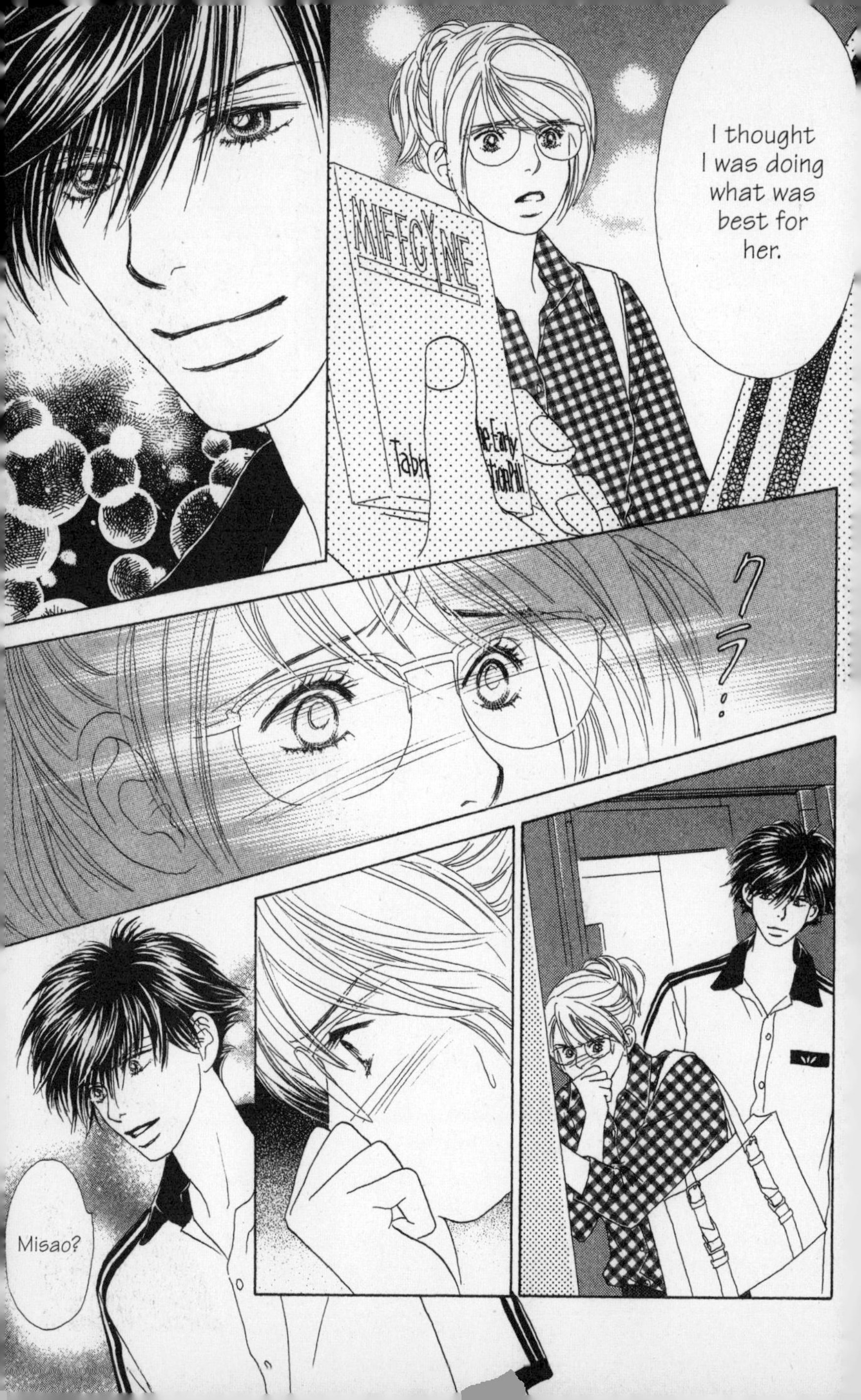
I thought I was doing what was best for her.
クラ
Misao?

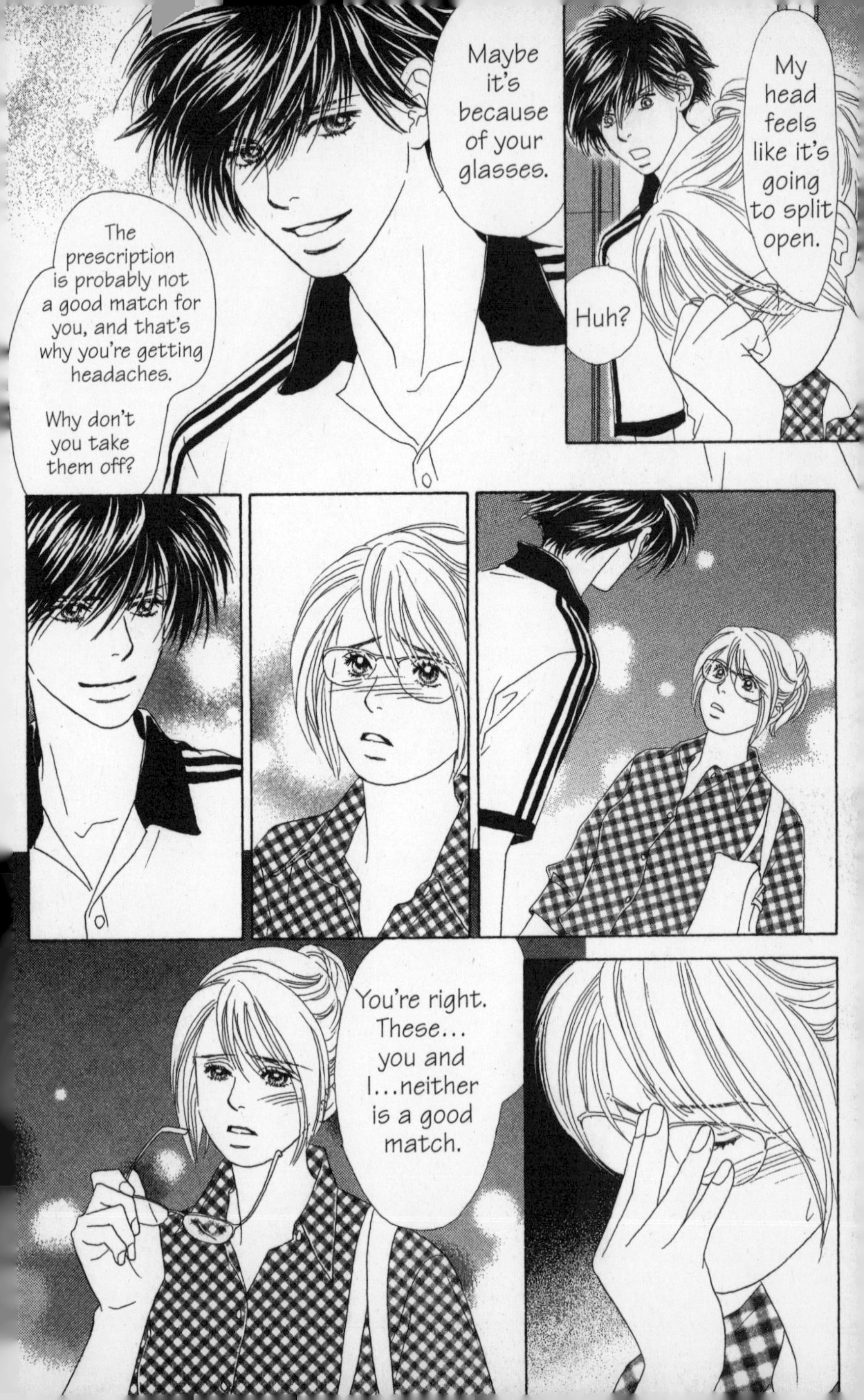
My head feels like it's going to split open.
Huh?
Maybe it's because of your glasses.
The prescription is probably not a good match for you, and that's why you're getting headaches.
Why don't you take them off?
You're right. These... you and I...neither is a good match.

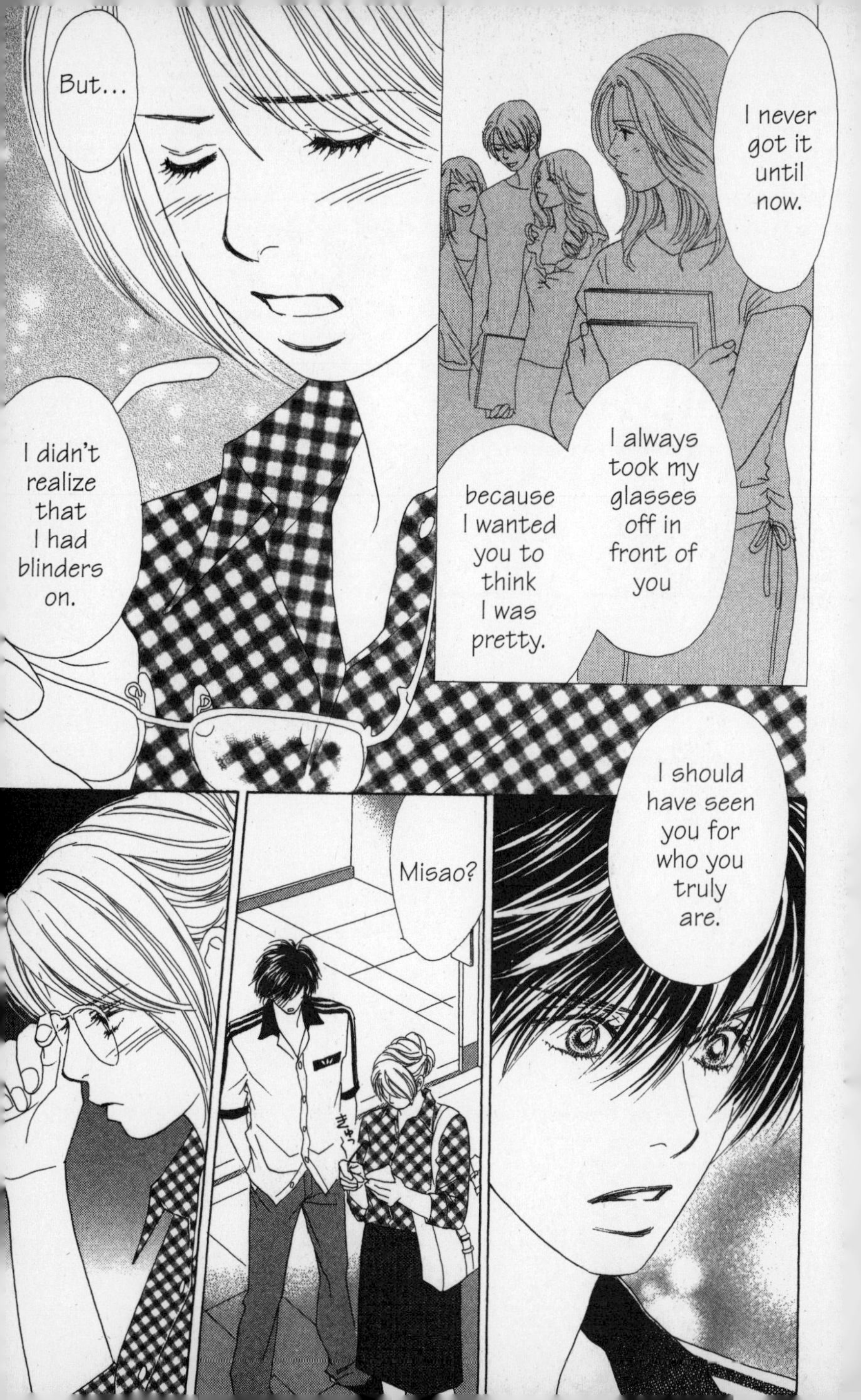
I never got it until now.
I always took my glasses off in front of you
because I wanted you to think I was pretty.
But…
I didn't realize that I had blinders on.
I should have seen you for who you truly are.
Misao?

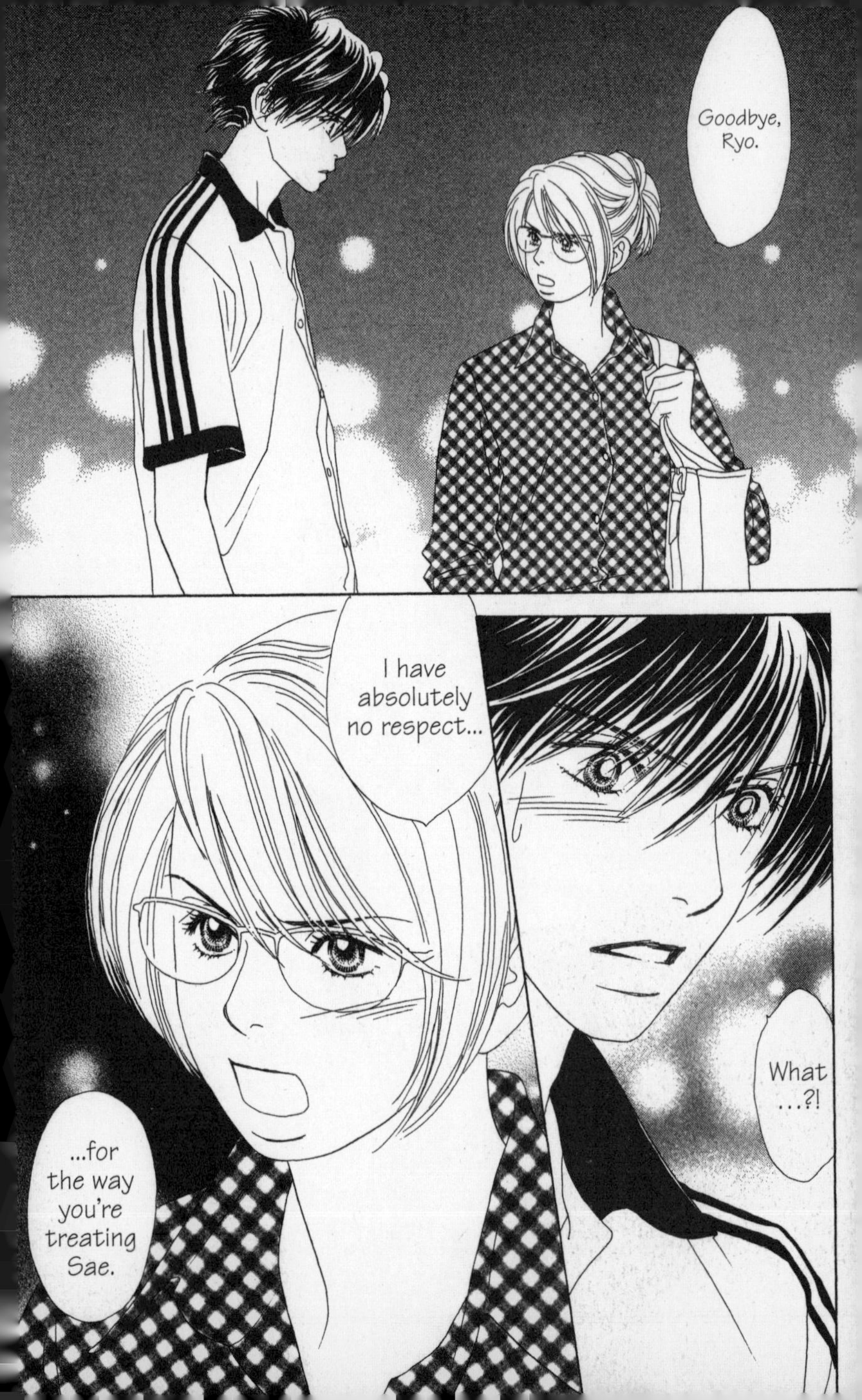
Goodbye, Ryo.
I have absolutely no respect...
What ...?!
...for the way you're treating Sae.

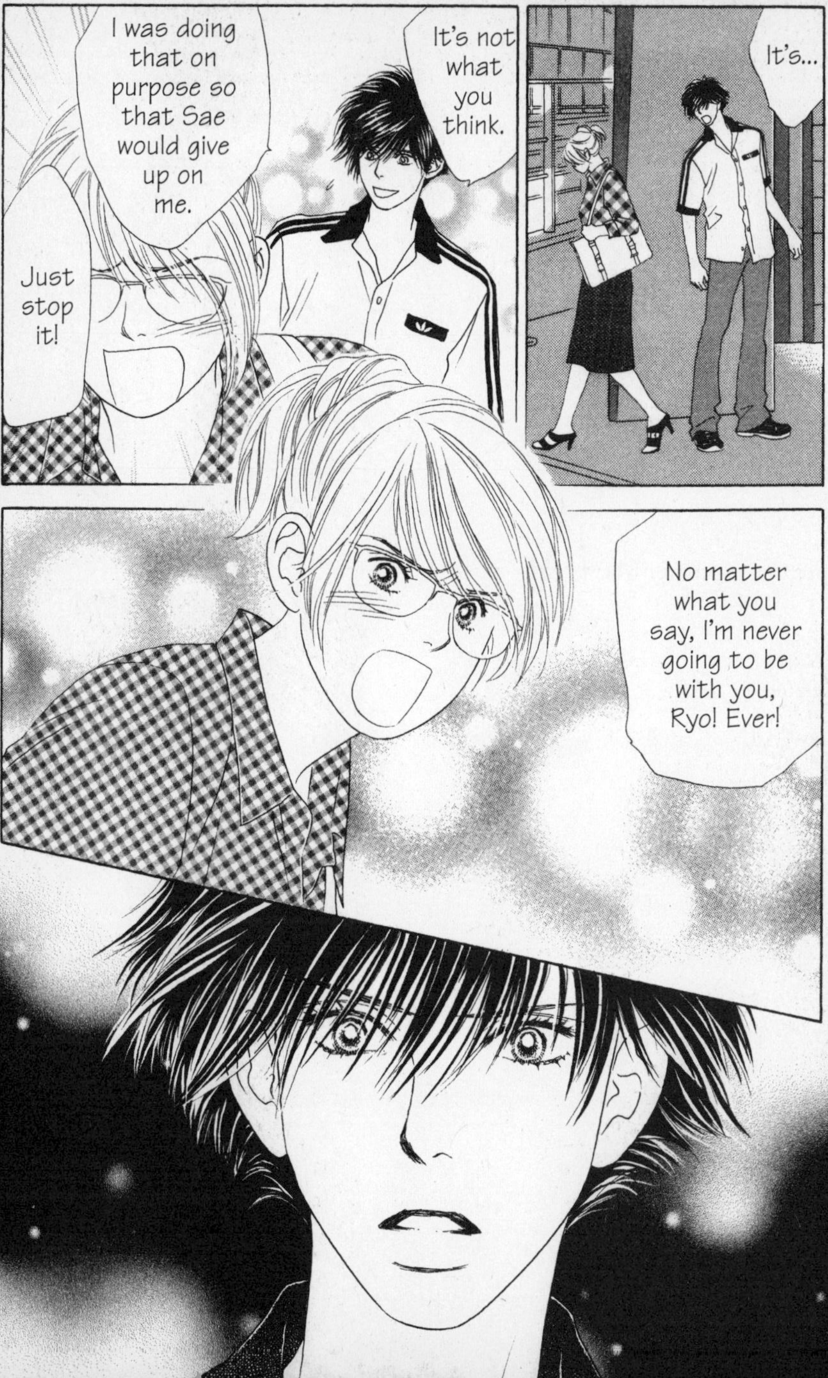

It's...
It's not what you think.
I was doing that on purpose so that Sae would give up on me.
Just stop it!
No matter what you say, I'm never going to be with you, Ryo! Ever!

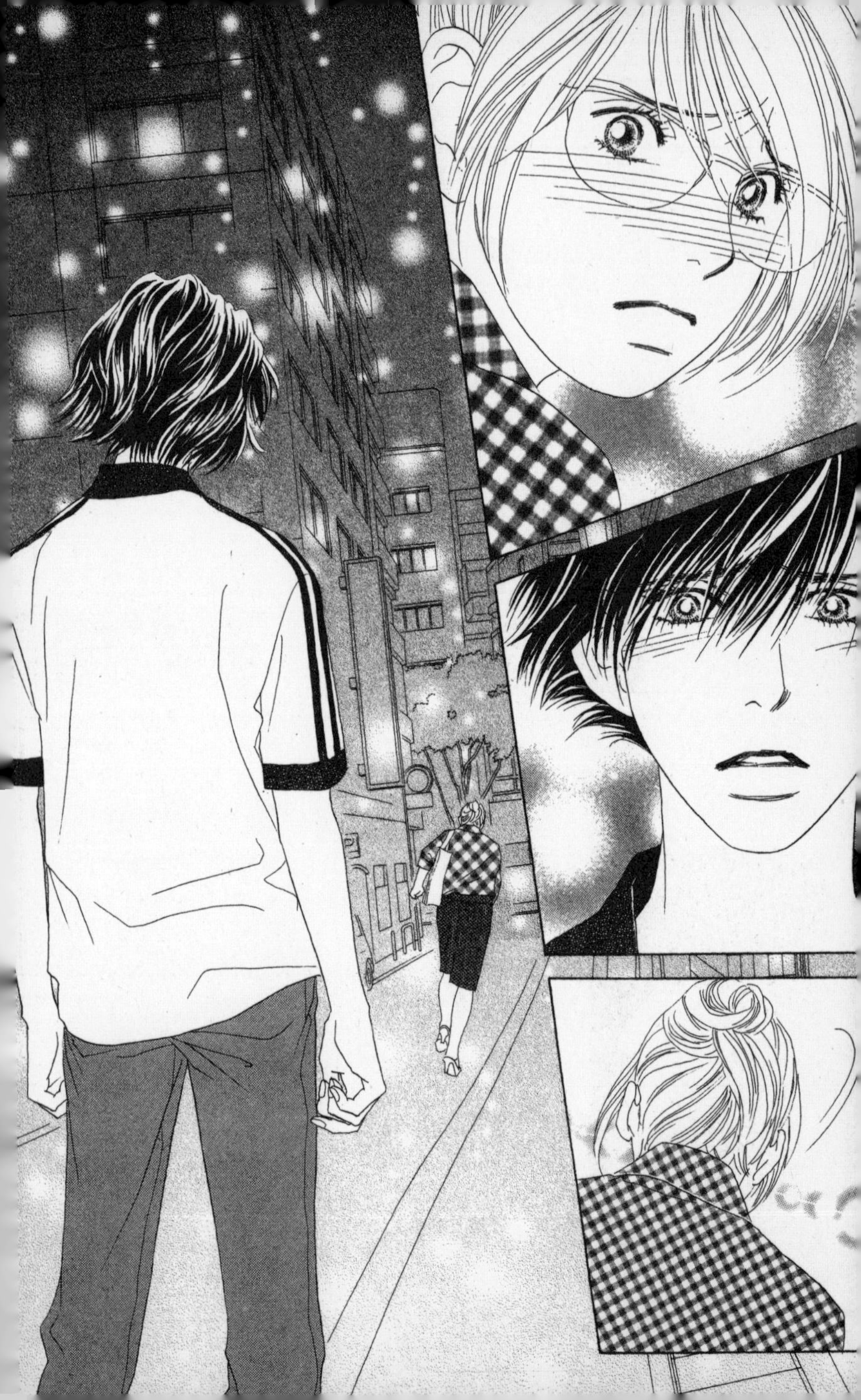

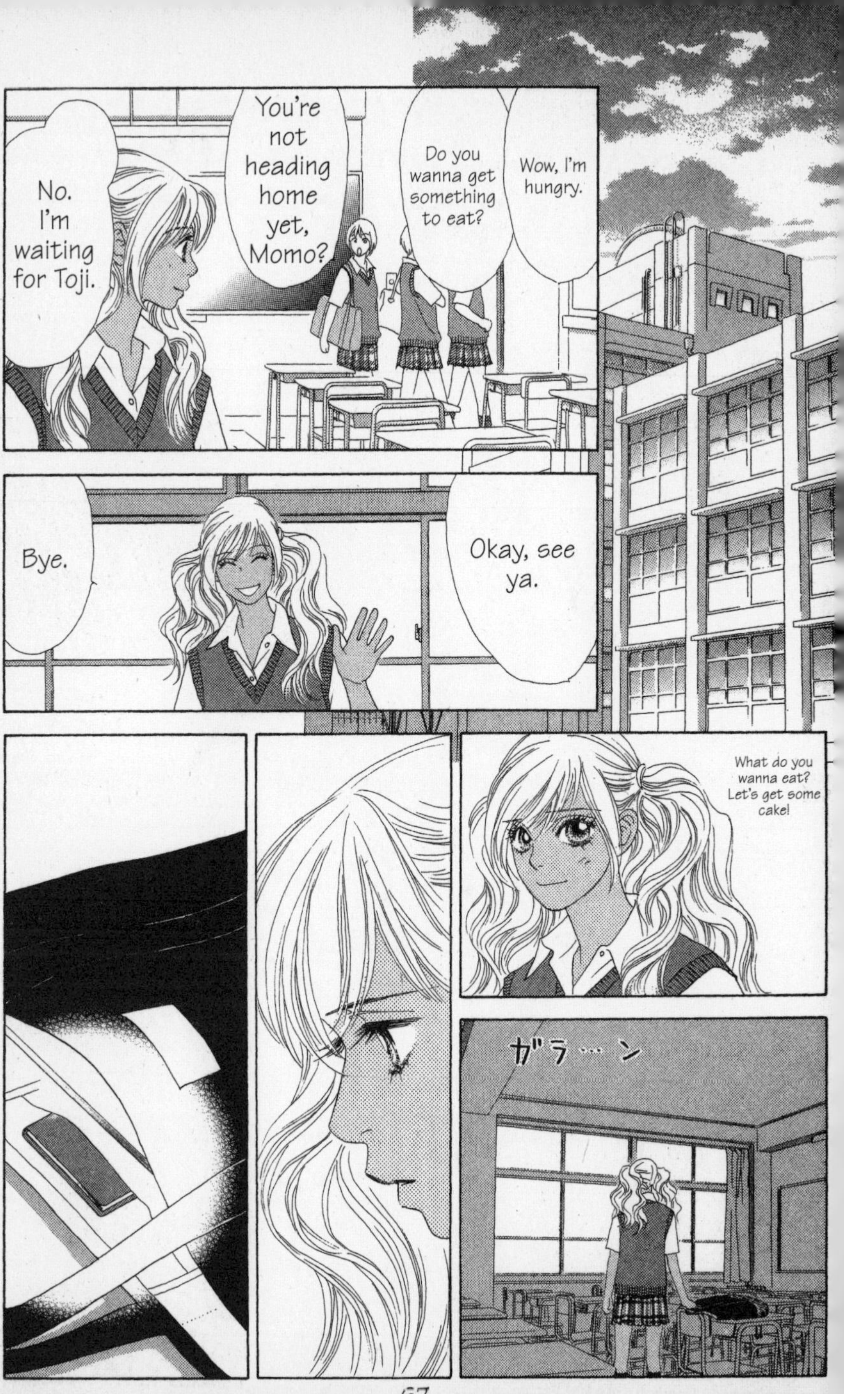
Wow, I'm hungry.
Do you wanna get something to eat?
You're not heading home yet, Momo?
No. I'm waiting for Toji.
Okay, see ya.
Bye.
What do you wanna eat? Let's get some cake!
ガラ…ン

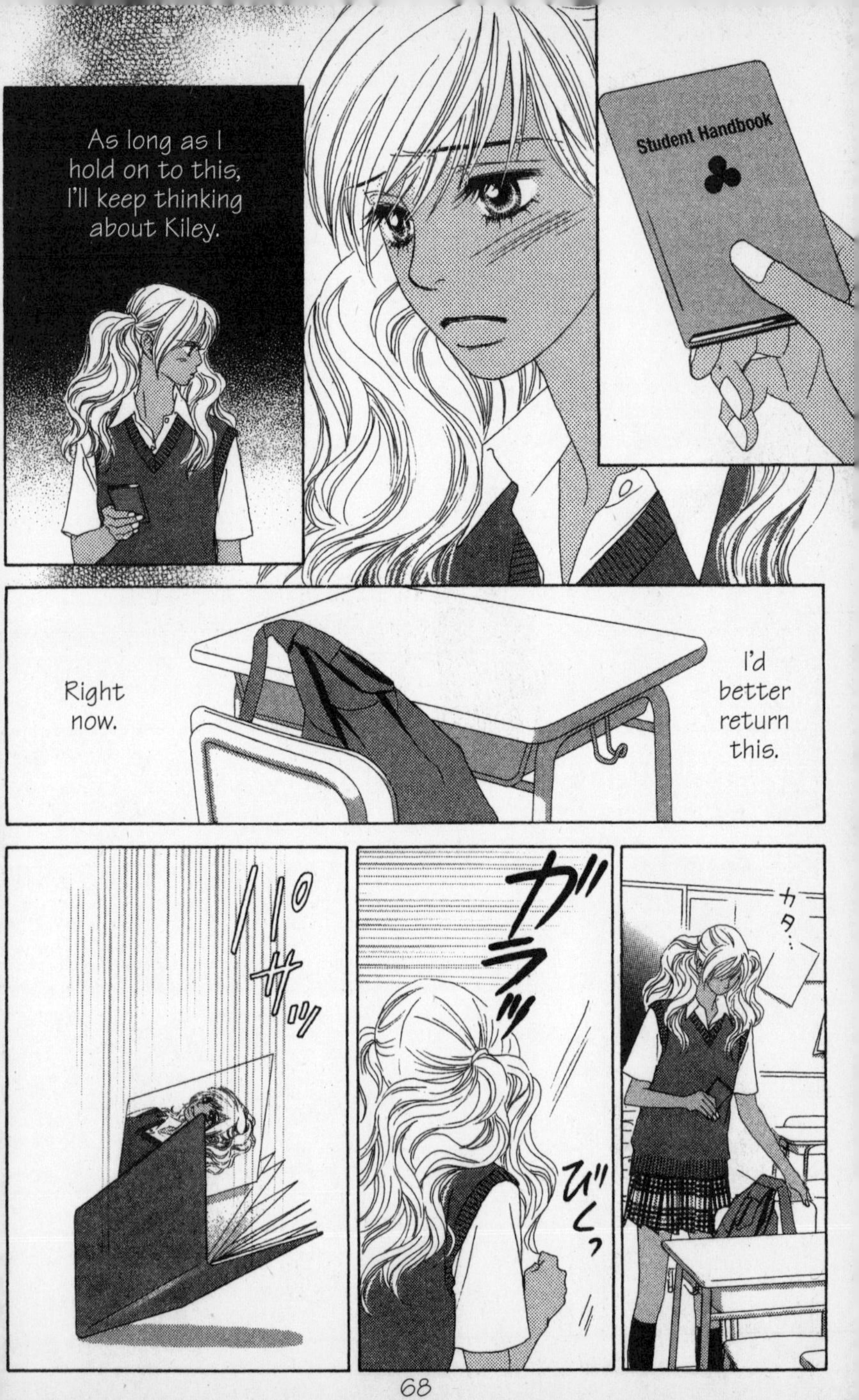
Student Handbook
As long as I hold on to this, I'll keep thinking about Kiley.
I'd better return this.
Right now.
カタ…
ガラッ
びくっ
パサッ

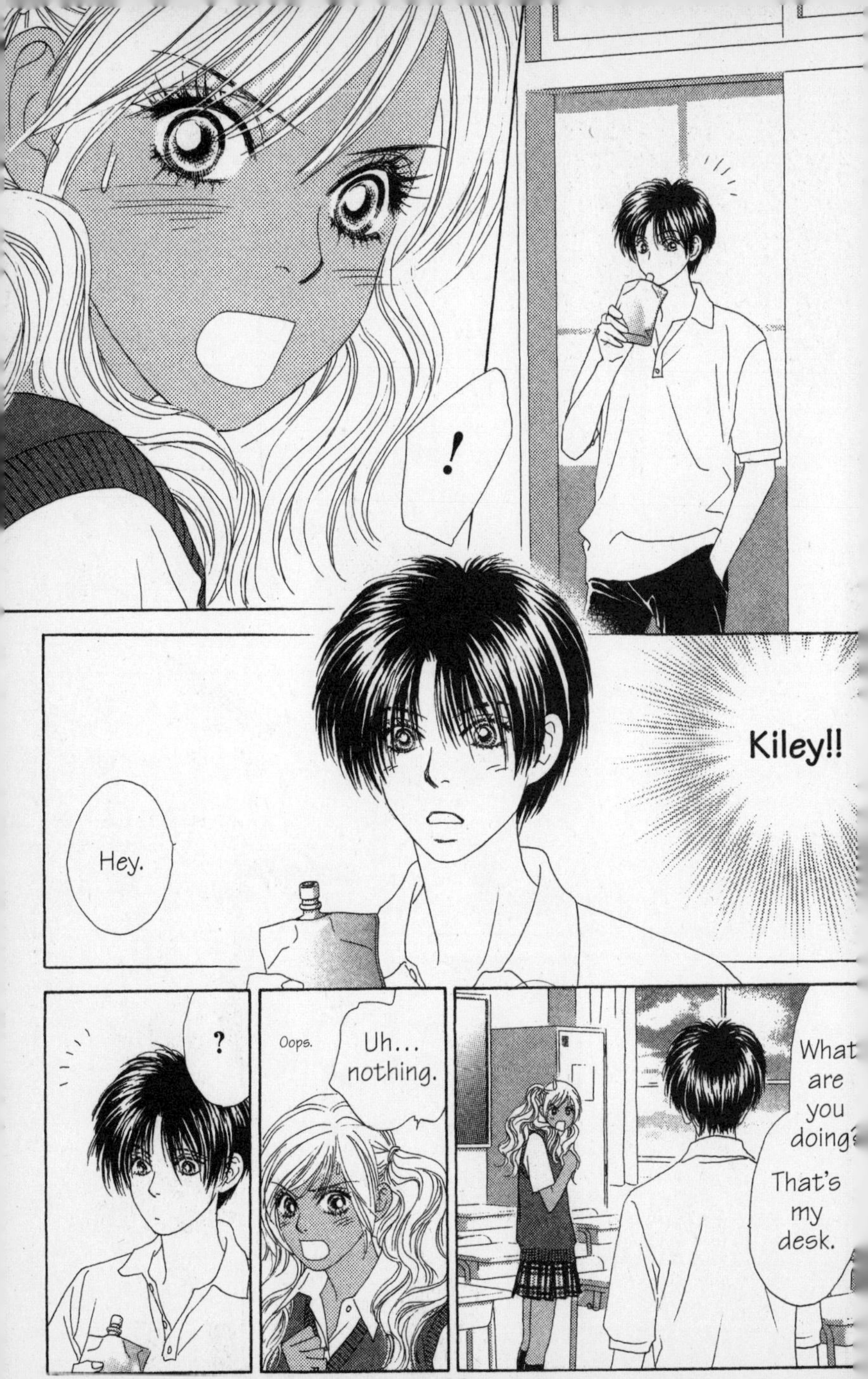
!
Kiley!!
Hey.
What are you doing?
That's my desk.
Uh... nothing.
Oops.
?

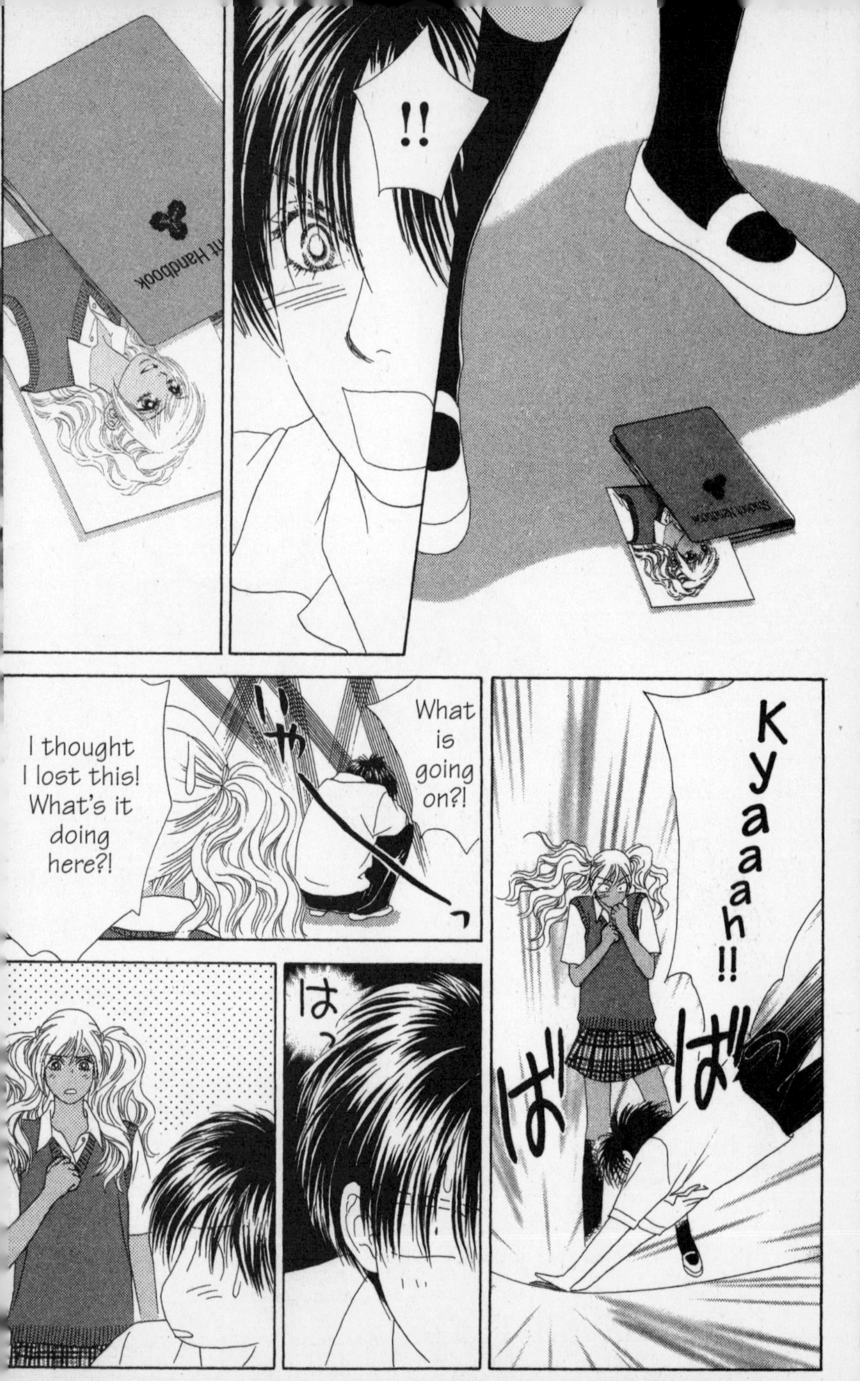
!!
Kyaaah!!
ぱっ ぱっ
いやっ
What is going on?!
I thought I lost this! What's it doing here?!
はっ

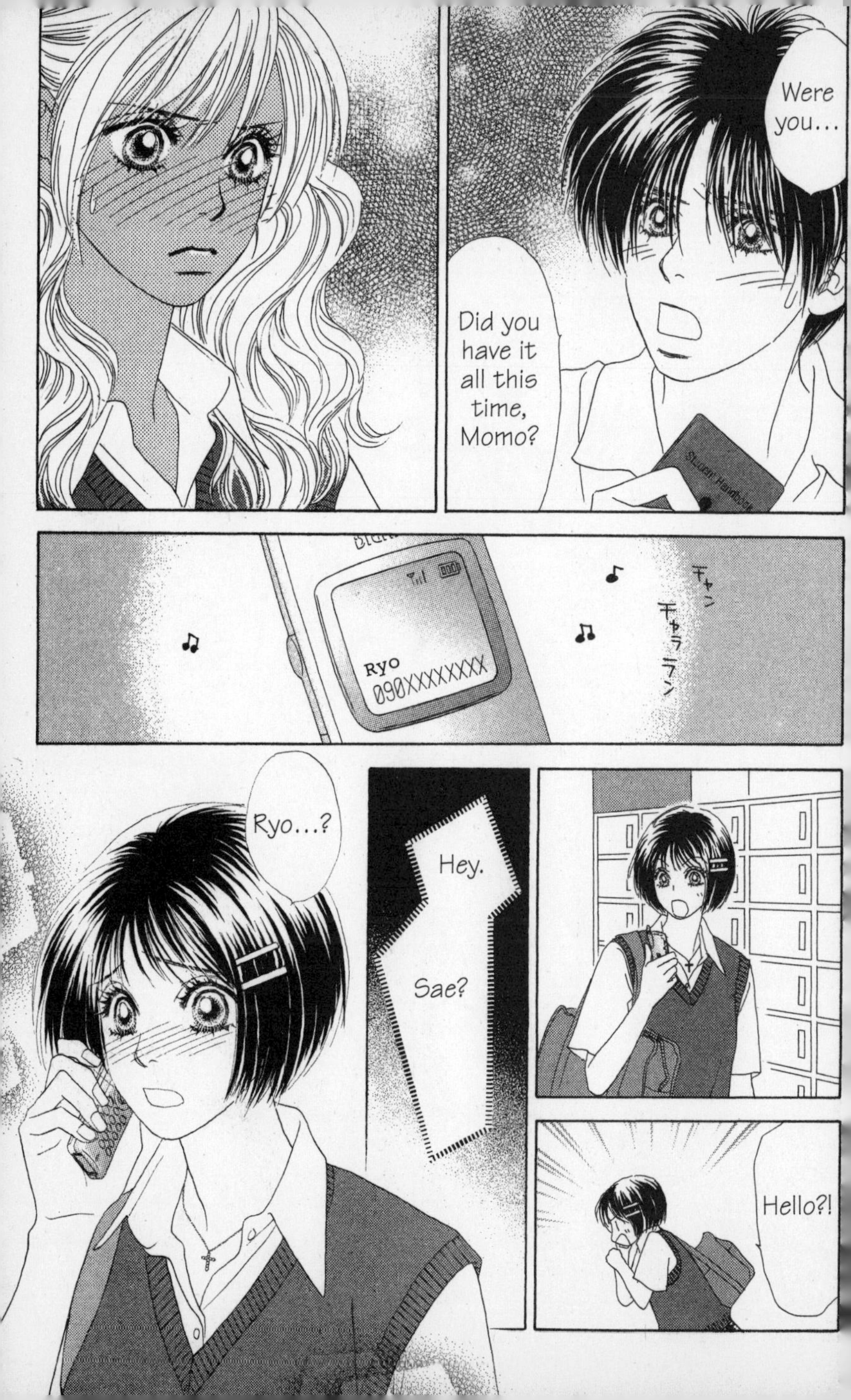
Were you...
Did you have it all this time, Momo?
Student Handbook
Ryo
090XXXXXXXX
チャン
チャラ ラン
Hey.
Sae?
Ryo...?
Hello?!

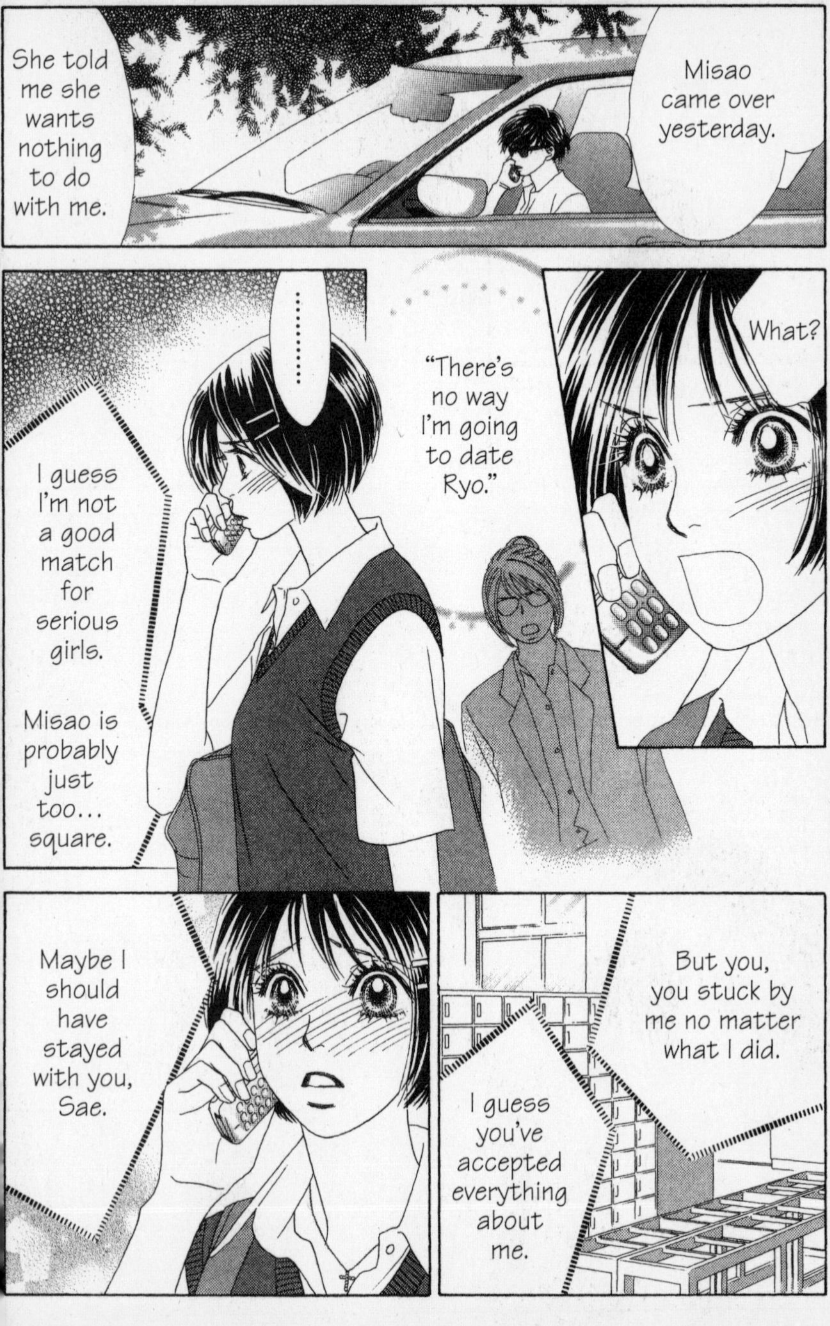
Misao came over yesterday.
She told me she wants nothing to do with me.
What?
"There's no way I'm going to date Ryo."
......
I guess I'm not a good match for serious girls.
Misao is probably just too... square.
But you, you stuck by me no matter what I did.
I guess you've accepted everything about me.
Maybe I should have stayed with you, Sae.

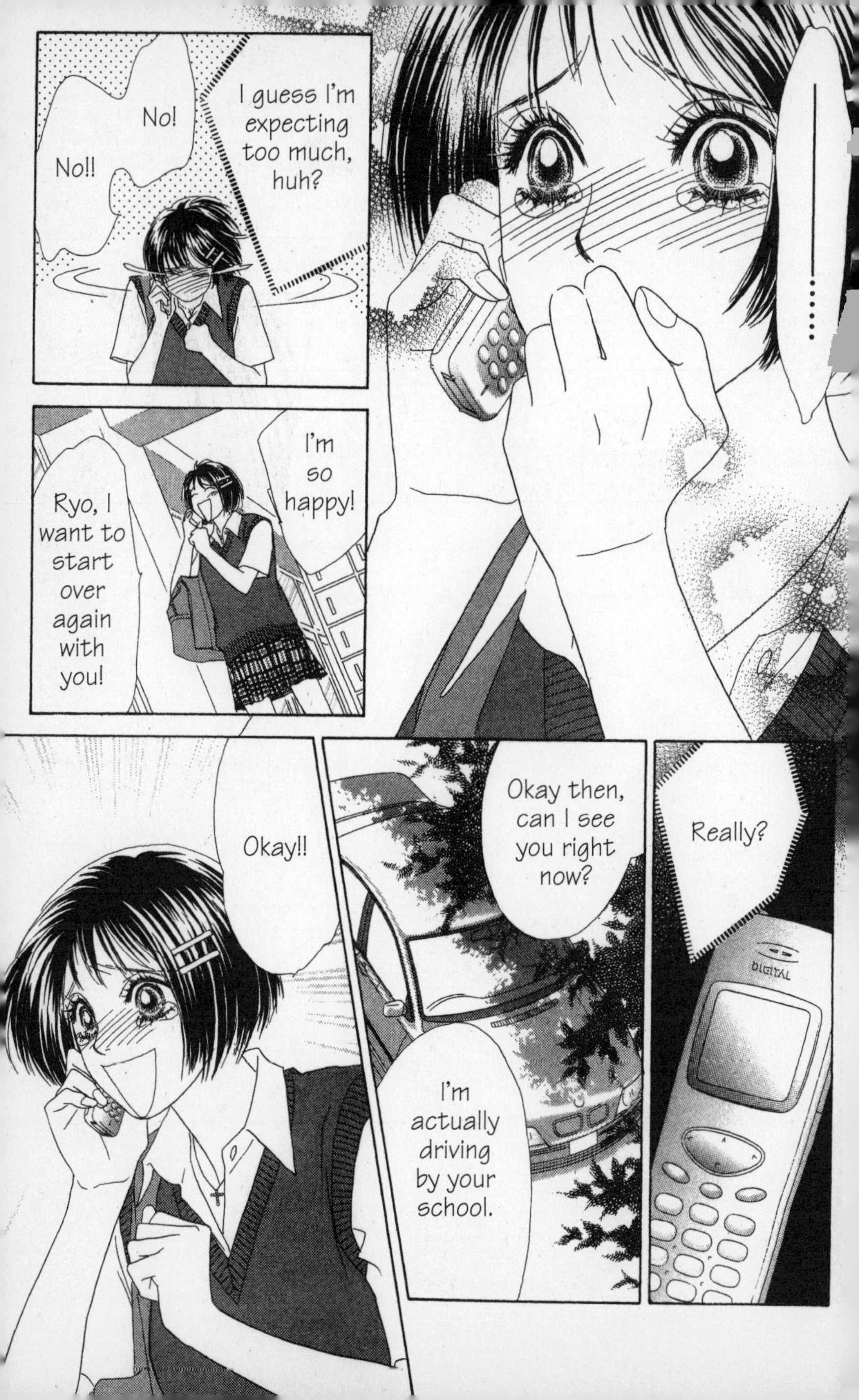
I guess I'm expecting too much, huh?
No!
No!!
I'm so happy!
Ryo, I want to start over again with you!
Really?
DIGITAL
Okay then, can I see you right now?
I'm actually driving by your school.
Okay!!

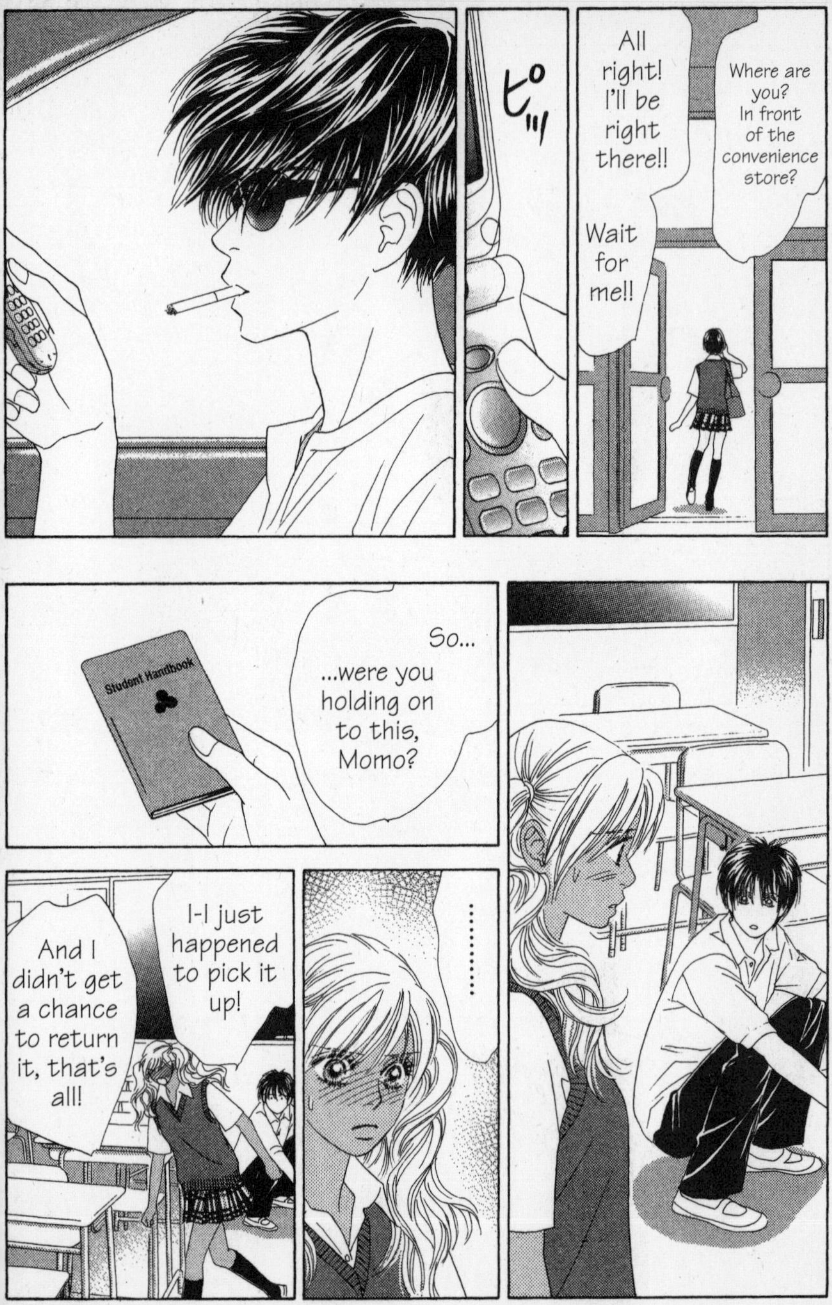
Where are you? In front of the convenience store?
All right! I'll be right there!!
Wait for me!!
ピッ
Student Handbook
So...
...were you holding on to this, Momo?
......
I-I just happened to pick it up!
And I didn't get a chance to return it, that's all!

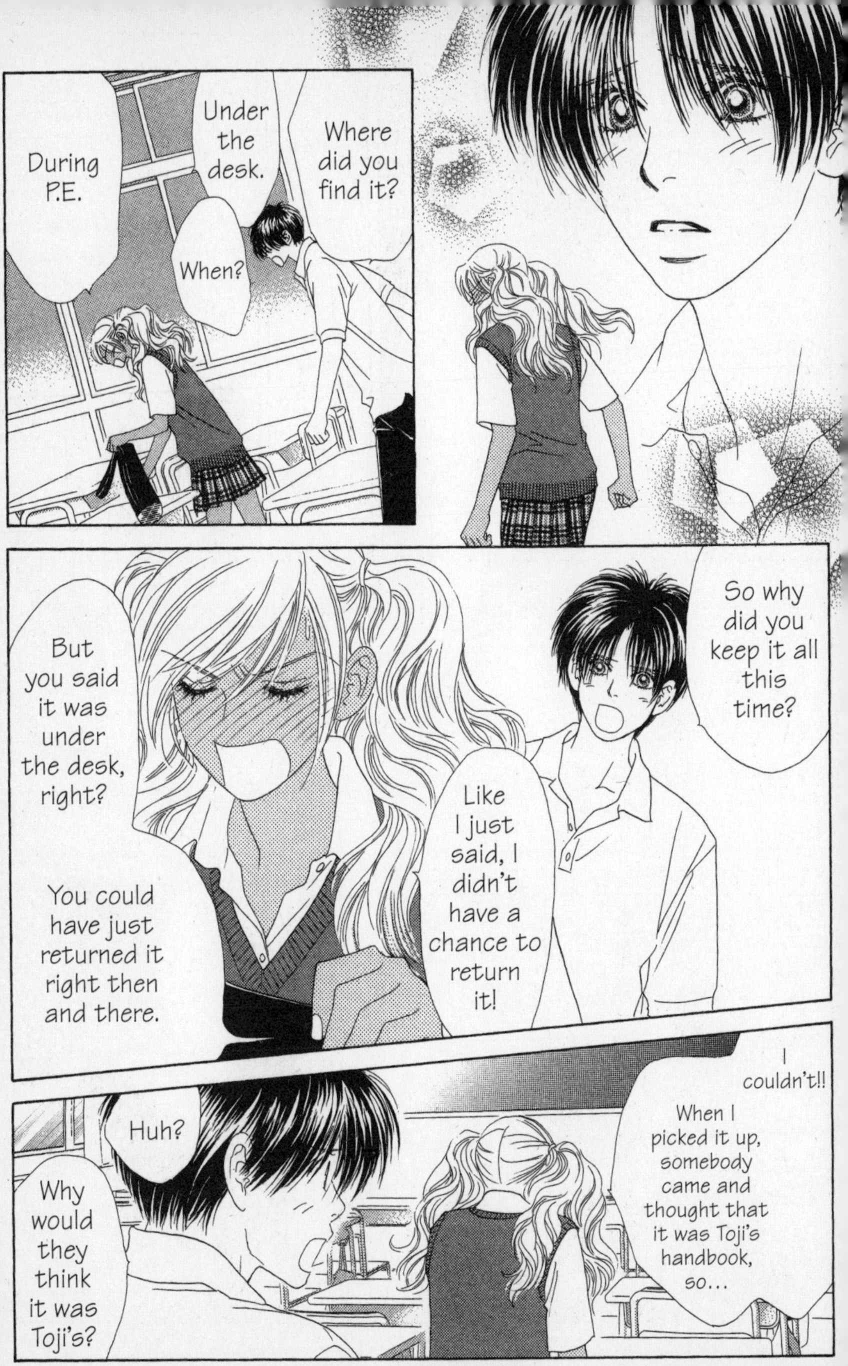
Where did you find it?
Under the desk.
When?
During P.E.
So why did you keep it all this time?
Like I just said, I didn't have a chance to return it!
But you said it was under the desk, right?
You could have just returned it right then and there.
I couldn't!!
When I picked it up, somebody came and thought that it was Toji's handbook, so...
Huh?
Why would they think it was Toji's?

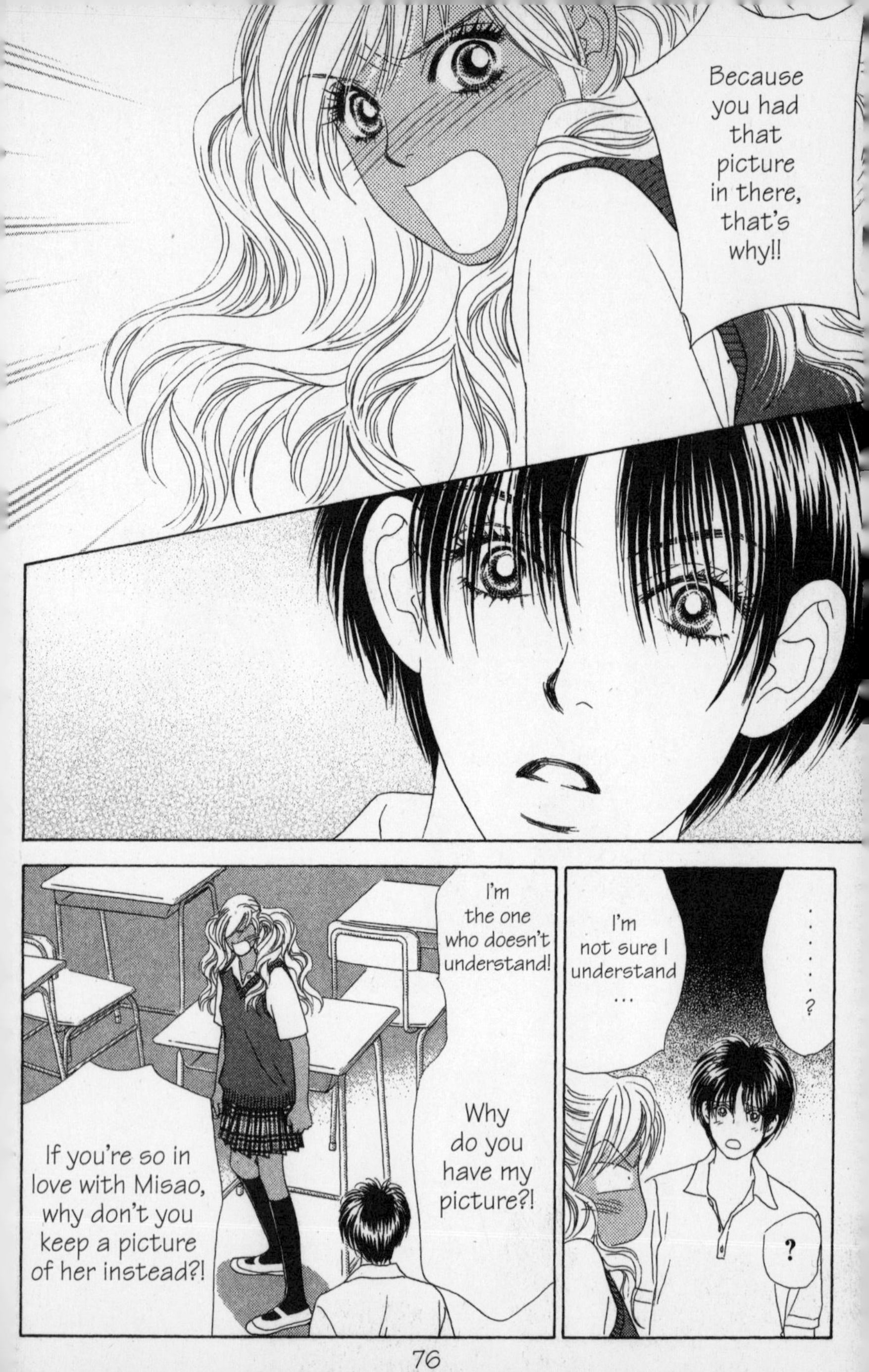
Because you had that picture in there, that's why!!
. . . . . . ?
I'm not sure I understand . . .
?
I'm the one who doesn't understand!
Why do you have my picture?!
If you're so in love with Misao, why don't you keep a picture of her instead?!

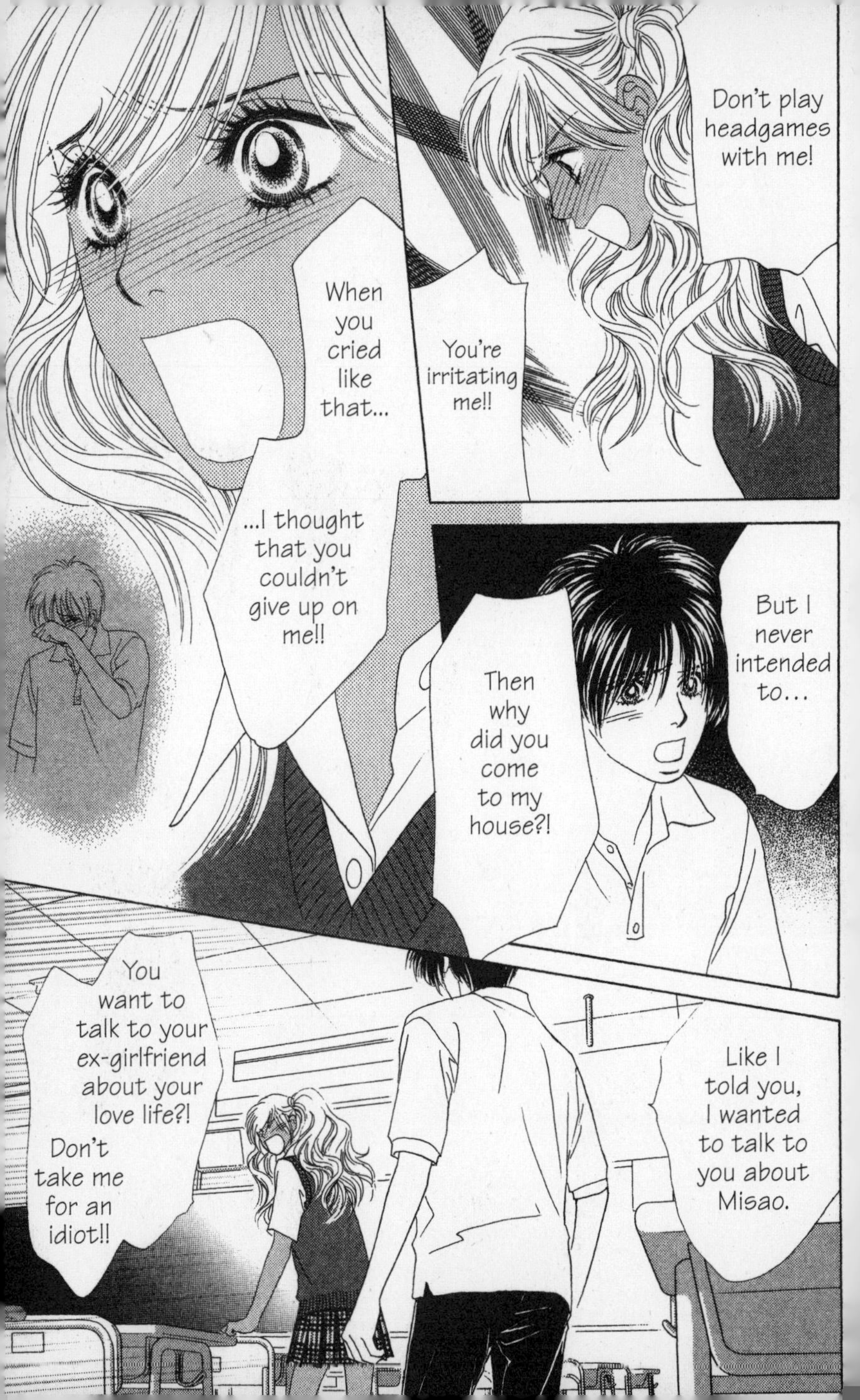
Don't play headgames with me!
You're irritating me!!
But I never intended to…
Then why did you come to my house?!
When you cried like that...
...I thought that you couldn't give up on me!!
Like I told you, I wanted to talk to you about Misao.
You want to talk to your ex-girlfriend about your love life?!
Don't take me for an idiot!!

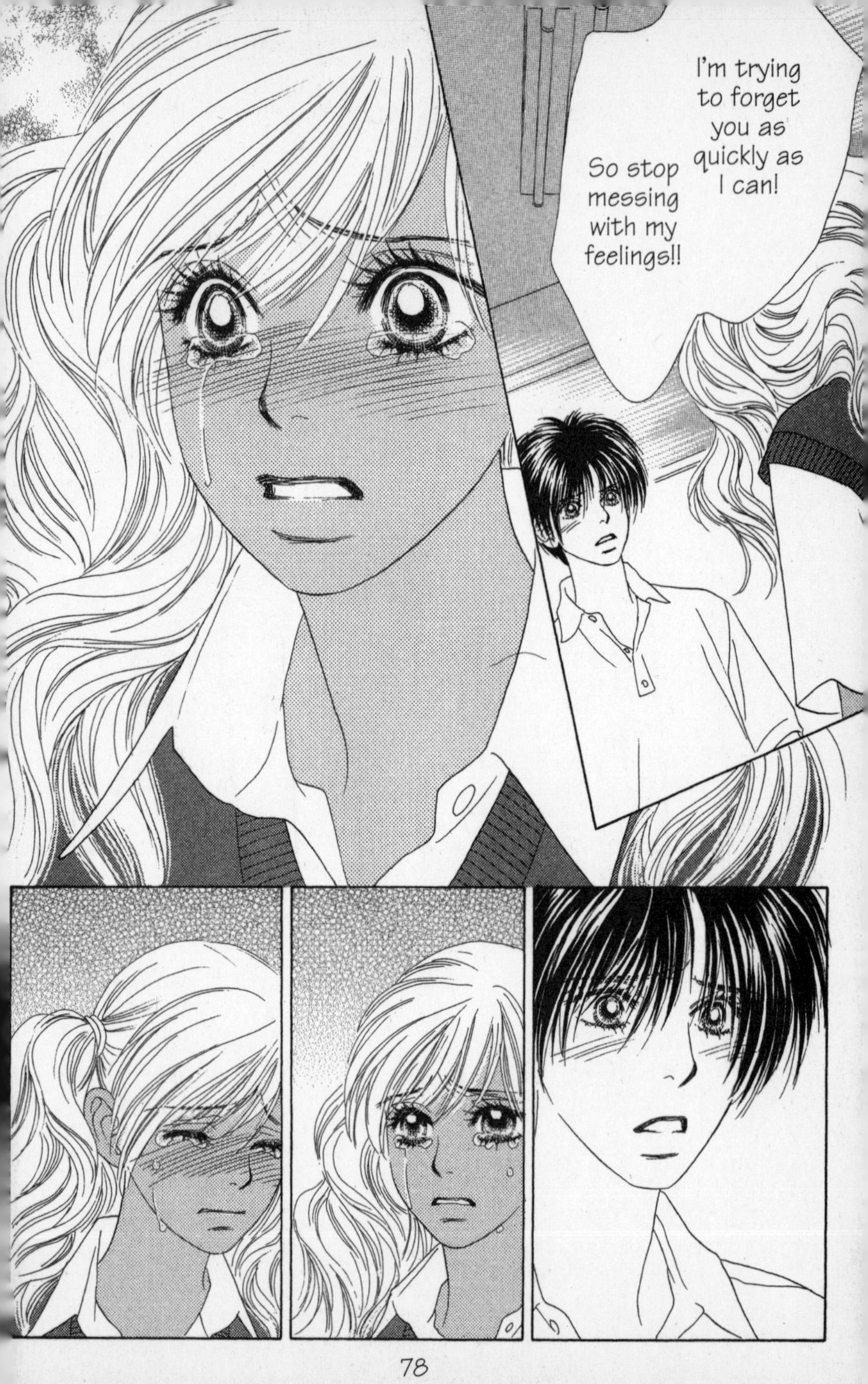
I'm trying to forget you as quickly as I can!
So stop messing with my feelings!!

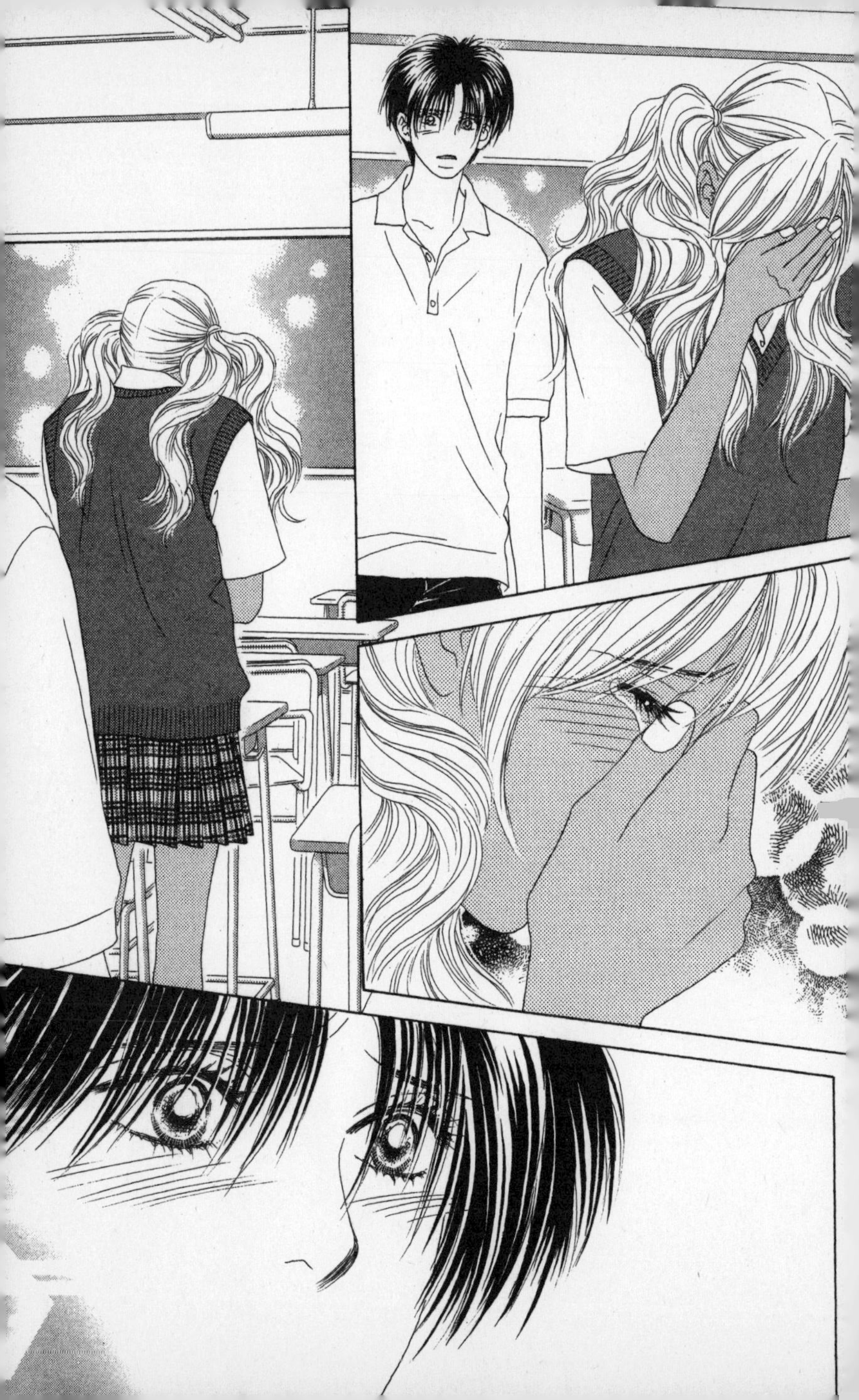

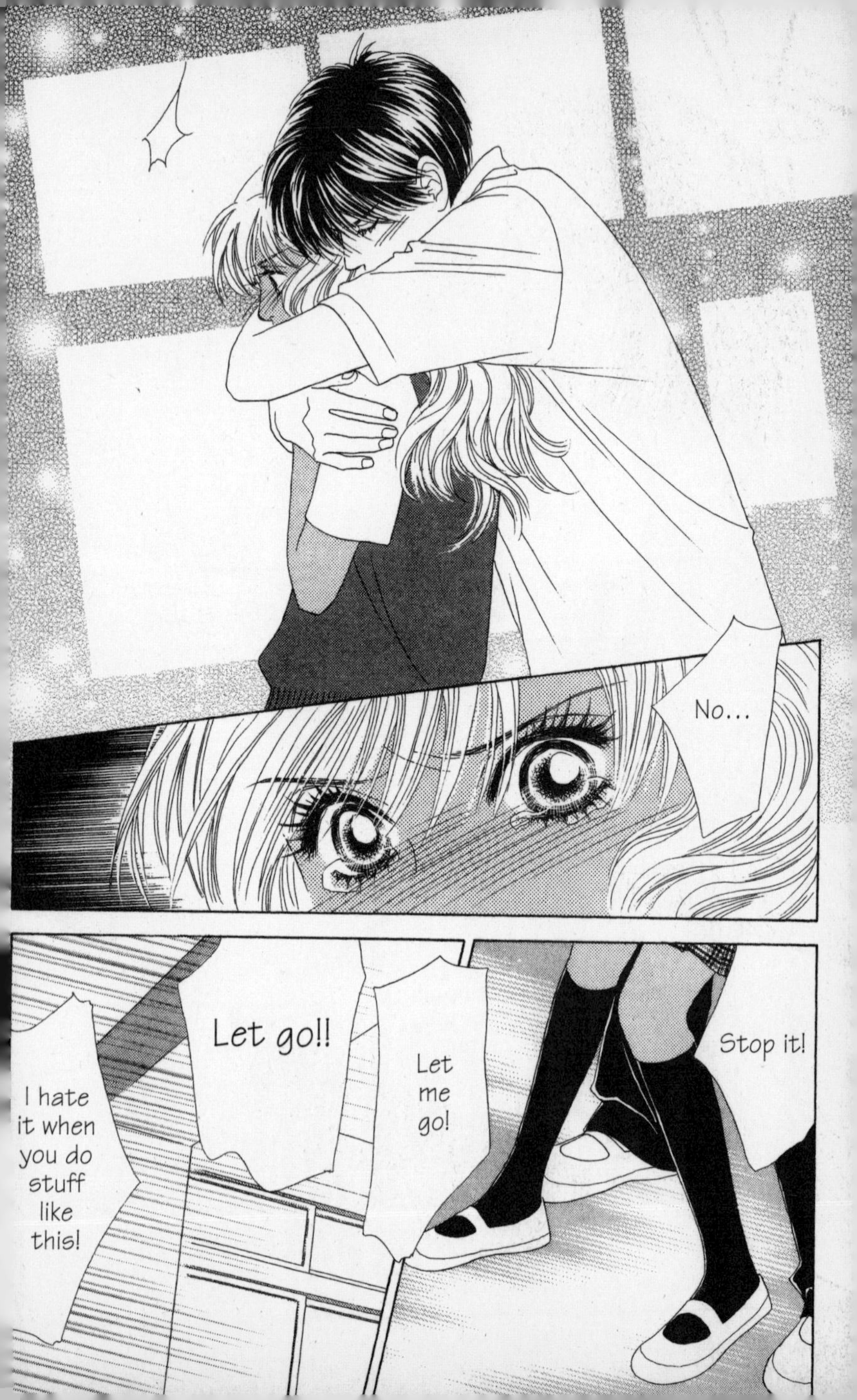
No...
Stop it!
Let me go!
Let go!!
I hate it when you do stuff like this!

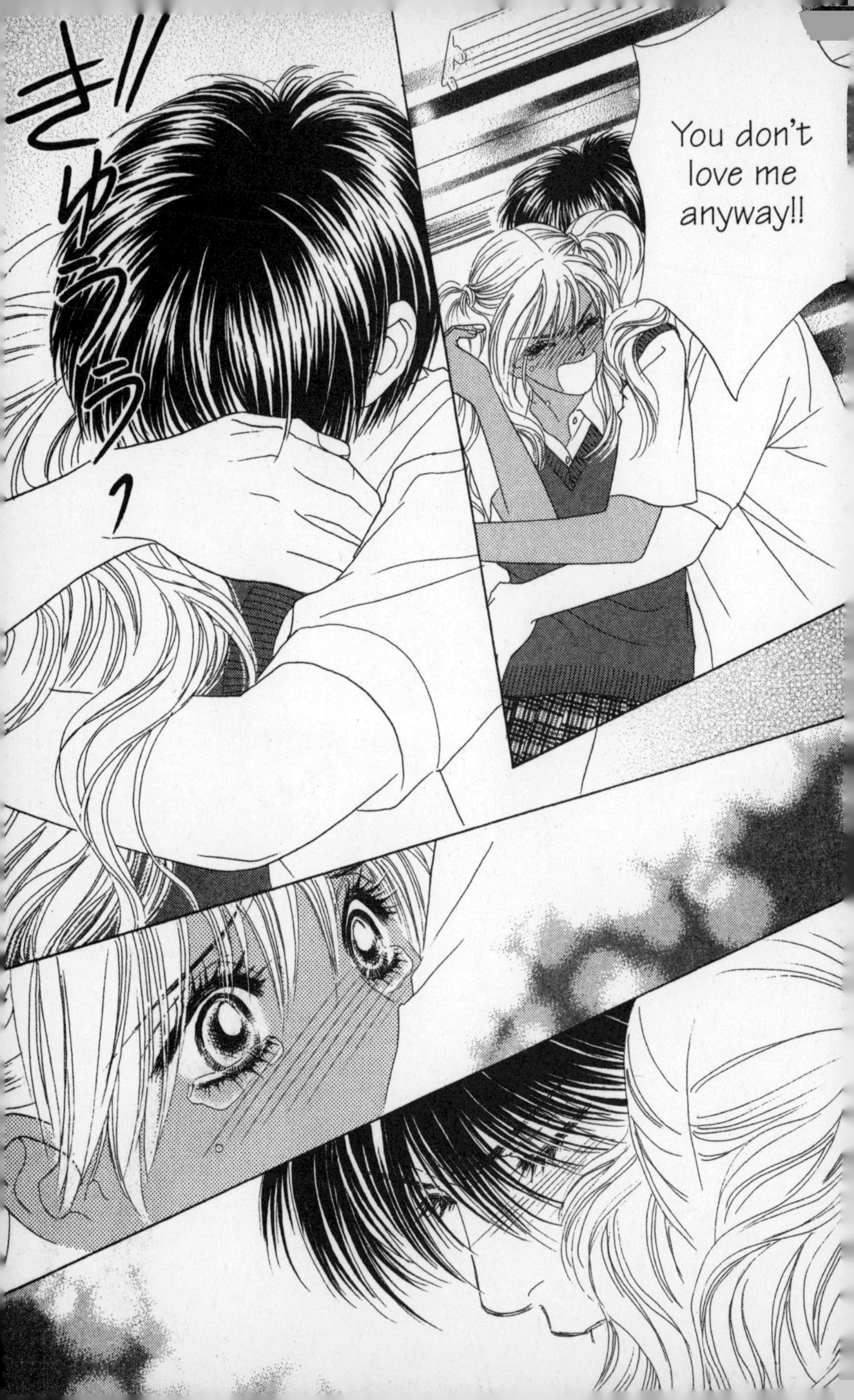
You don't love me anyway!!
ぎゅうう

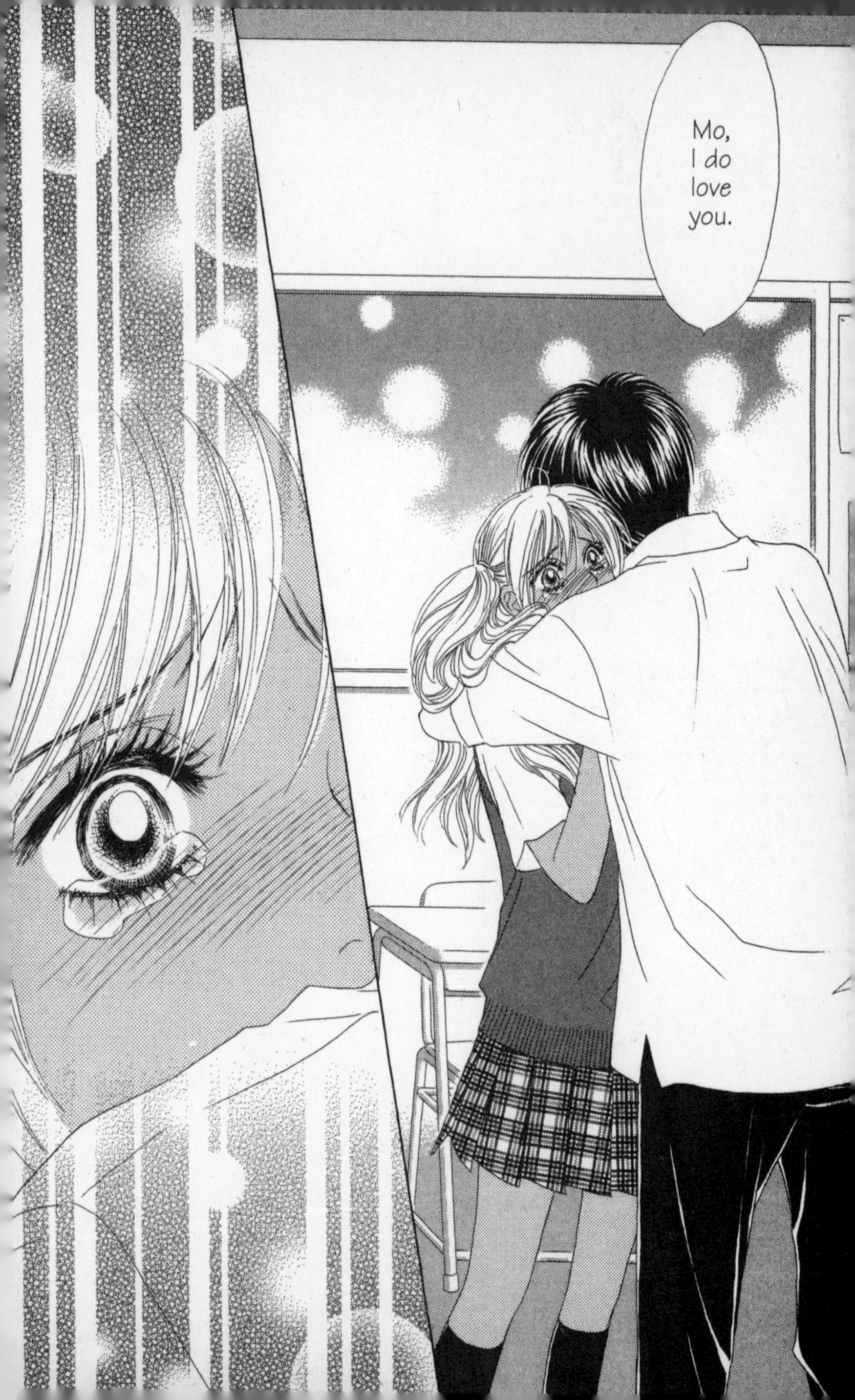
Mo, I do love you.

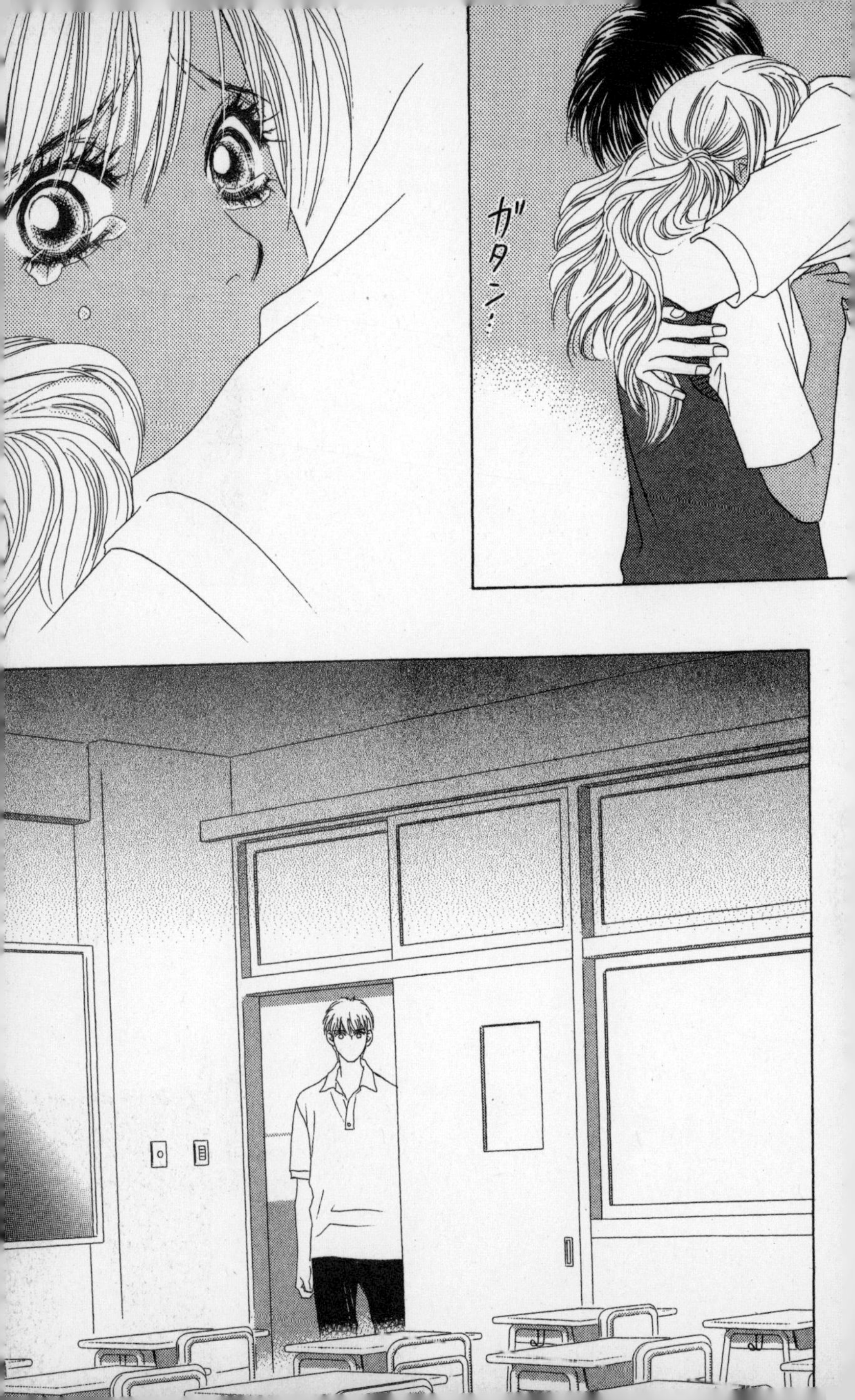
ガタン…

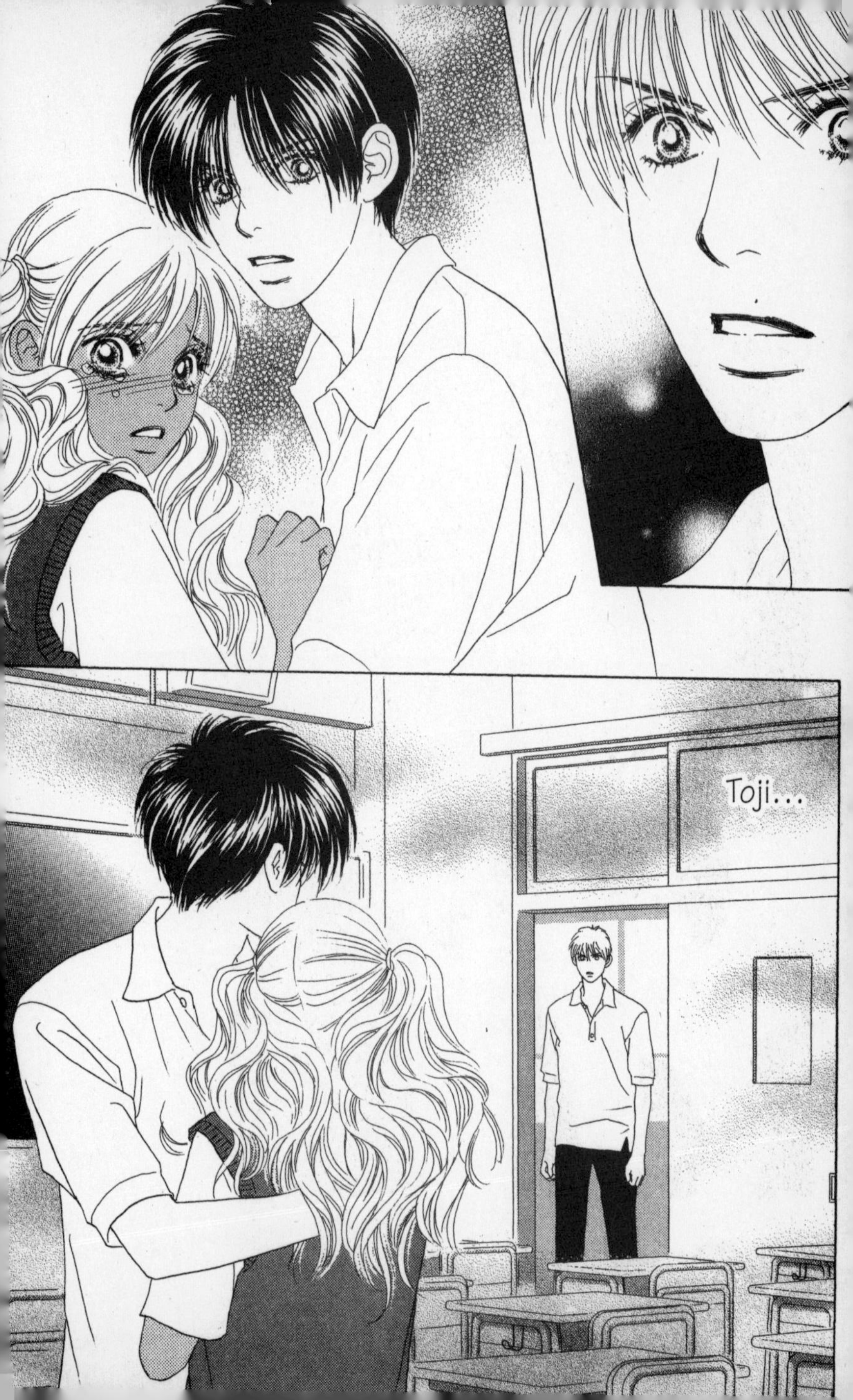
Toji...

ピーチガール

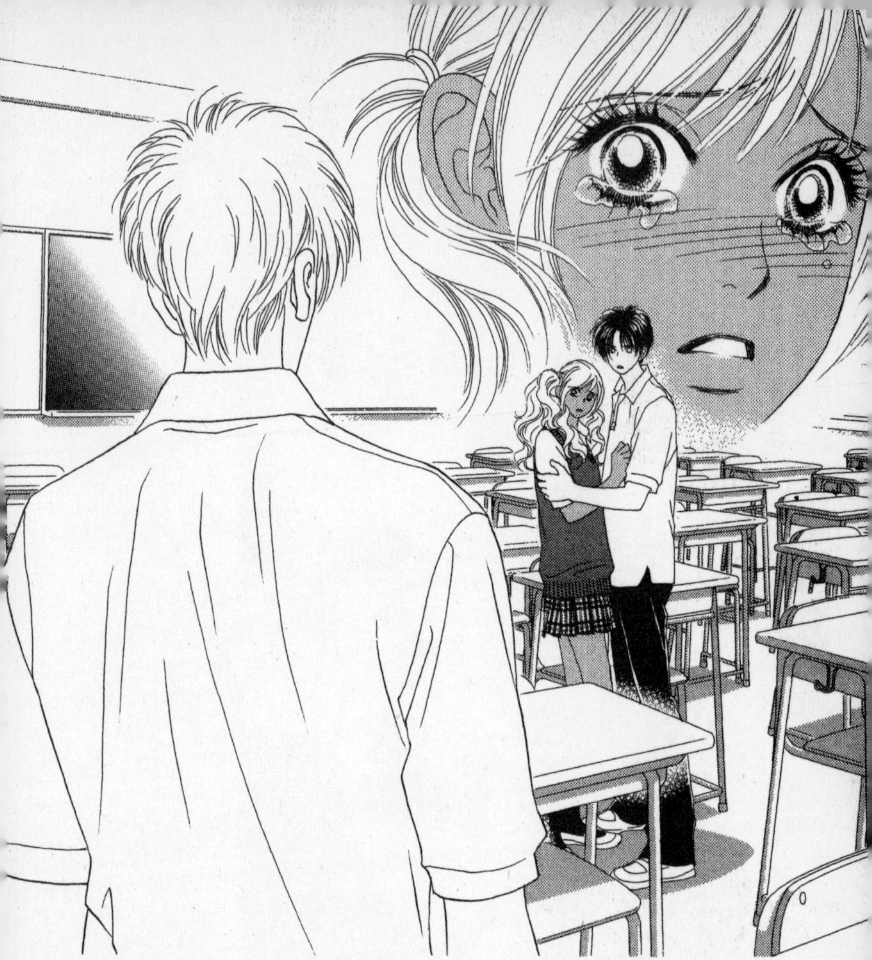

PEACH CLUB

I get sweaty very easily, so I have a hard time during summer, but I love fireworks and summer festivals. I get all giddy from them. These days, whenever festival season rolls around, I start to see young girls wearing their yukatas. It's always nice to see girls with their hair up, wearing colorful yukatas and walking around. It's totally a summer-in-Japan thing. Every year, I miss out on buying a yukata, but this time I went shopping early and got one—black with a lily pattern and very chic! I was all happy and wore it to go see the fireworks, but then it rained. A total downpour!! My yukata got so muddy! Ugh! But bravo to the city of Kameoka for going on with the fireworks display even through the rain!! It was a wonderful show! --Miwa

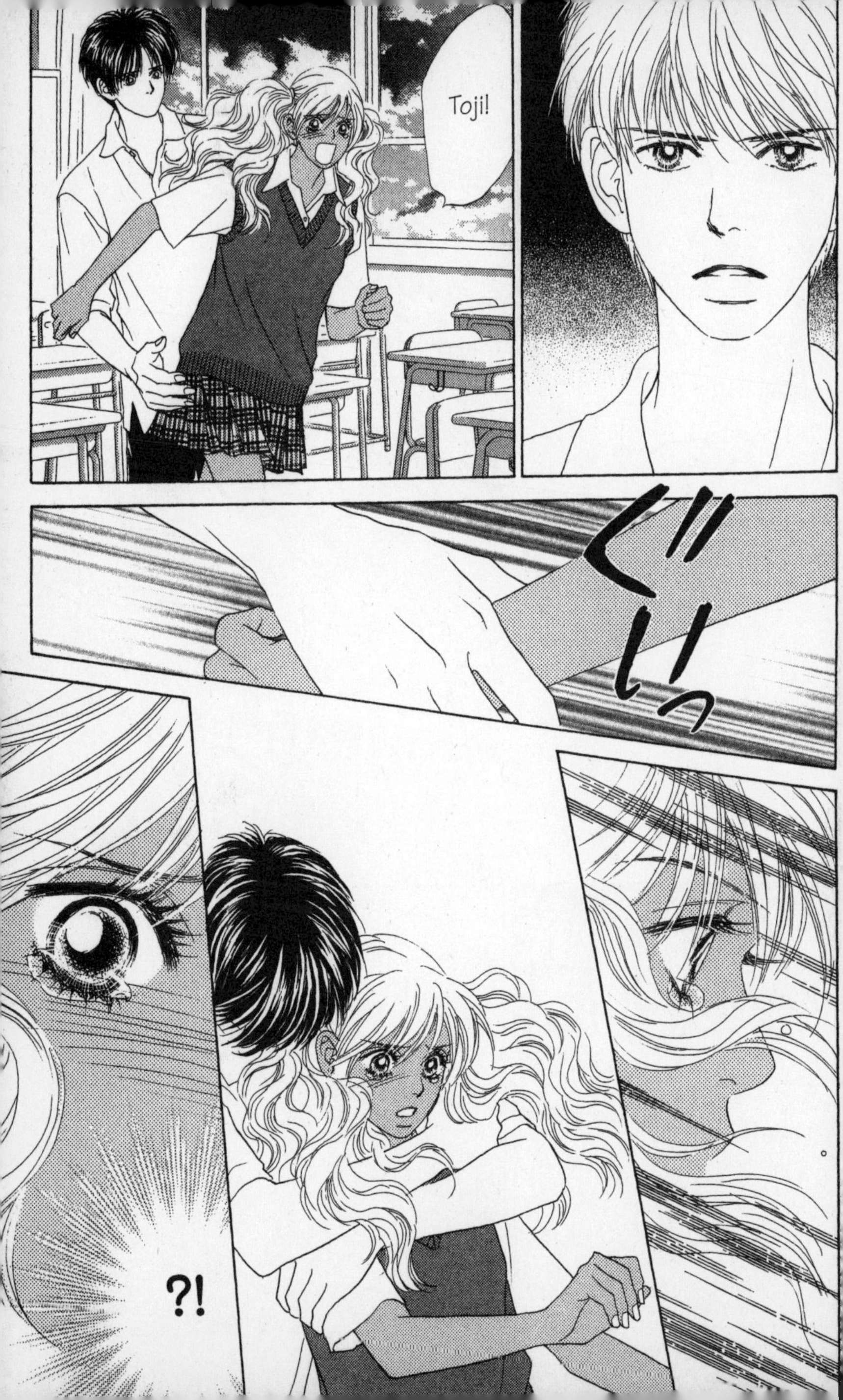
Toji!
ぐいっ
?!

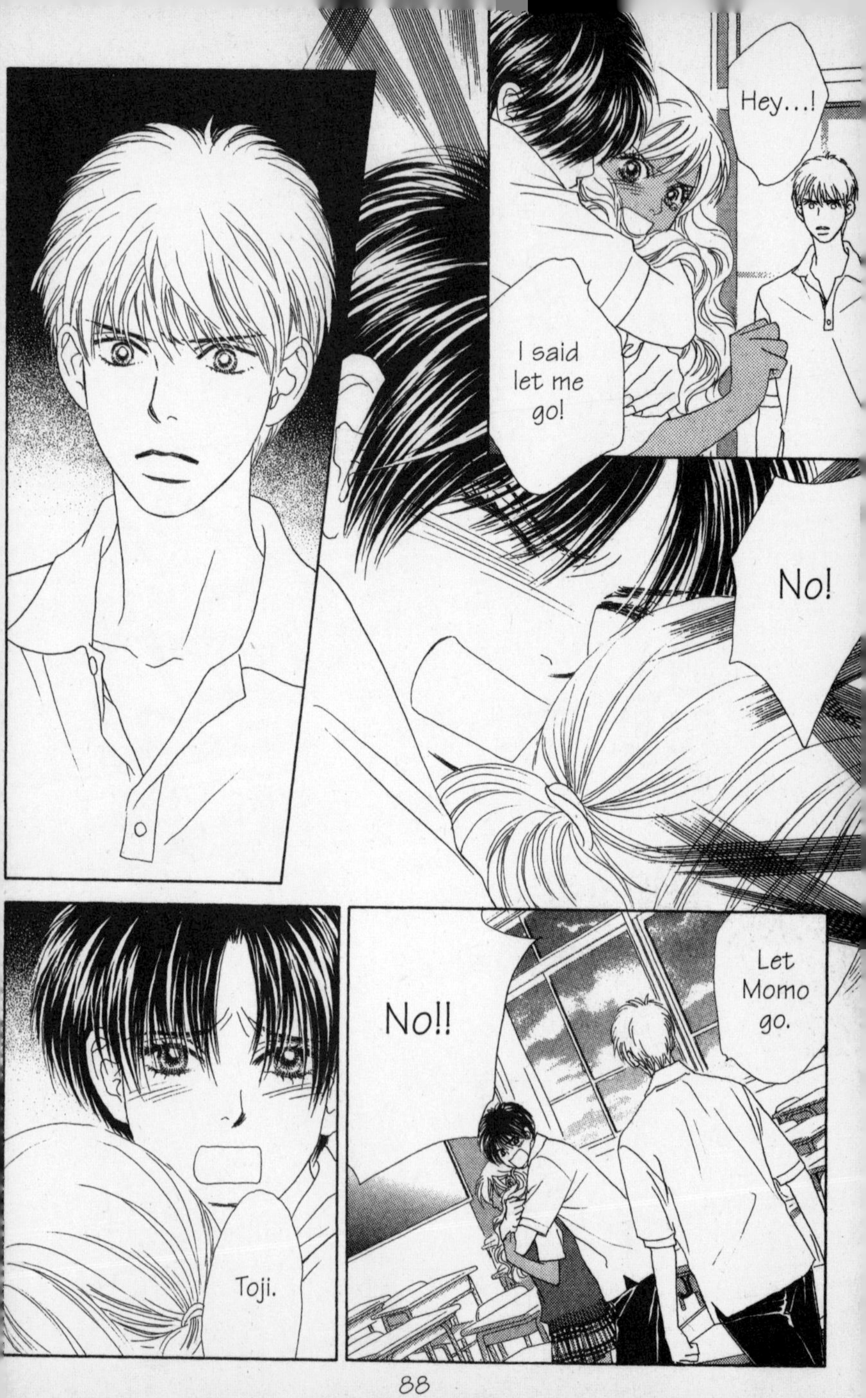
Hey...!
I said let me go!
No!
Let Momo go.
No!!
Toji.

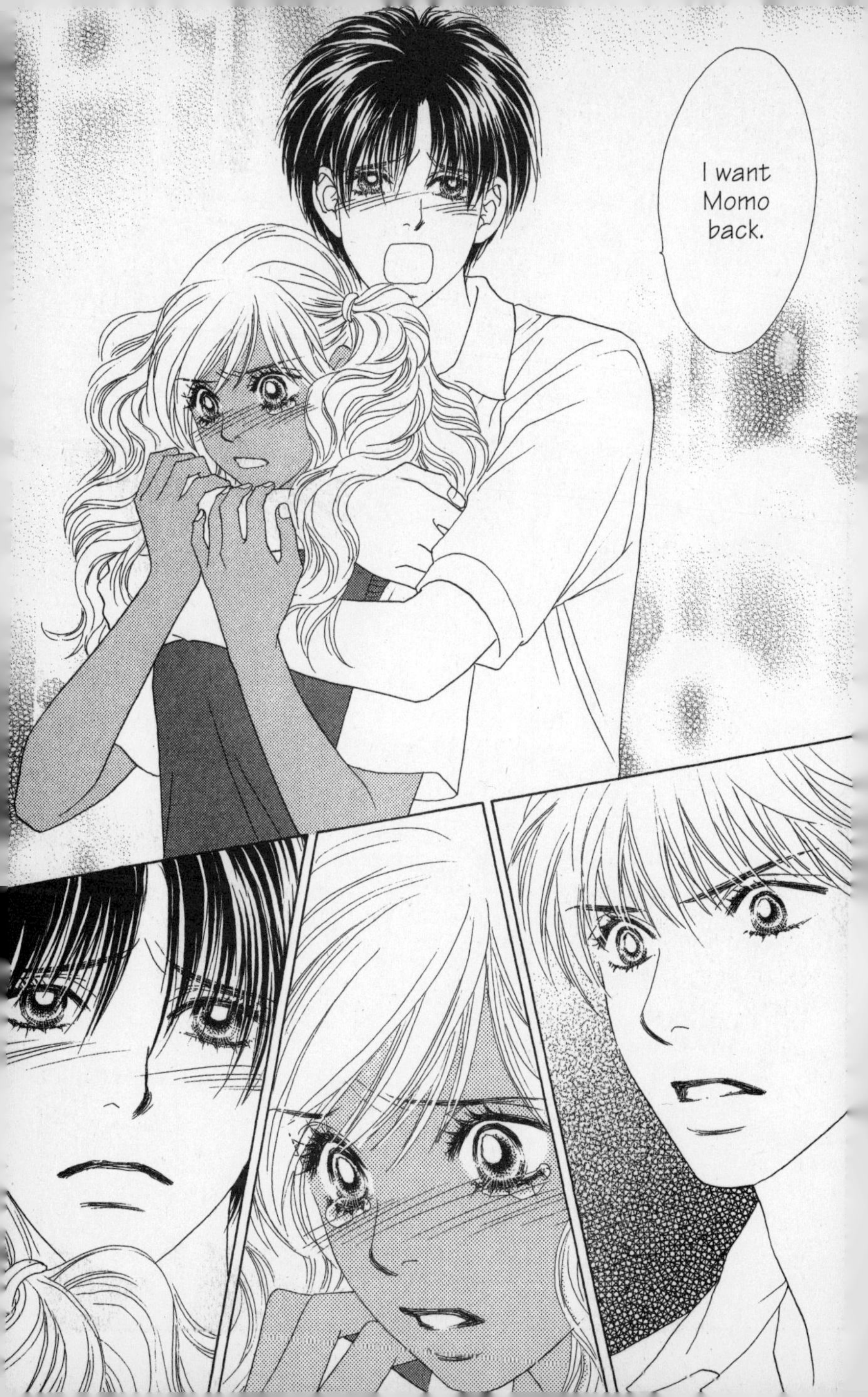
I want Momo back.

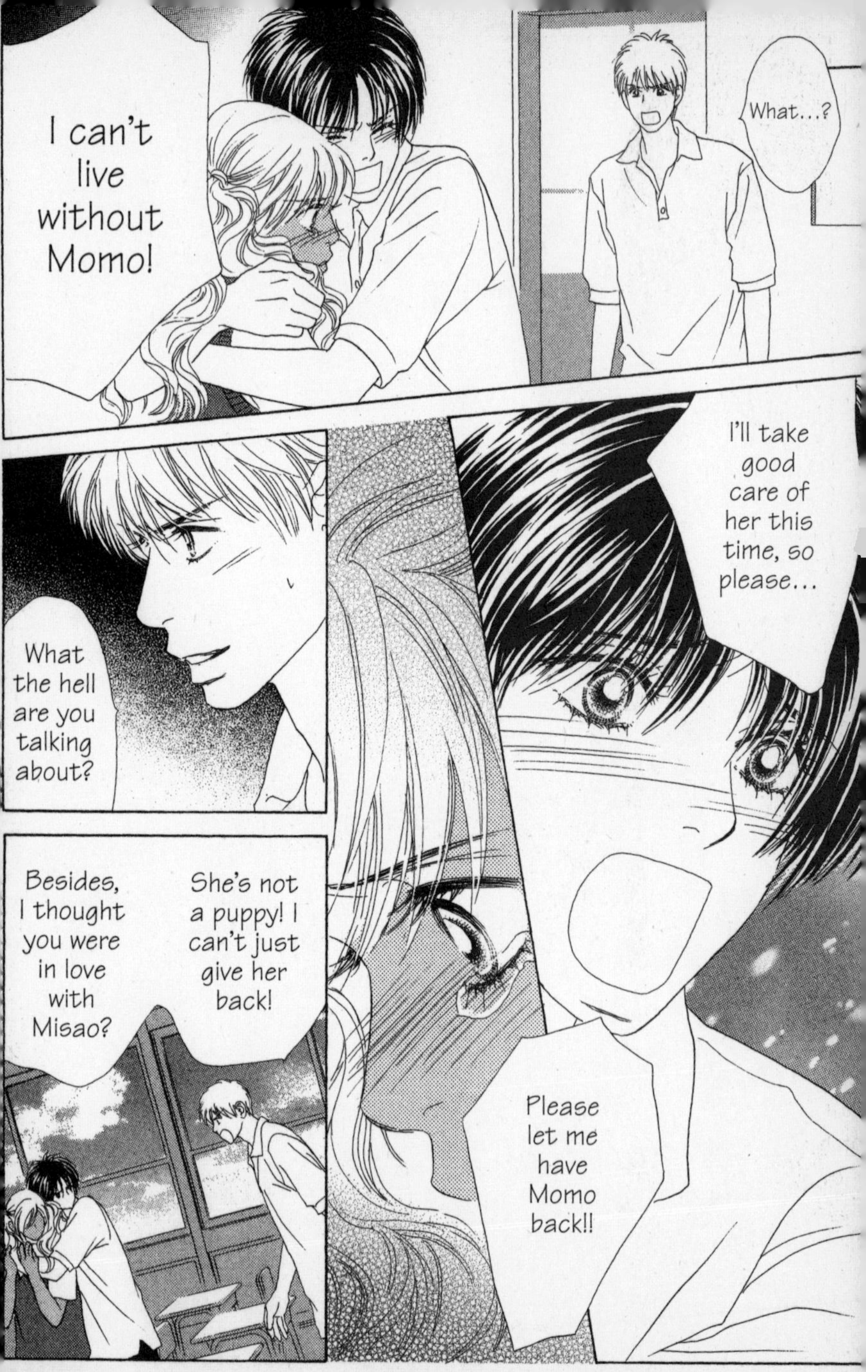
What...?
I can't live without Momo!
I'll take good care of her this time, so please...
Please let me have Momo back!!
What the hell are you talking about?
She's not a puppy! I can't just give her back!
Besides, I thought you were in love with Misao?

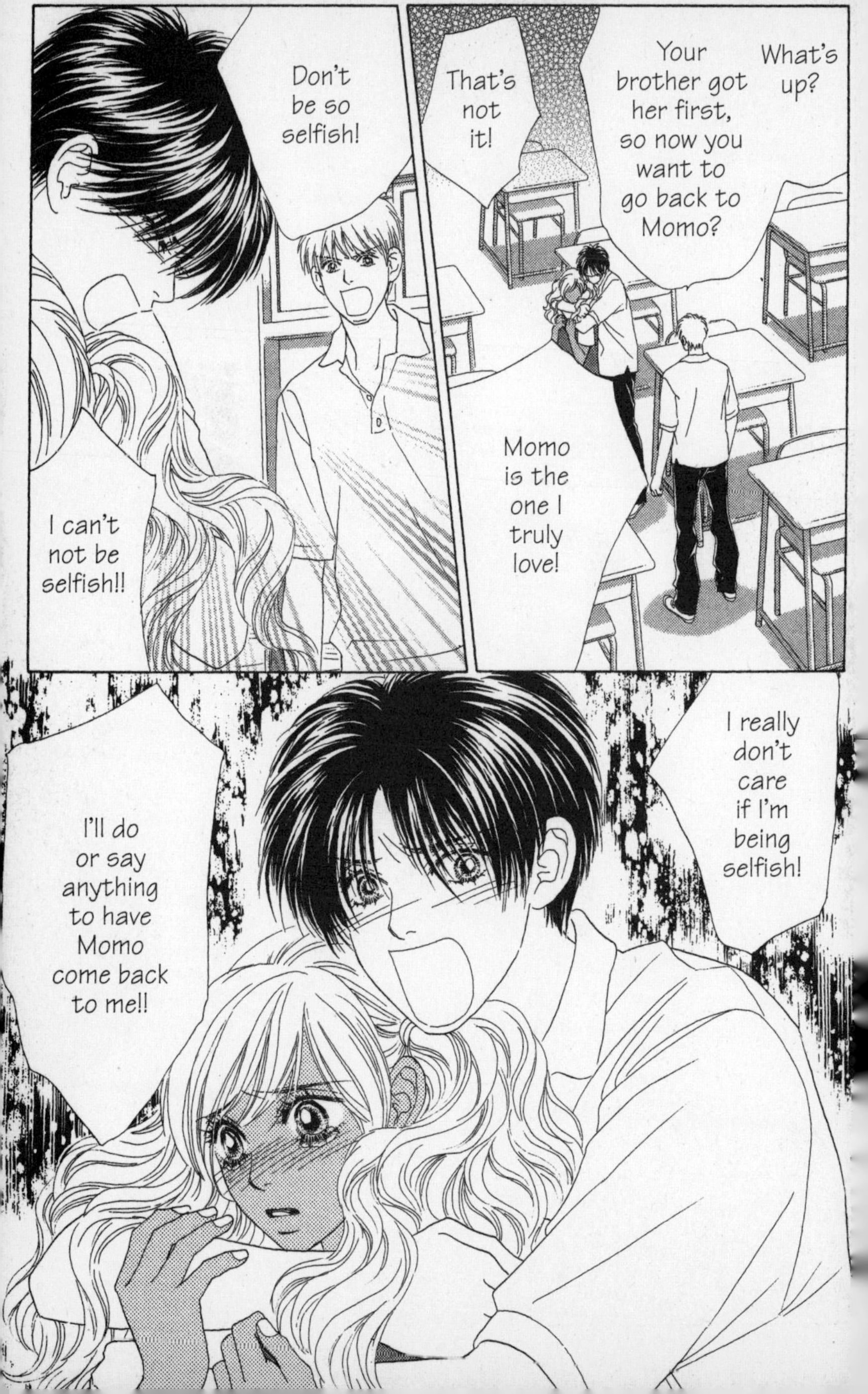
What's up?
Your brother got her first, so now you want to go back to Momo?
That's not it!
Momo is the one I truly love!
Don't be so selfish!
I can't not be selfish!!
I really don't care if I'm being selfish!
I'll do or say anything to have Momo come back to me!!

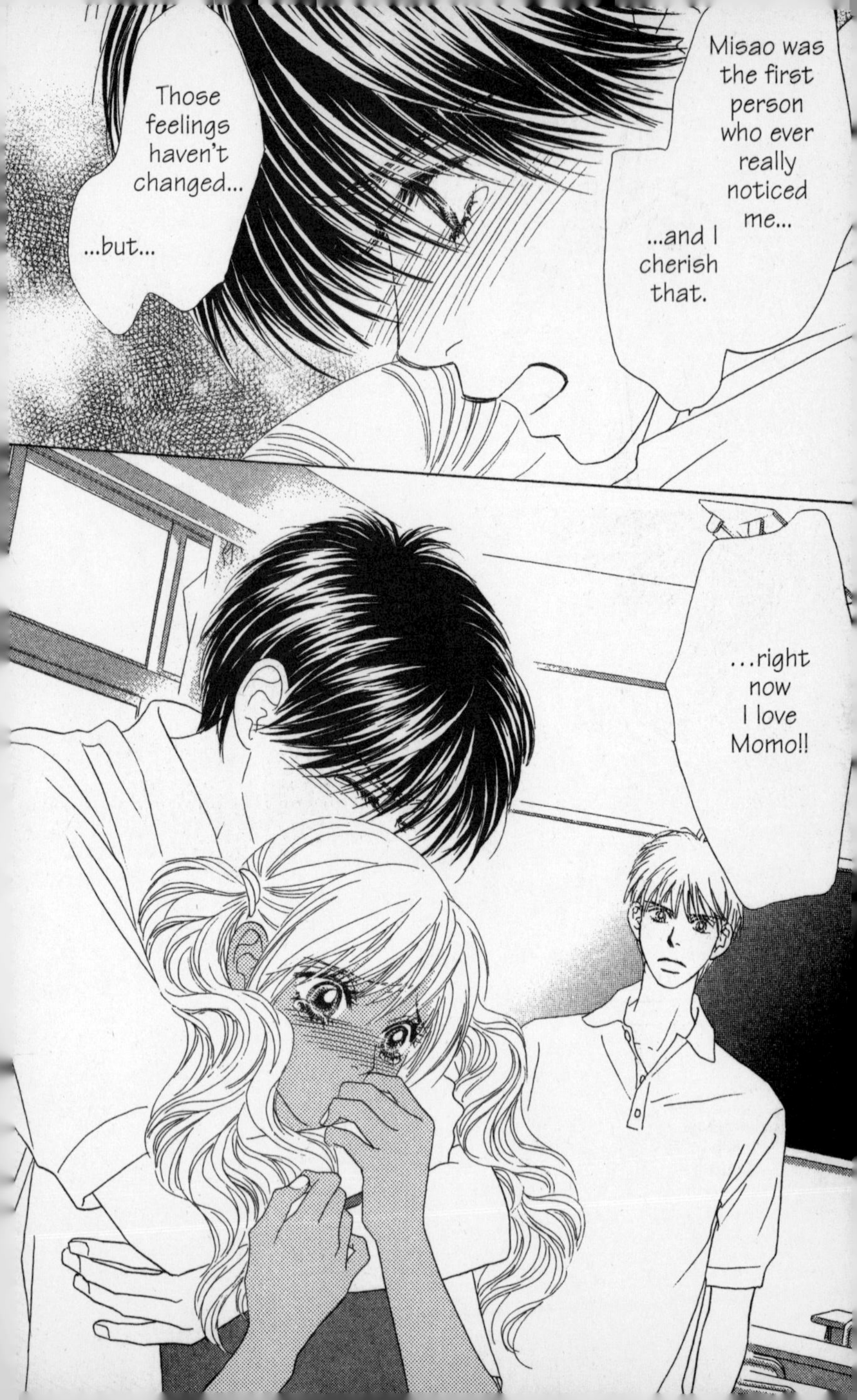
Misao was the first person who ever really noticed me...
...and I cherish that.
Those feelings haven't changed...
...but...
...right now I love Momo!!

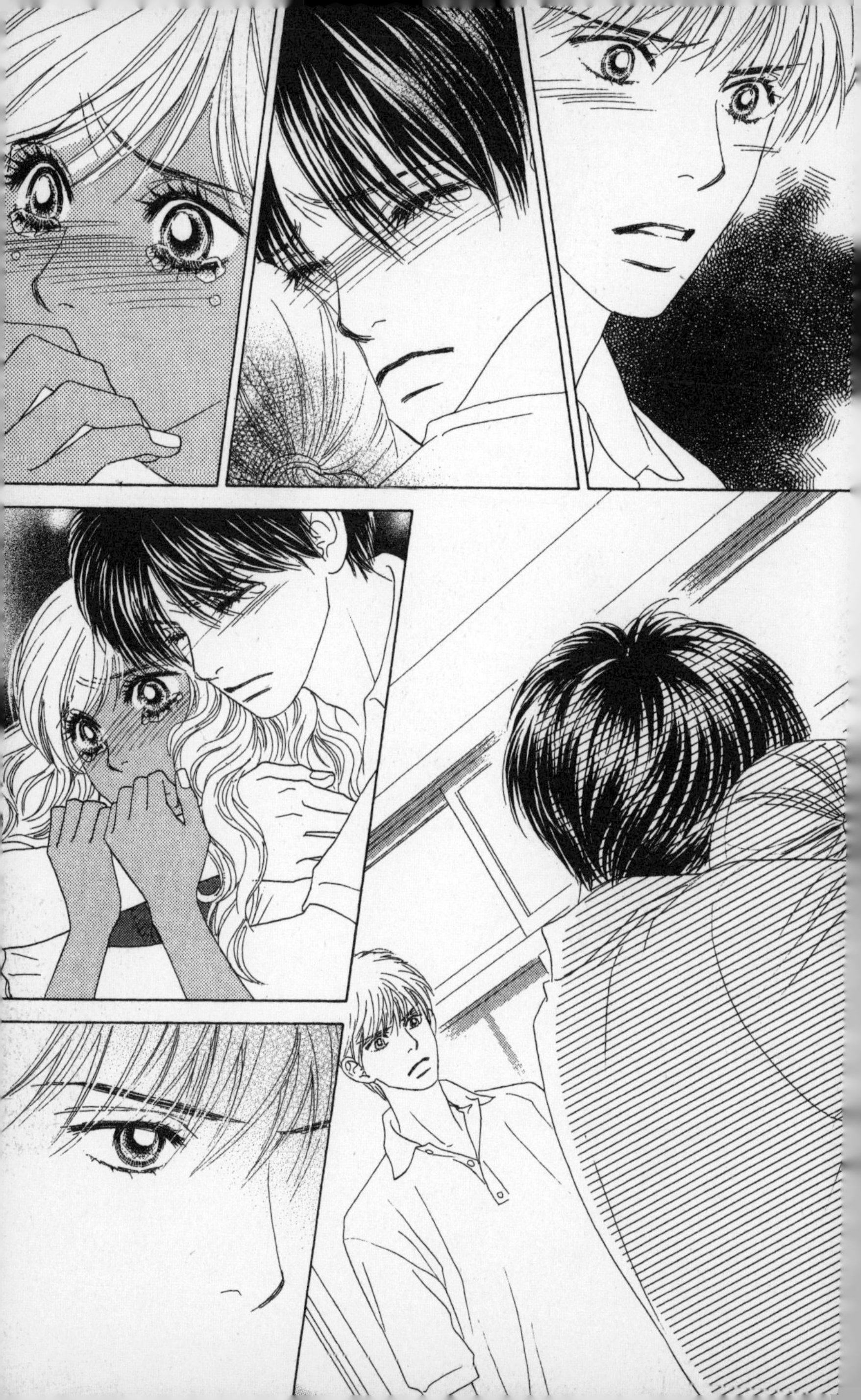

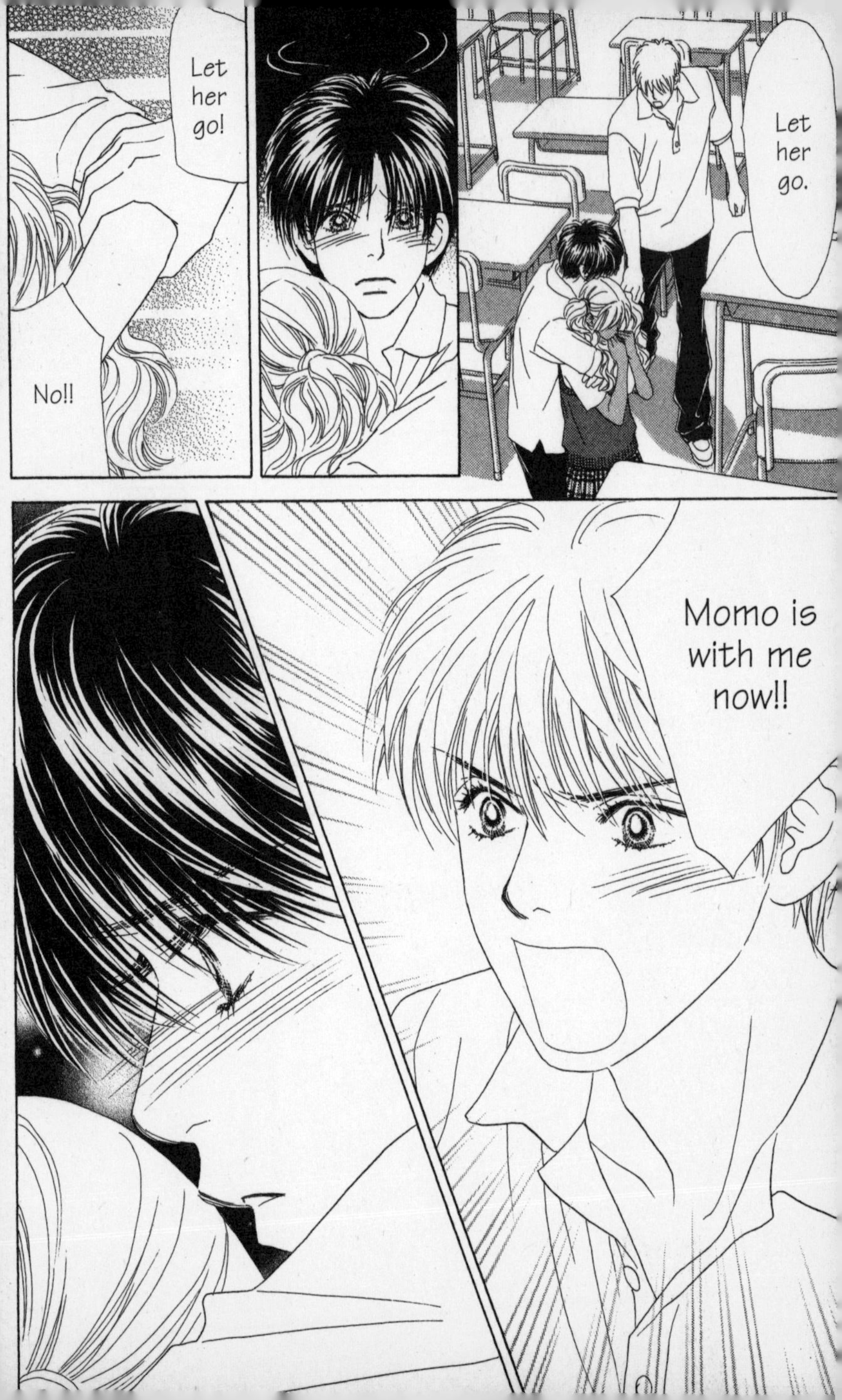
Let her go.
Let her go!
No!!
Momo is with me now!!

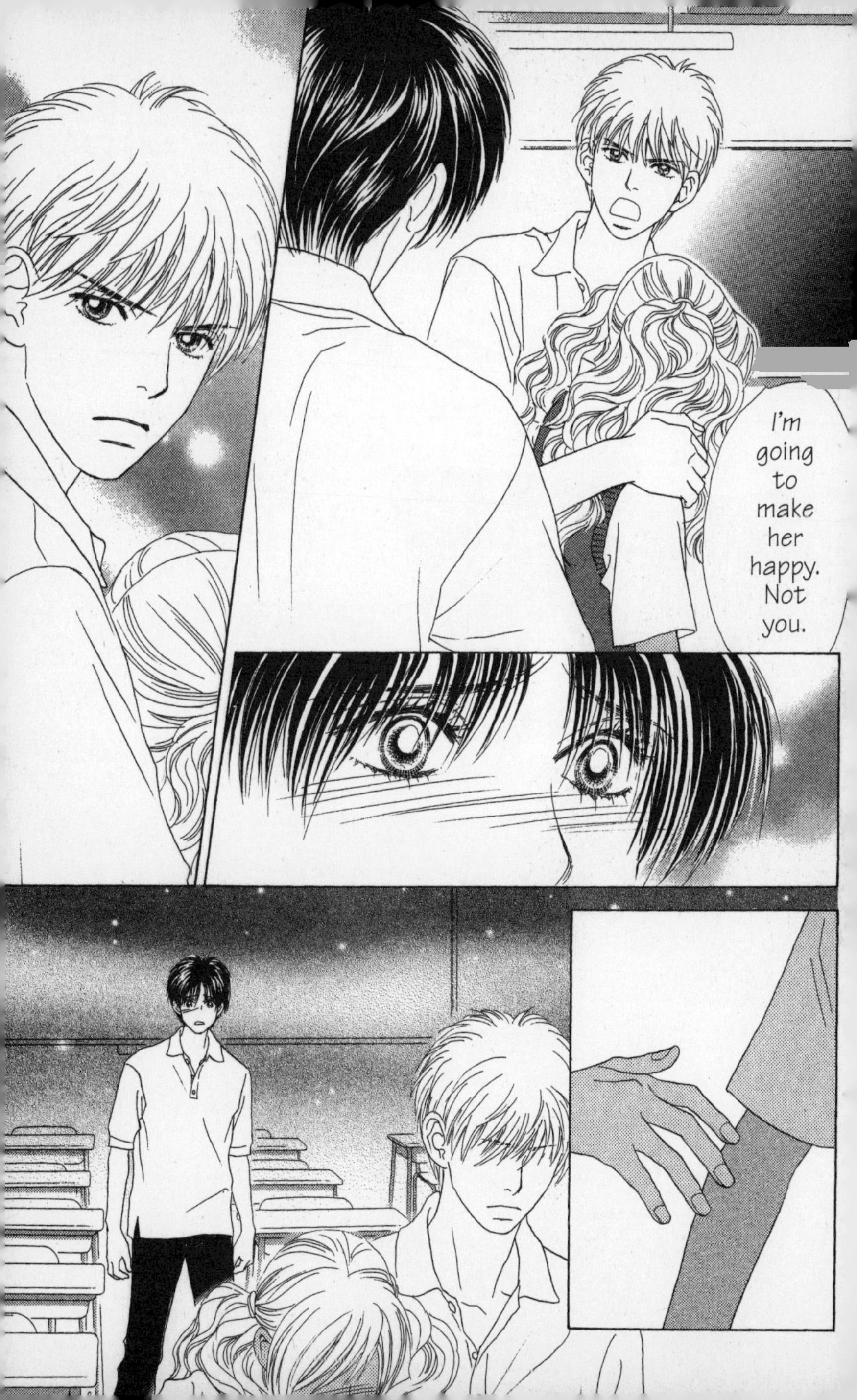
I'm going to make her happy. Not you.

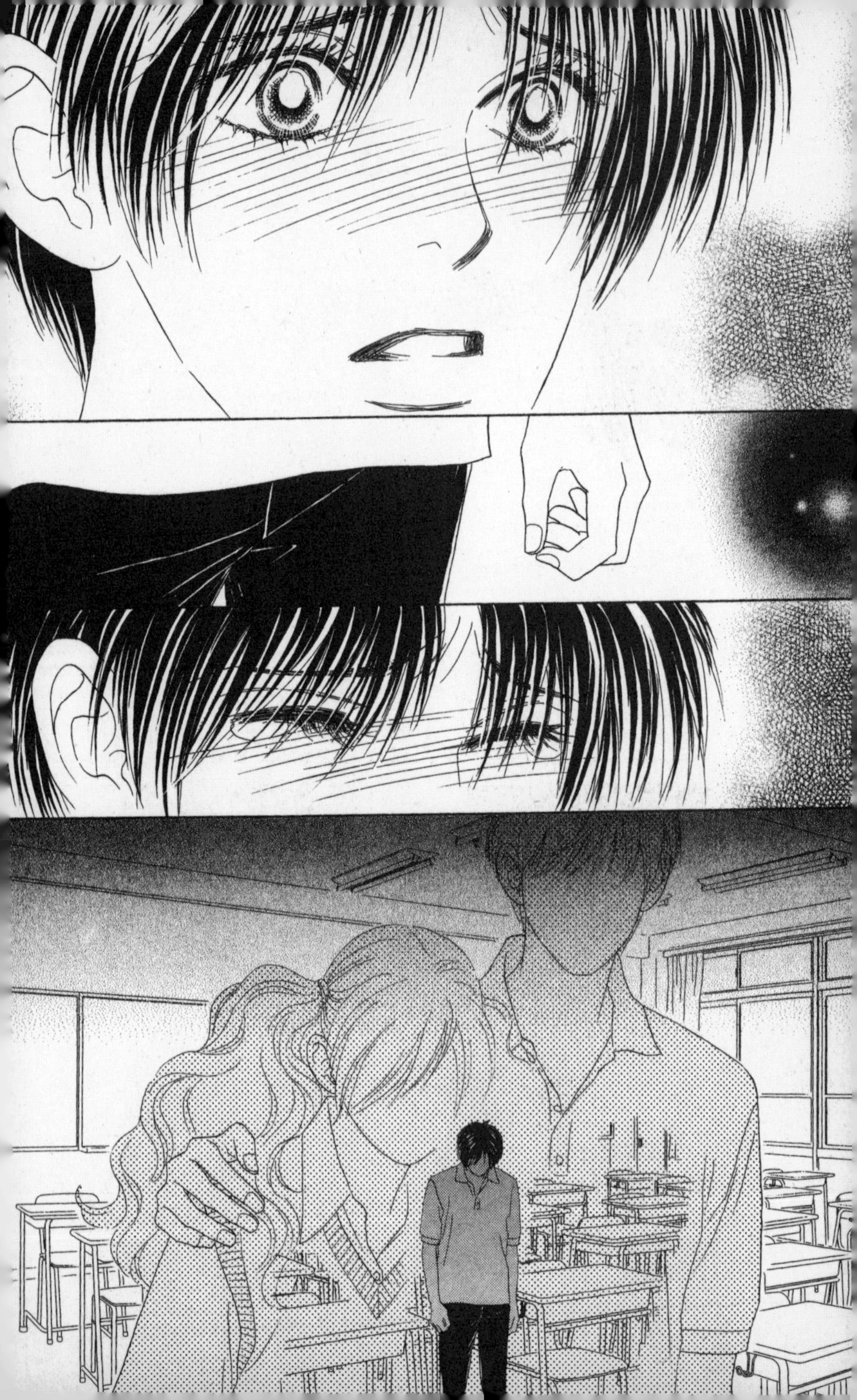

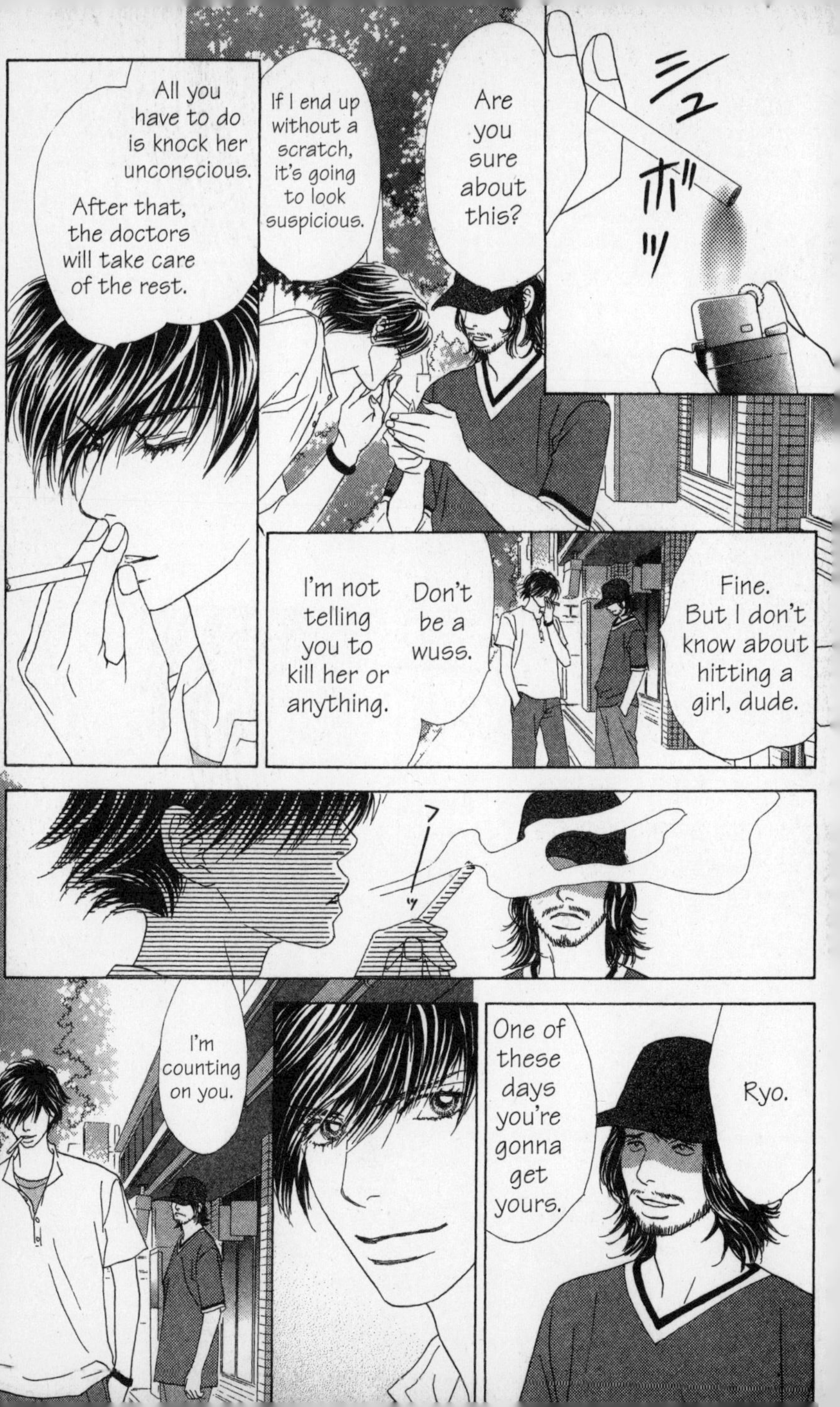
シュ
ボッ
Are you sure about this?
If I end up without a scratch, it's going to look suspicious.
Fine. But I don't know about hitting a girl, dude.
Don't be a wuss.
I'm not telling you to kill her or anything.
All you have to do is knock her unconscious.
After that, the doctors will take care of the rest.
Ryo.
One of these days you're gonna get yours.
I'm counting on you.

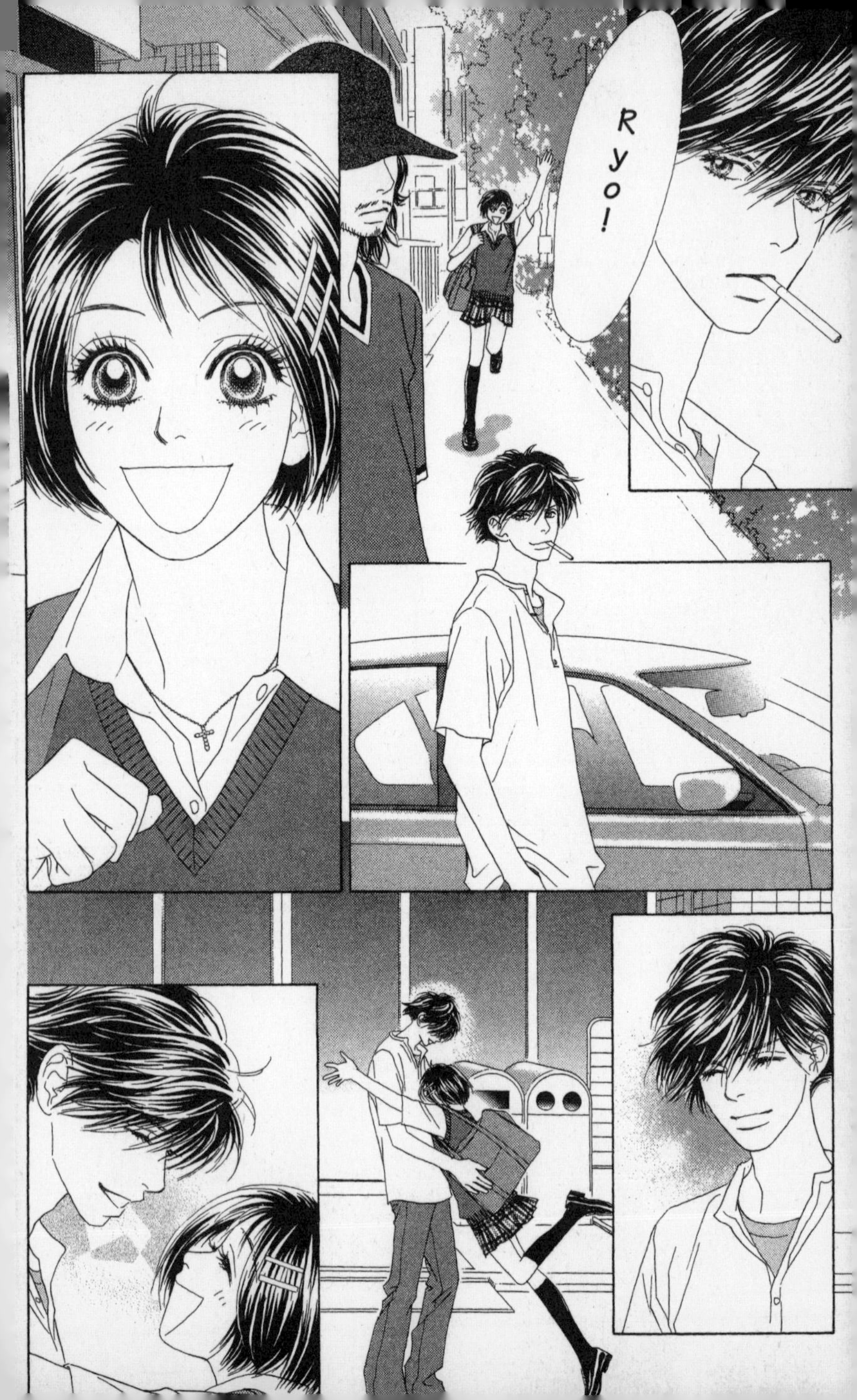
Ryo!

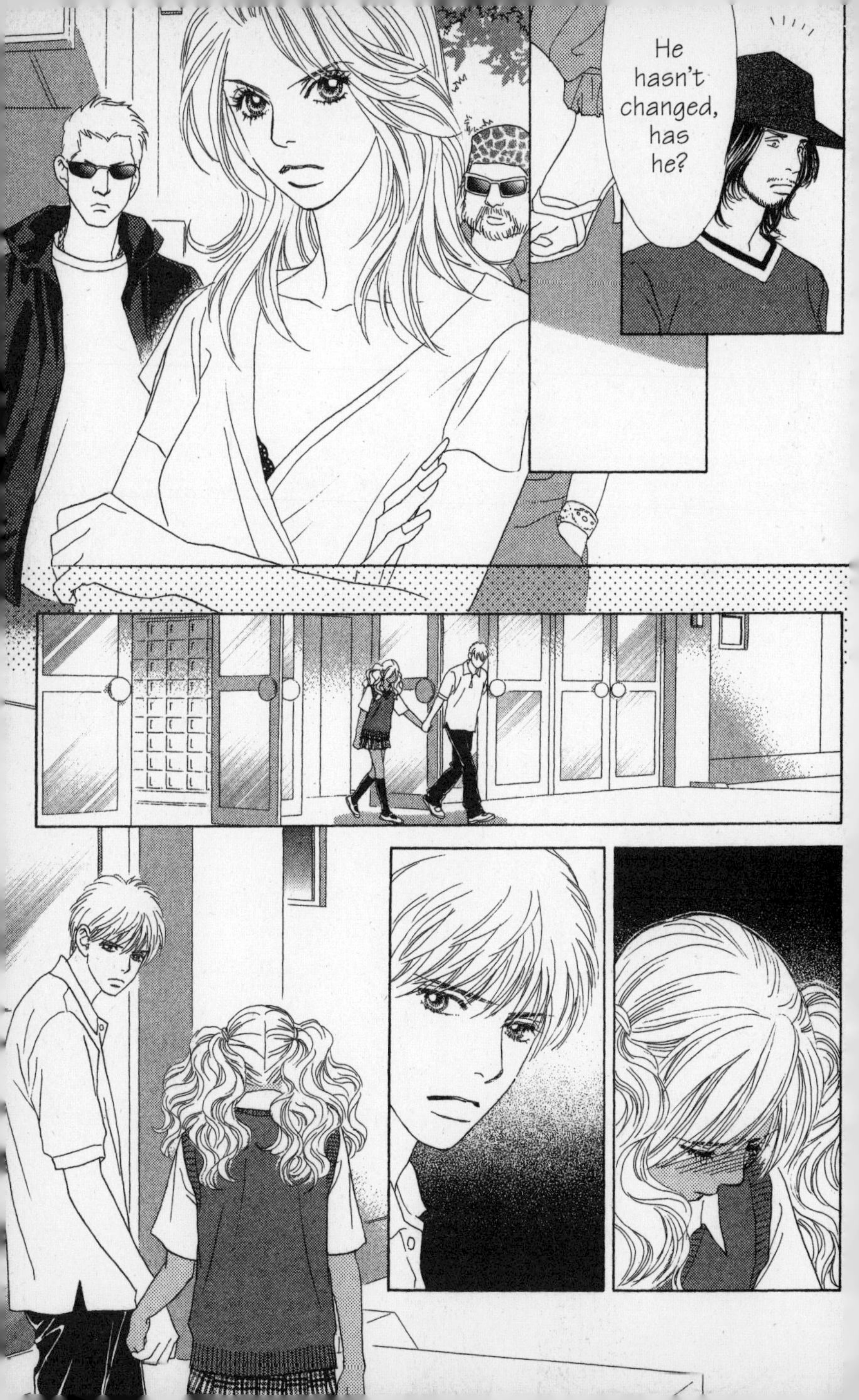
He hasn't changed, has he?

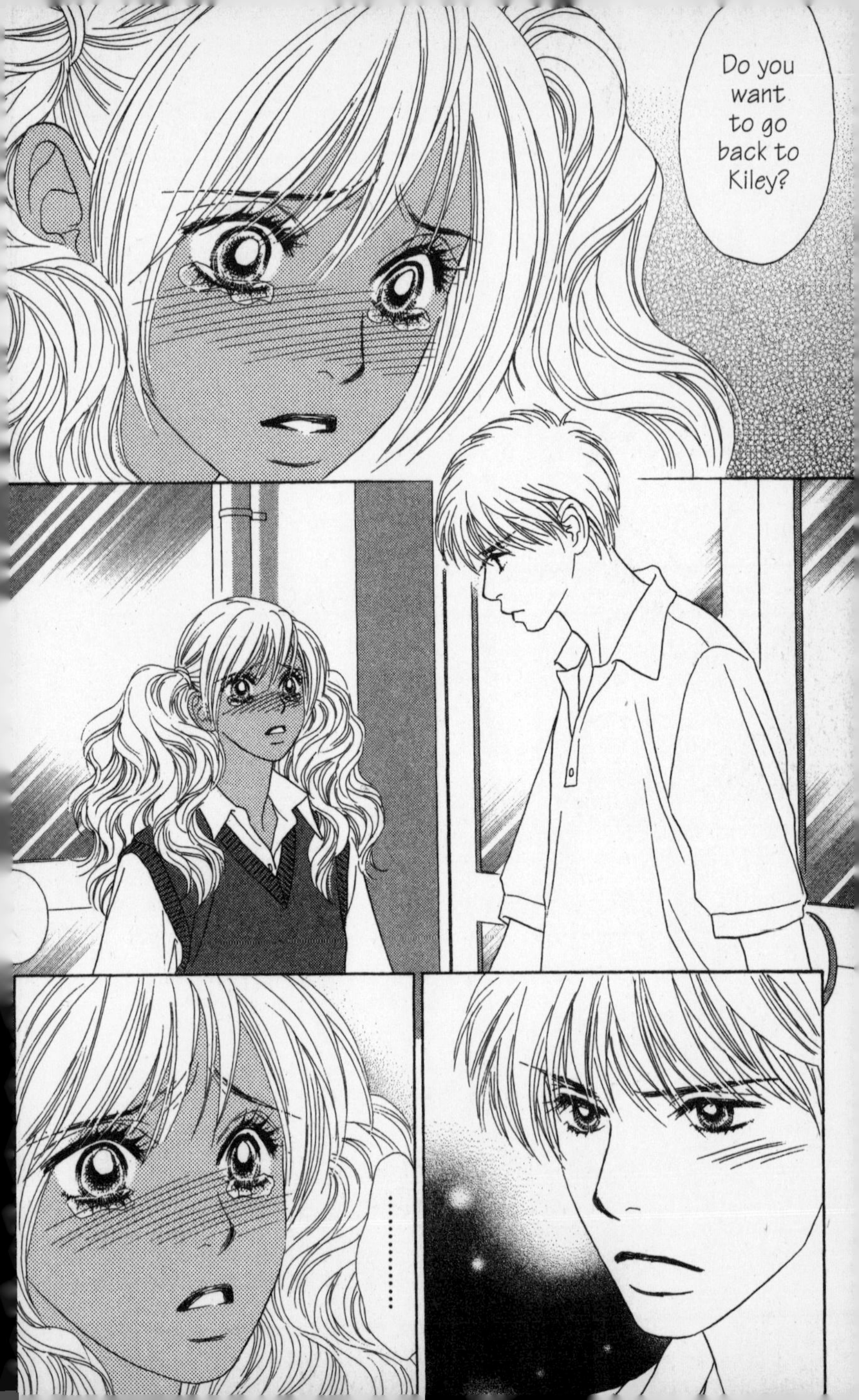
Do you want to go back to Kiley?
....

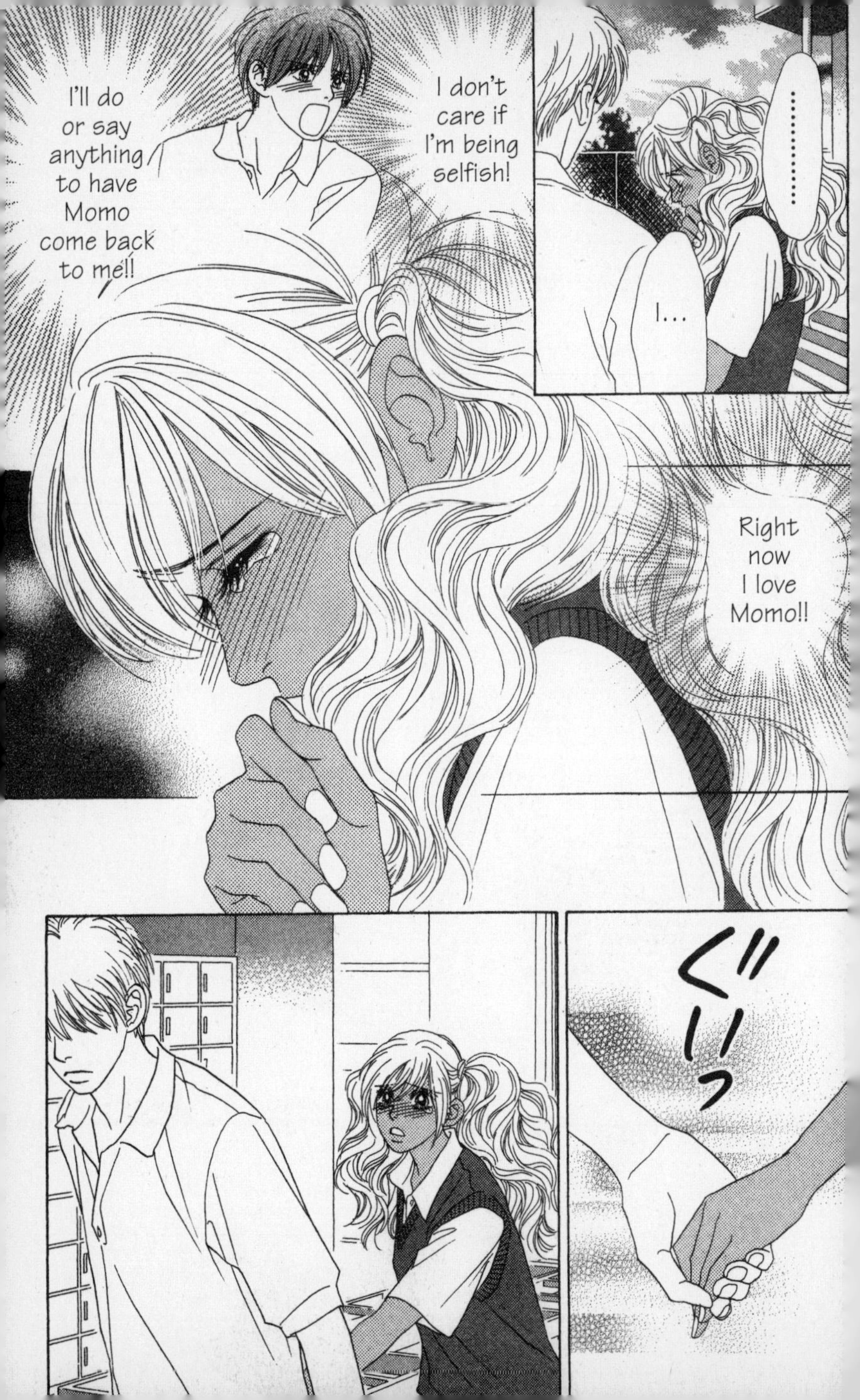
……
I…
I don't care if I'm being selfish!
I'll do or say anything to have Momo come back to me!!
Right now I love Momo!!
ぐいっ

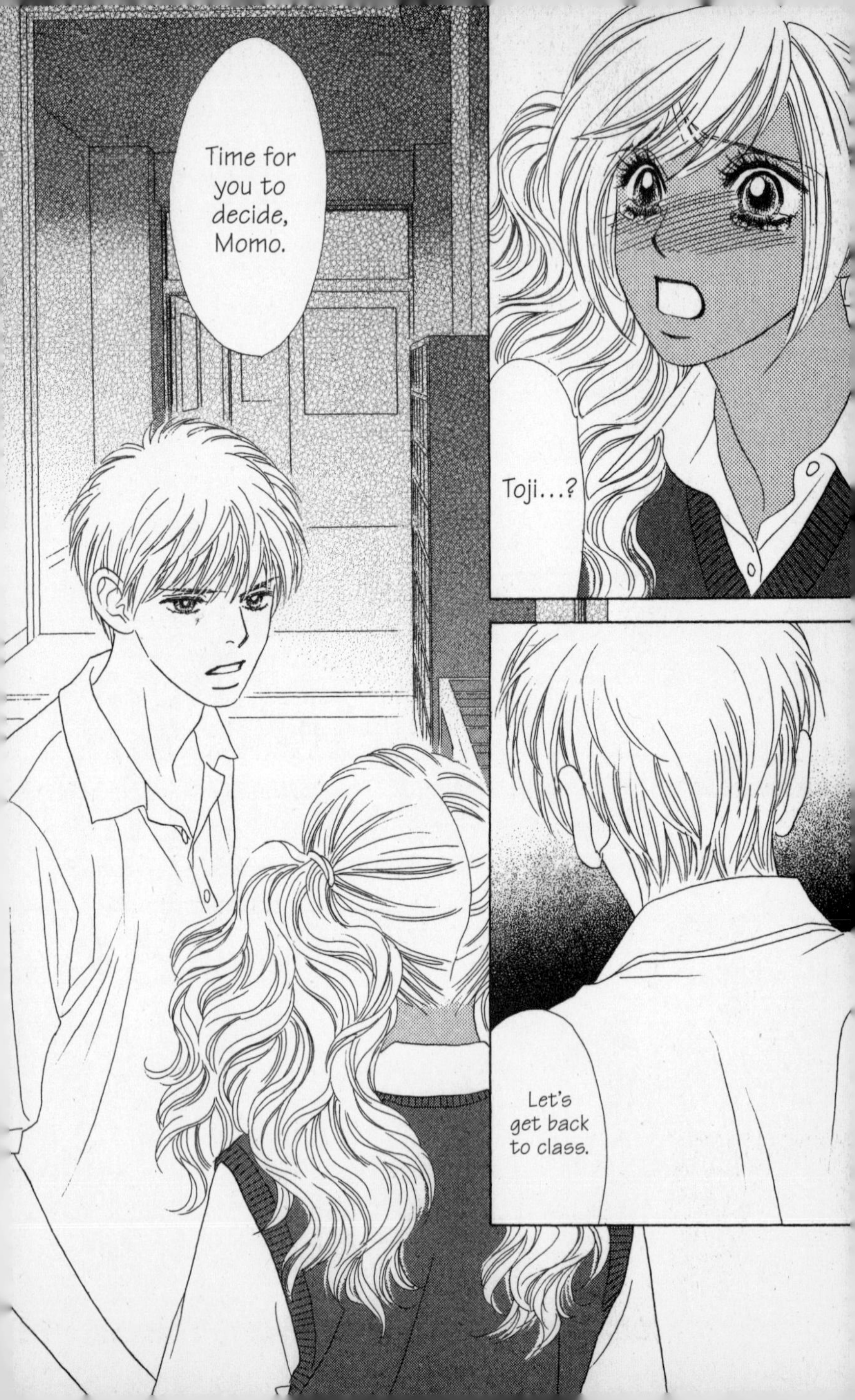
Toji...?
Let's get back to class.
Time for you to decide, Momo.

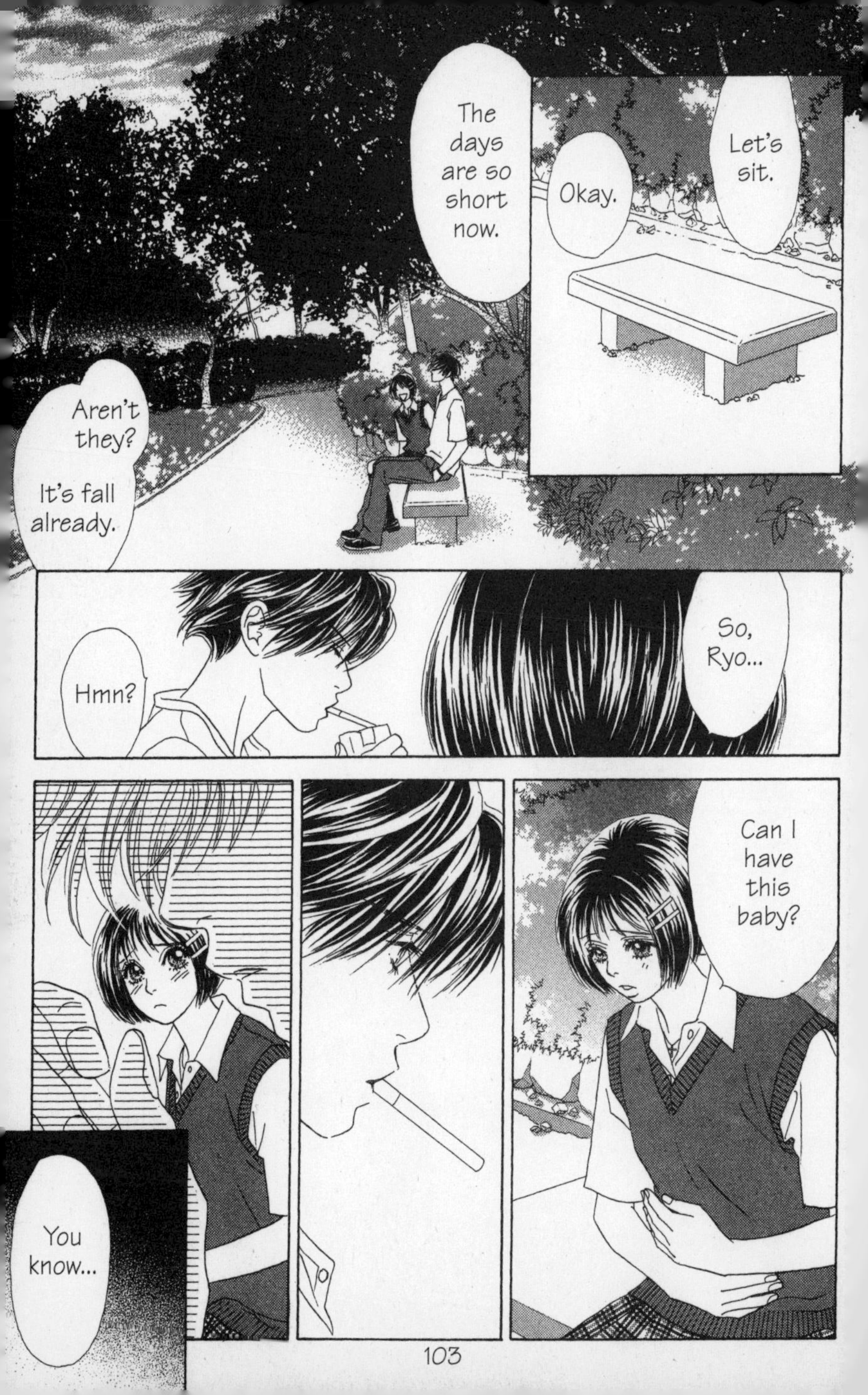
Let's sit.
Okay.
The days are so short now.
Aren't they?
It's fall already.
So, Ryo...
Hmn?
Can I have this baby?
You know...

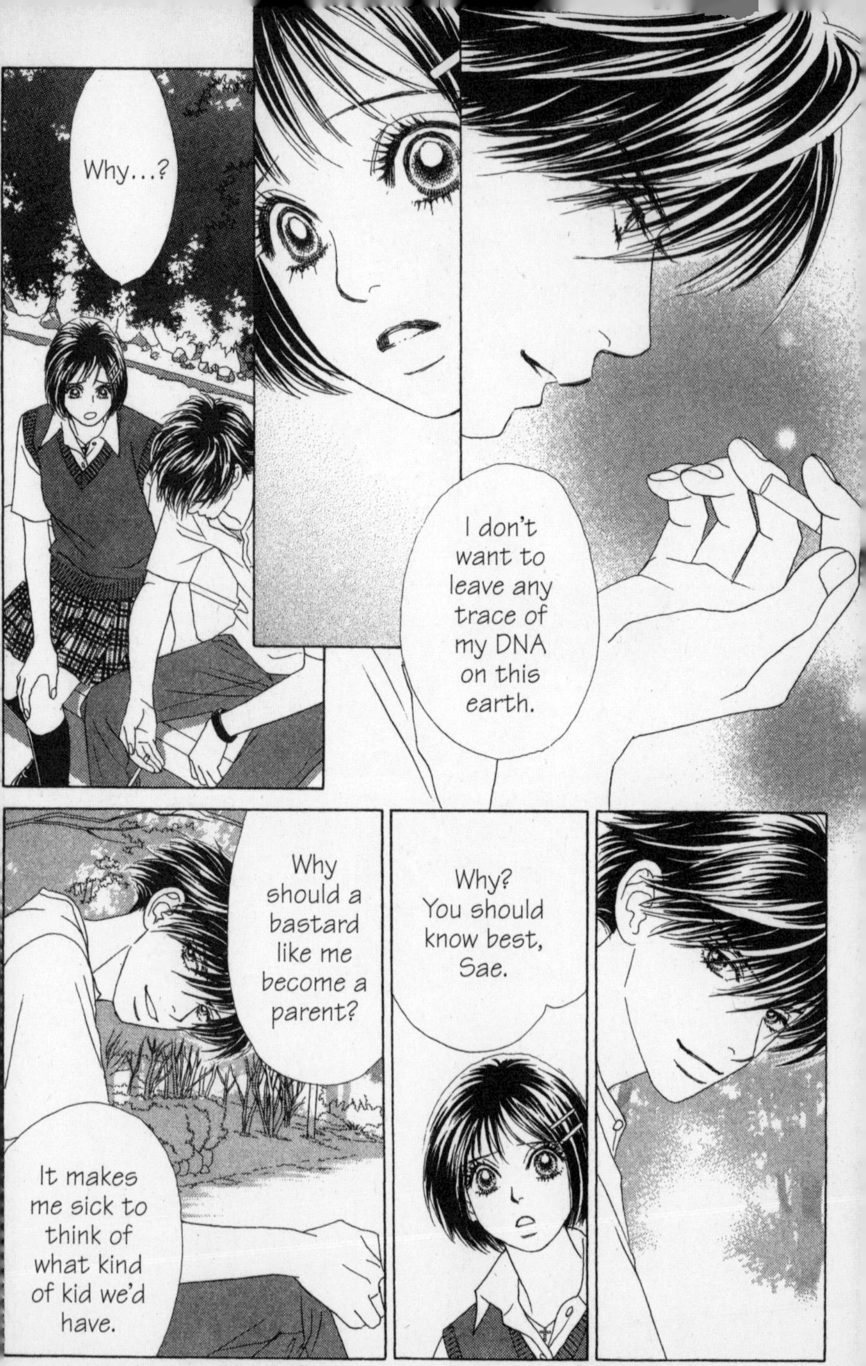
I don't want to leave any trace of my DNA on this earth.
Why...?
Why? You should know best, Sae.
Why should a bastard like me become a parent?
It makes me sick to think of what kind of kid we'd have.

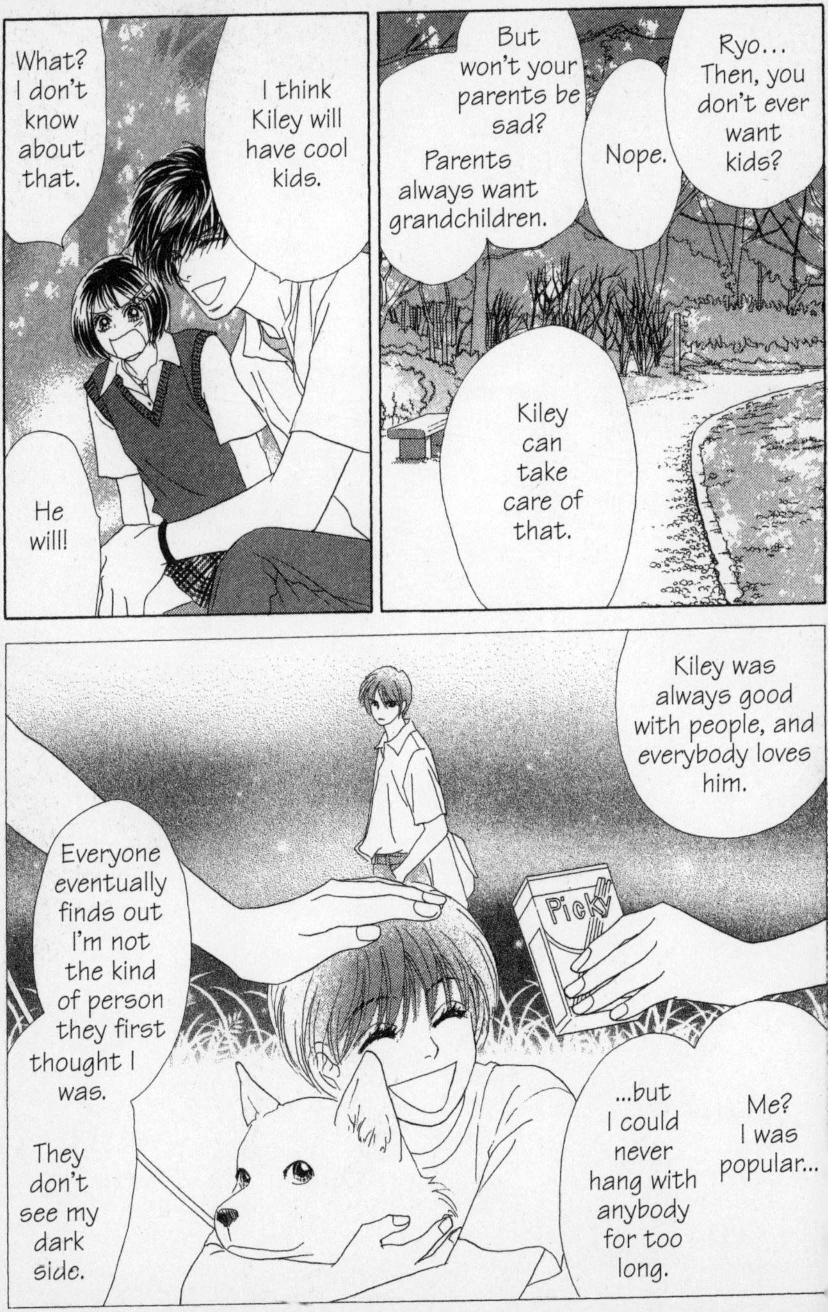
Ryo… Then, you don't ever want kids?
Nope.
But won't your parents be sad?
Parents always want grandchildren.
Kiley can take care of that.
I think Kiley will have cool kids.
What? I don't know about that.
He will!
Kiley was always good with people, and everybody loves him.
Me? I was popular...
...but I could never hang with anybody for too long.
Picky
Everyone eventually finds out I'm not the kind of person they first thought I was.
They don't see my dark side.

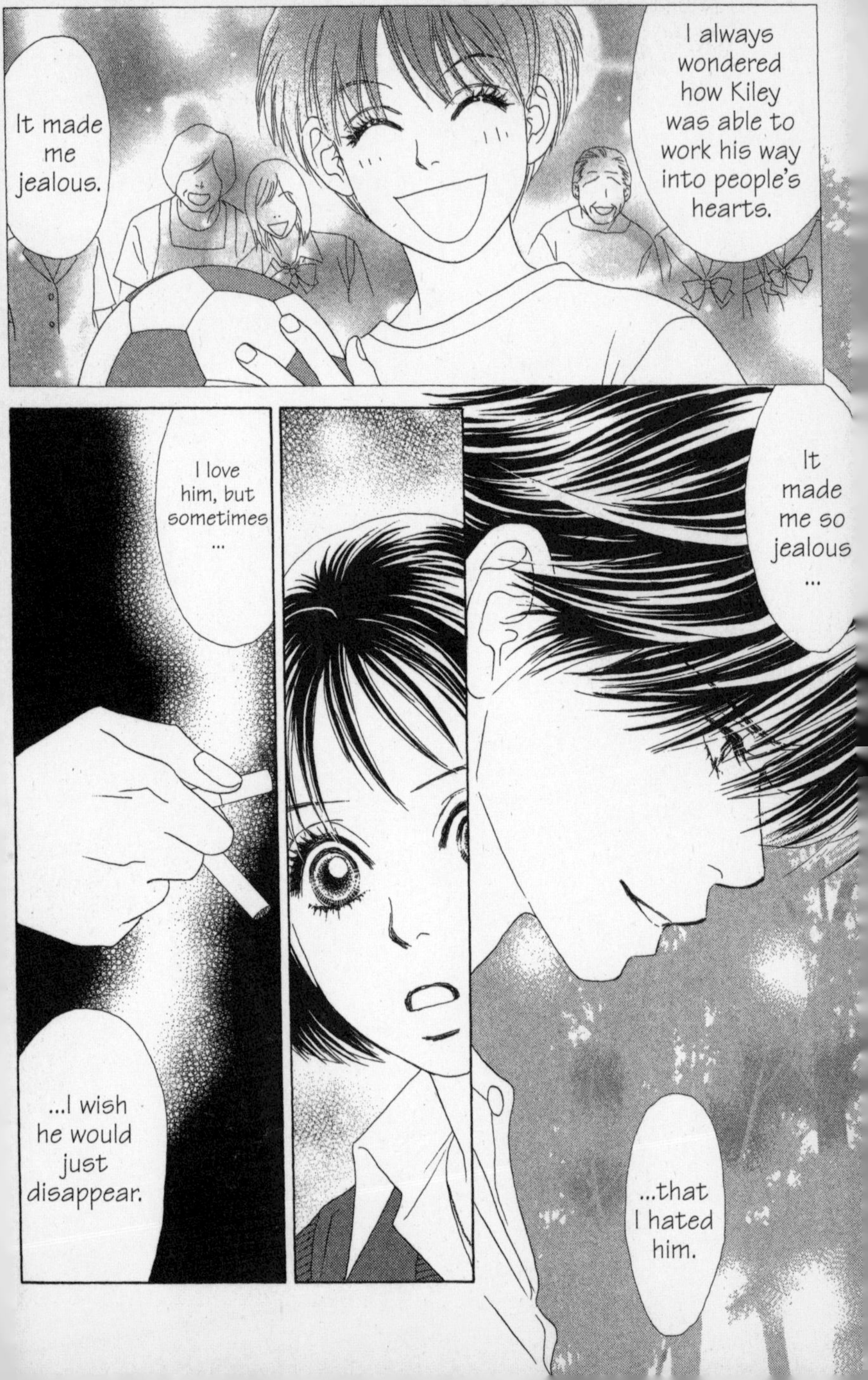
I always wondered how Kiley was able to work his way into people's hearts.
It made me jealous.
It made me so jealous ...
...that I hated him.
I love him, but sometimes ...
...I wish he would just disappear.

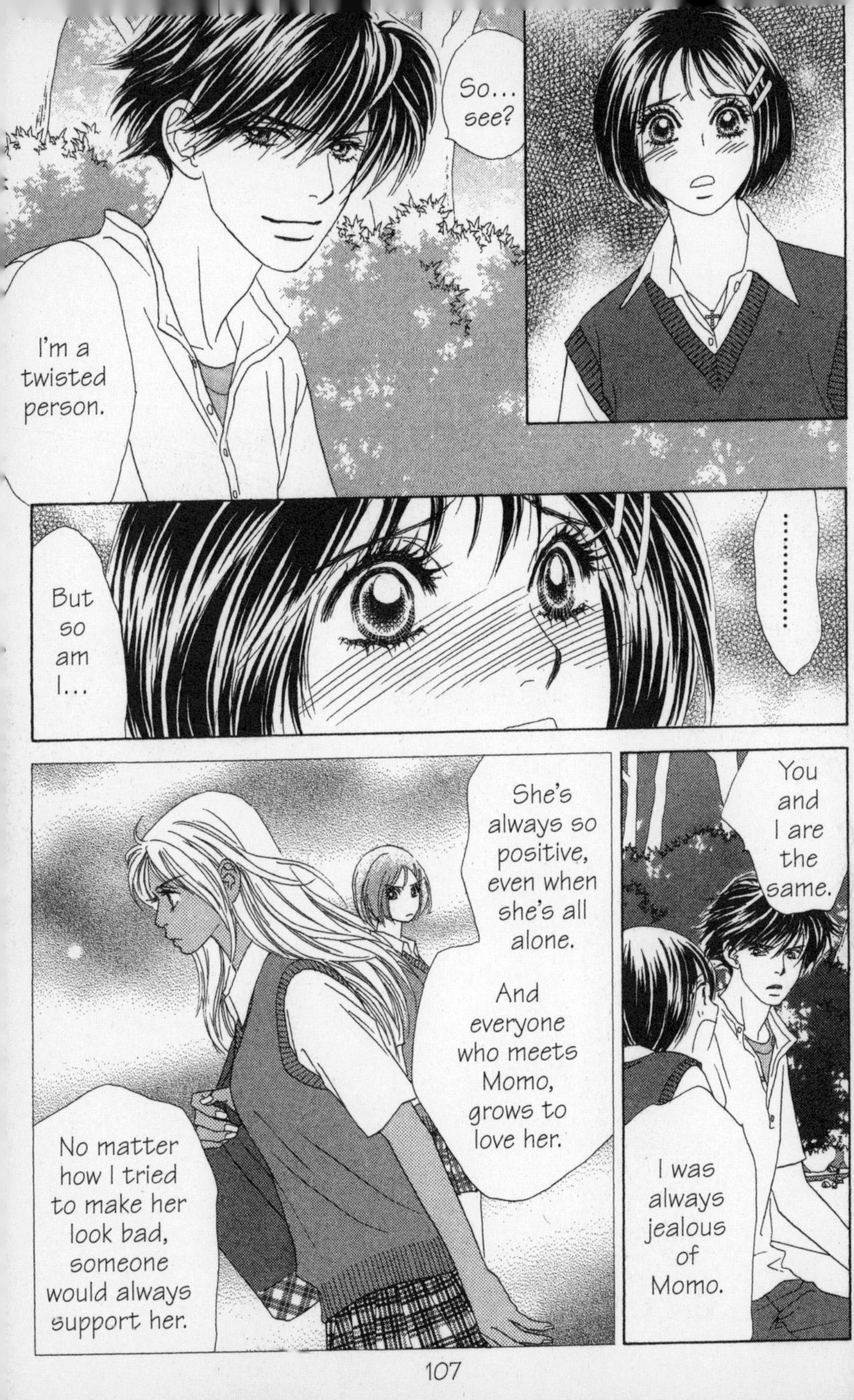

So… see?
I'm a twisted person.
……
But so am I…
You and I are the same.
I was always jealous of Momo.
She's always so positive, even when she's all alone.
And everyone who meets Momo, grows to love her.
No matter how I tried to make her look bad, someone would always support her.

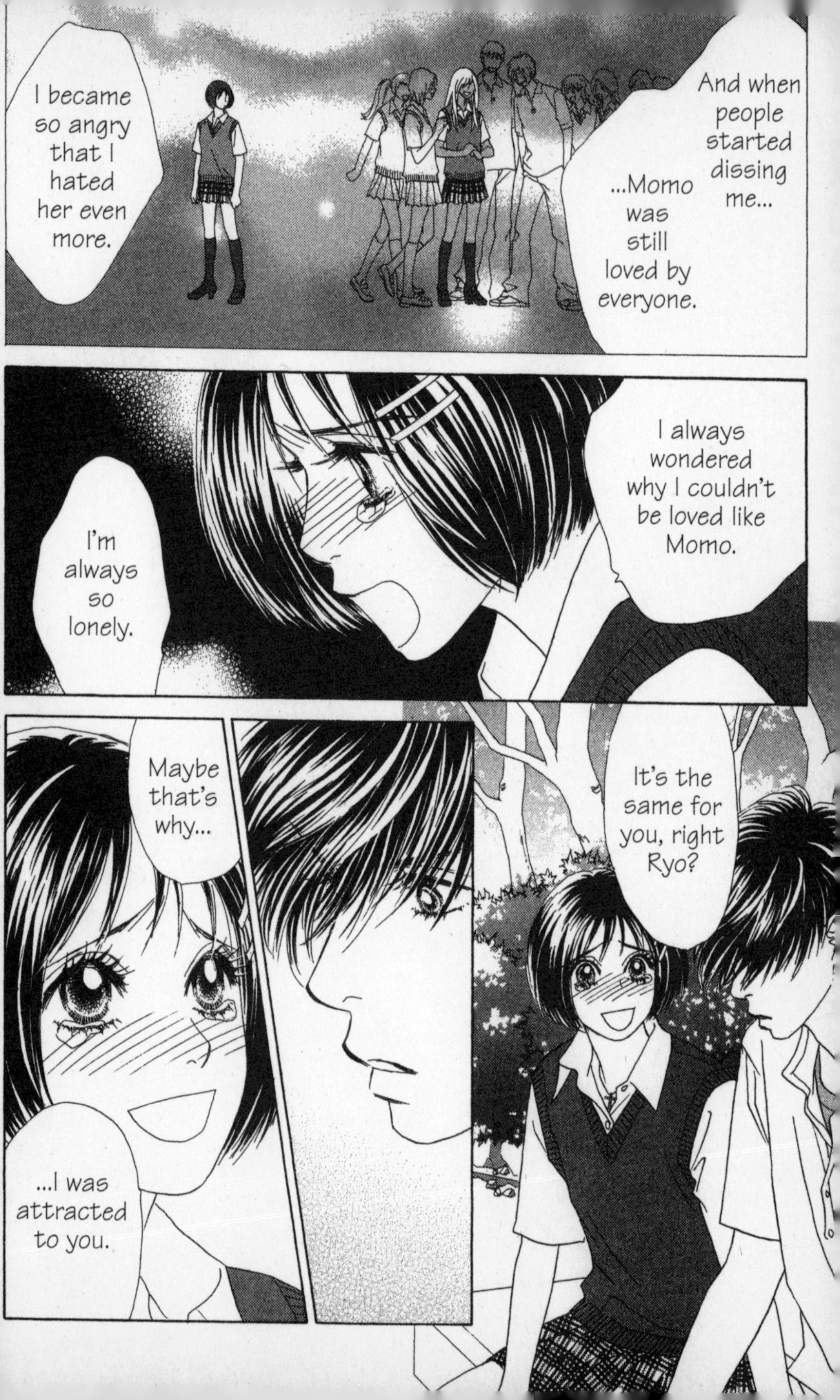
And when people started dissing me...
...Momo was still loved by everyone.
I became so angry that I hated her even more.
I always wondered why I couldn't be loved like Momo.
I'm always so lonely.
It's the same for you, right Ryo?
Maybe that's why...
...I was attracted to you.

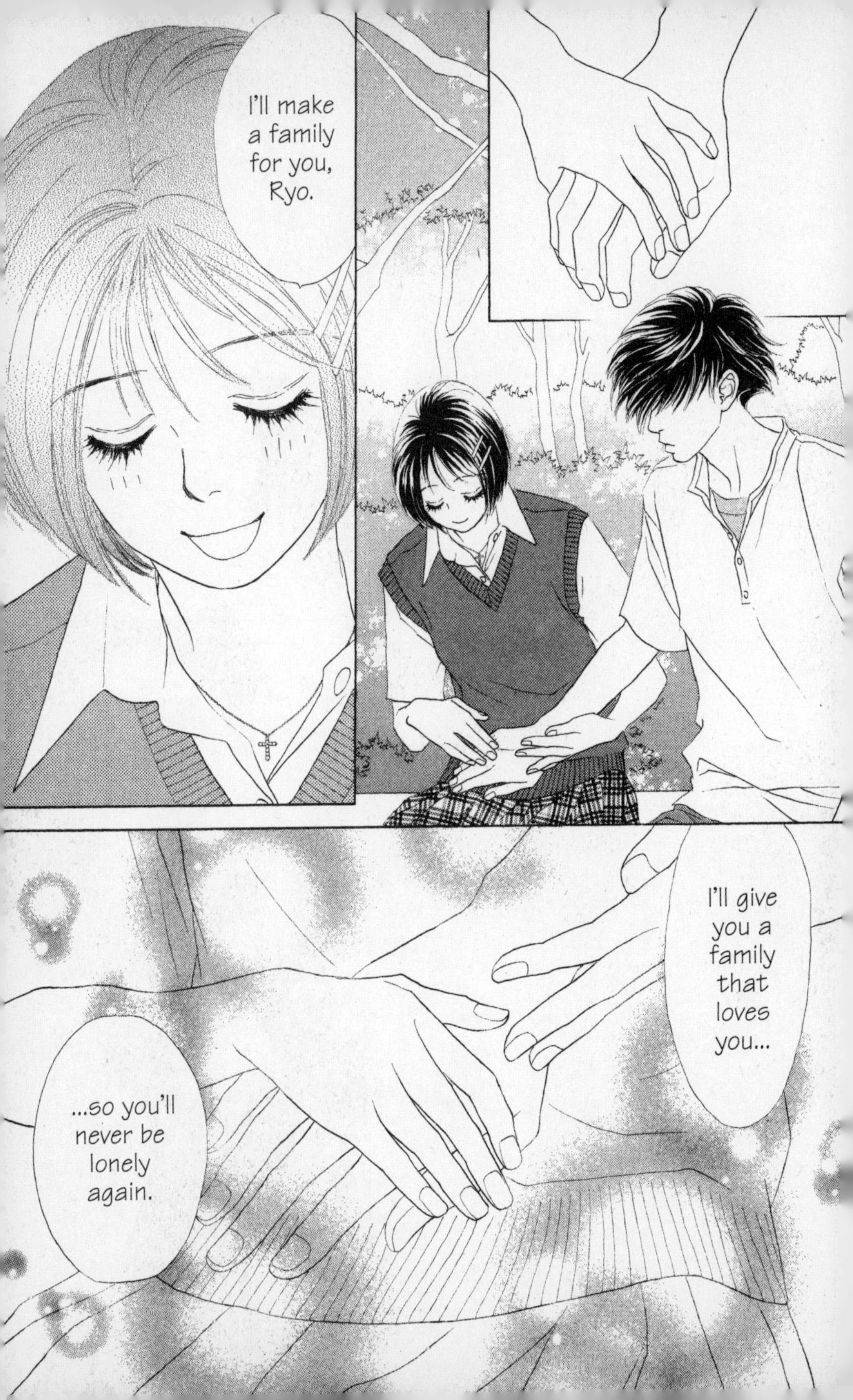
I'll make a family for you, Ryo.
I'll give you a family that loves you...
...so you'll never be lonely again.

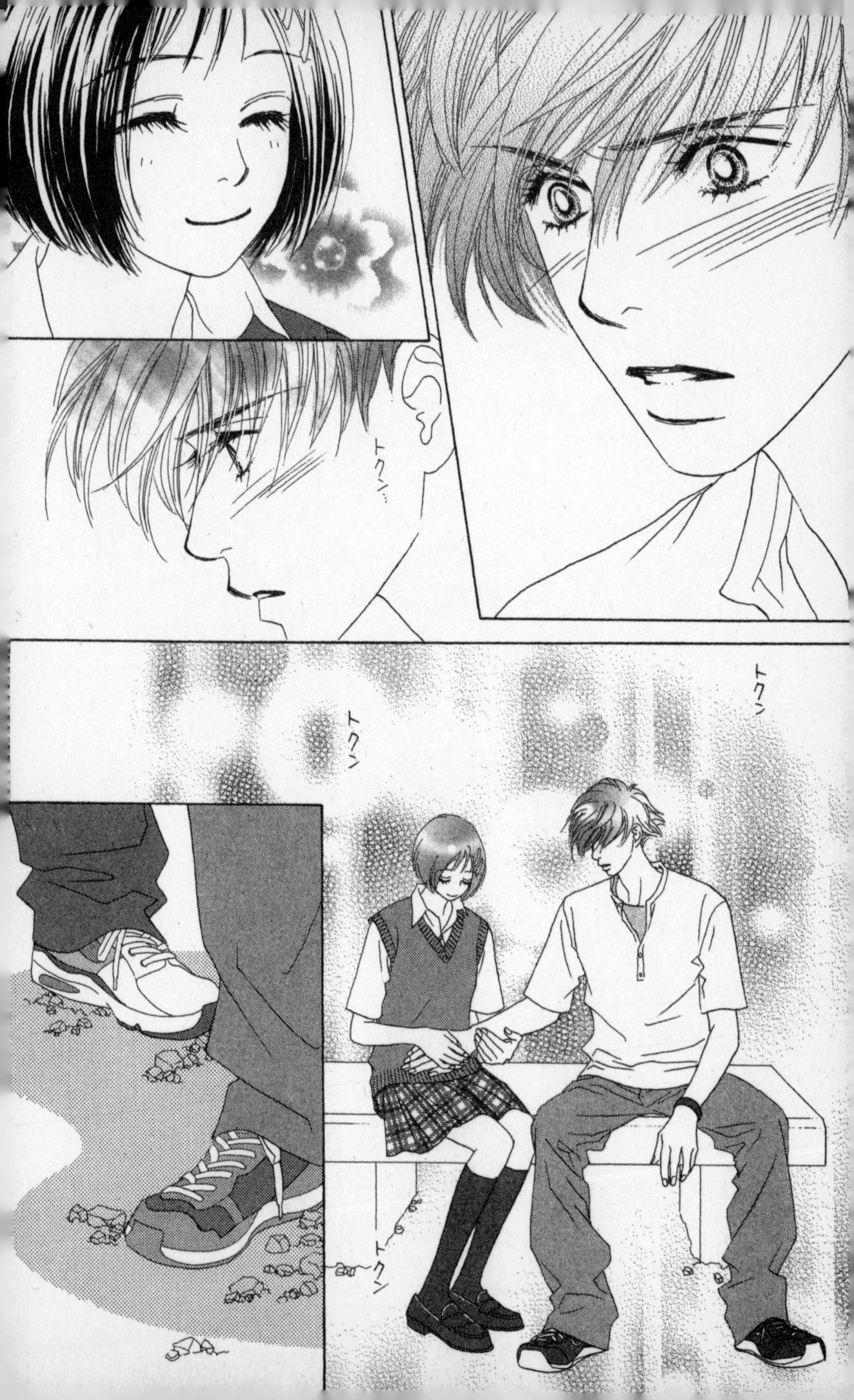
トクン…
トクン
トクン
トクン

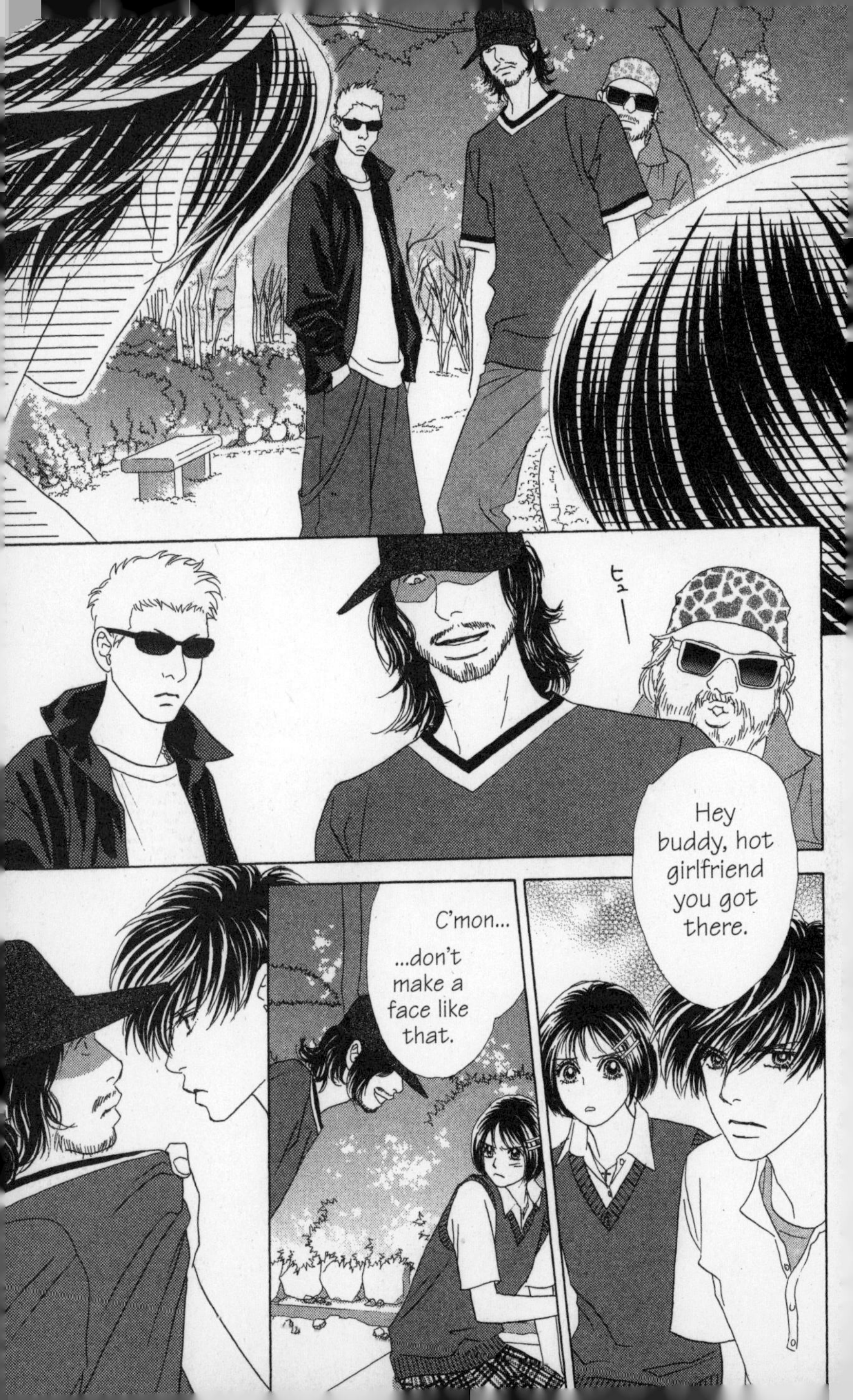
ヒュー
Hey buddy, hot girlfriend you got there.
C'mon...
...don't make a face like that.

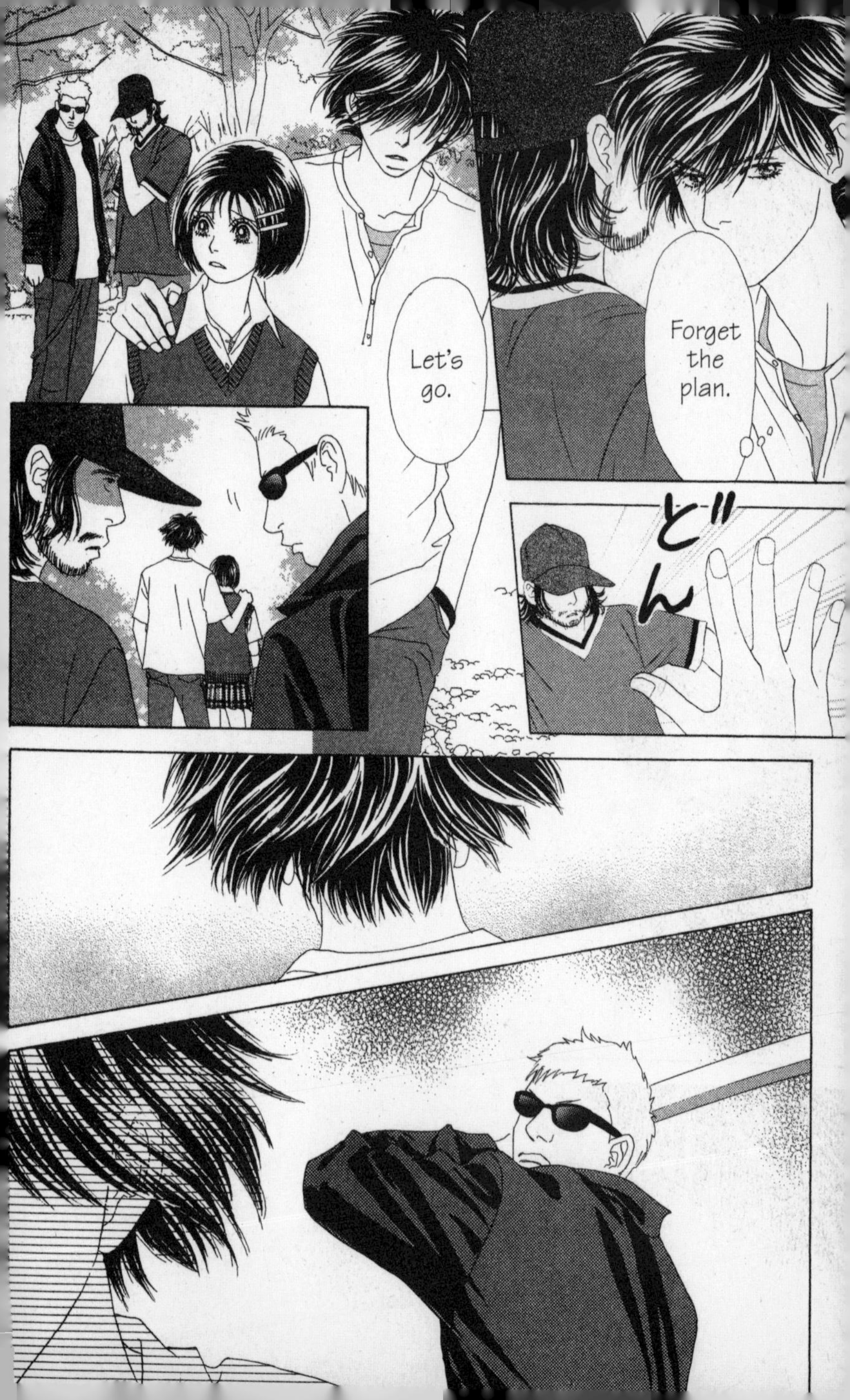
Forget the plan.
Let's go.
どん

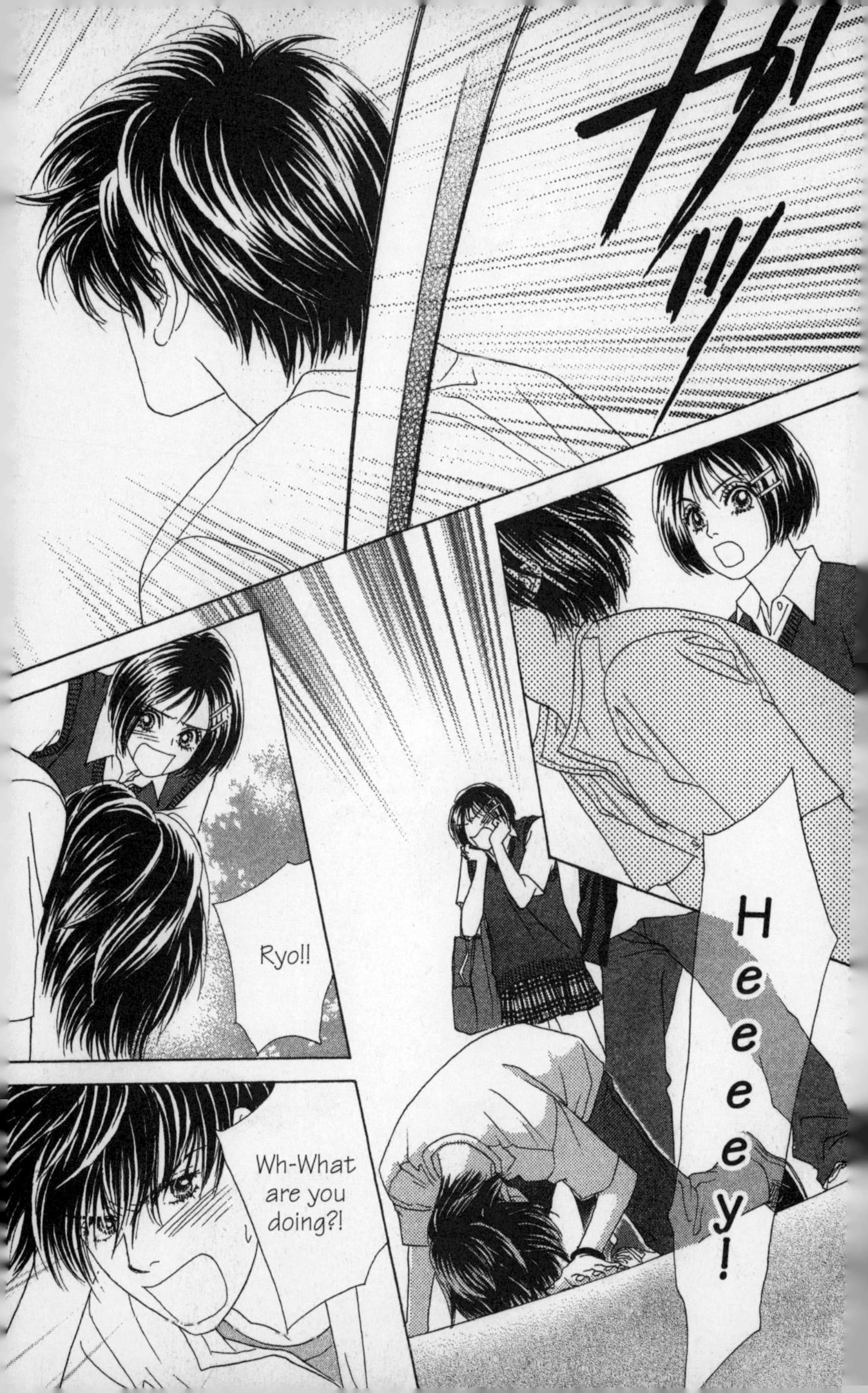
ガッ
Heeeey!
Ryo!!
Wh-What are you doing?!

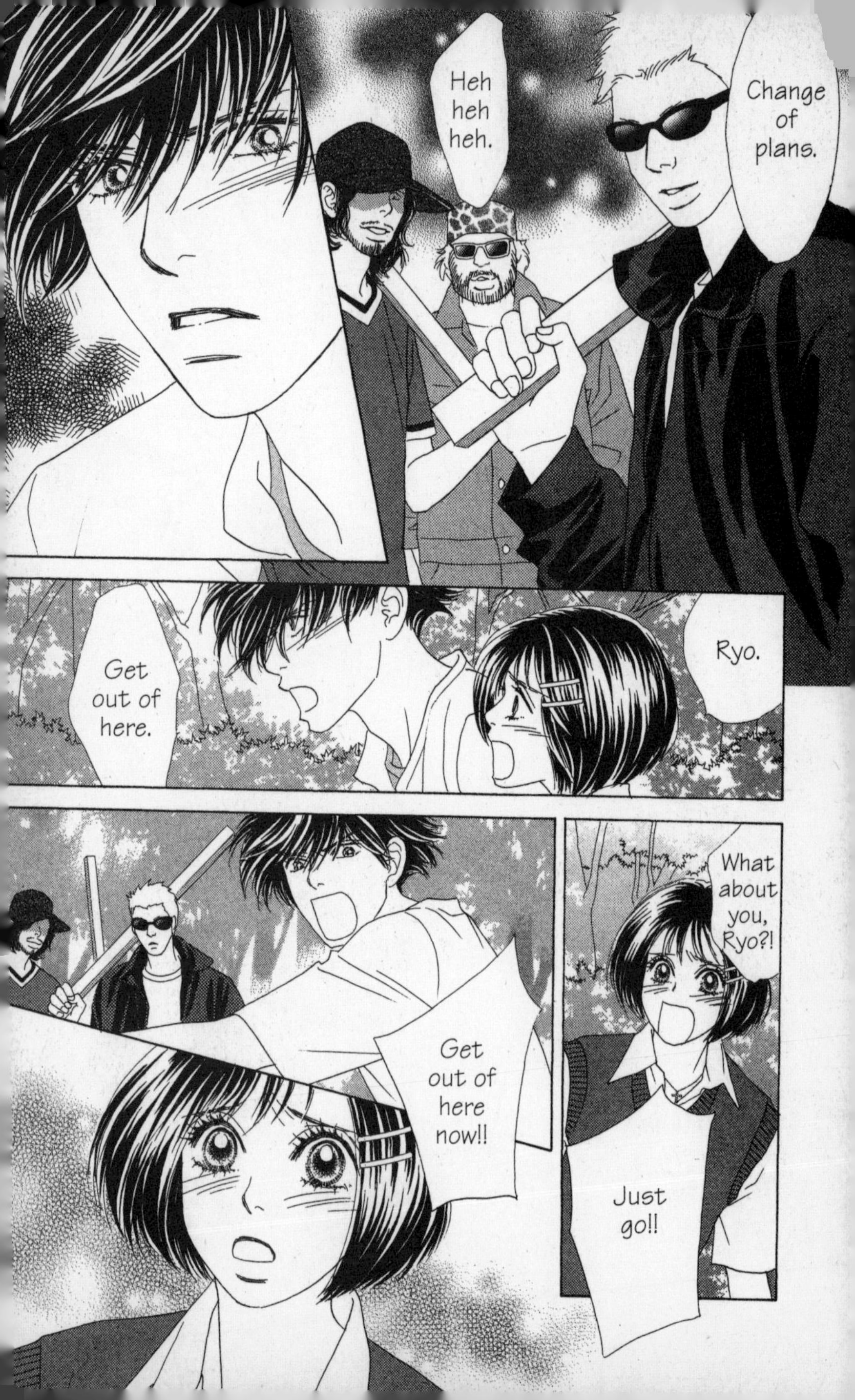
Change of plans.
Heh heh heh.
Ryo.
Get out of here.
What about you, Ryo?!
Just go!!
Get out of here now!!

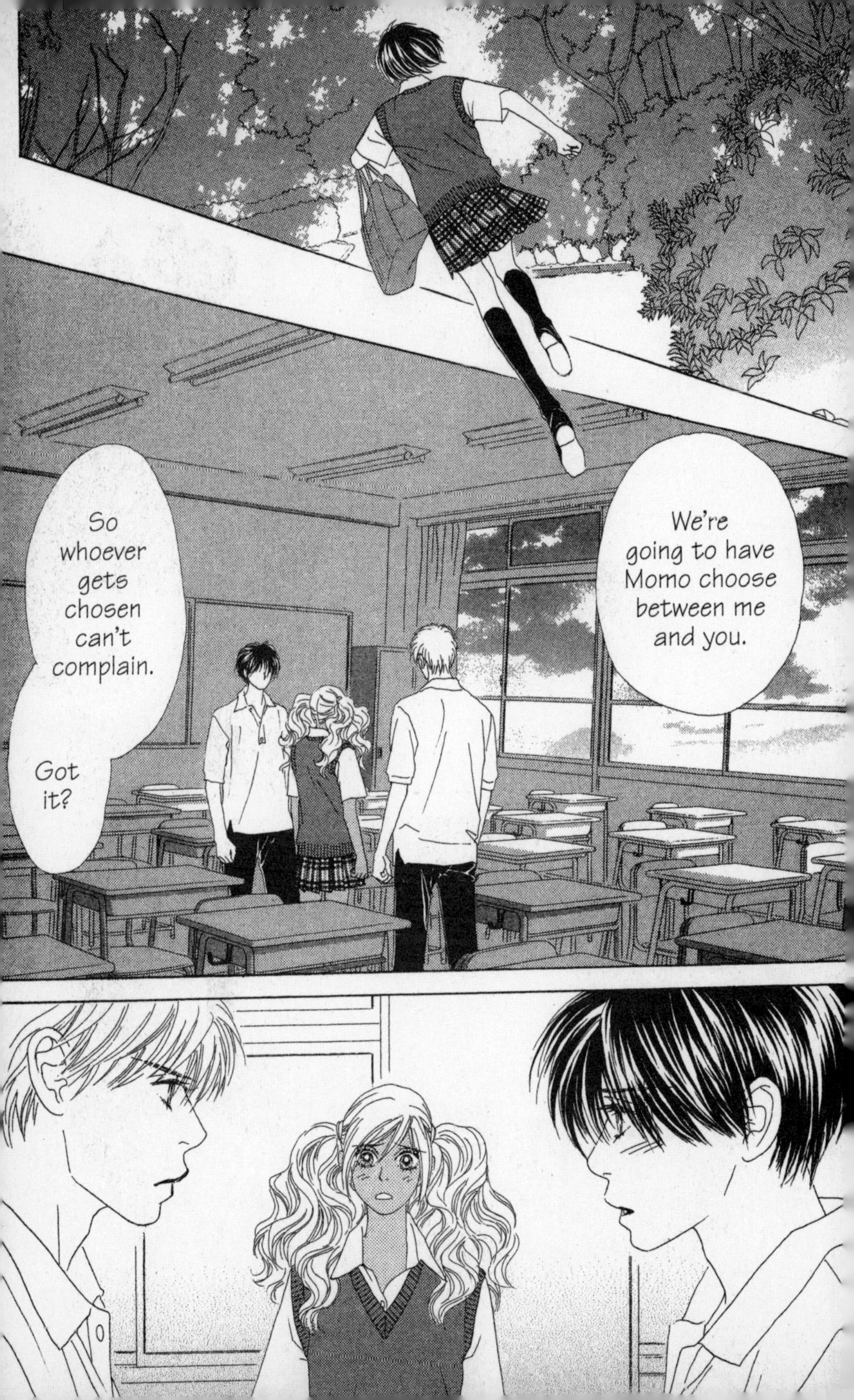
We're going to have Momo choose between me and you.
So whoever gets chosen can't complain.
Got it?

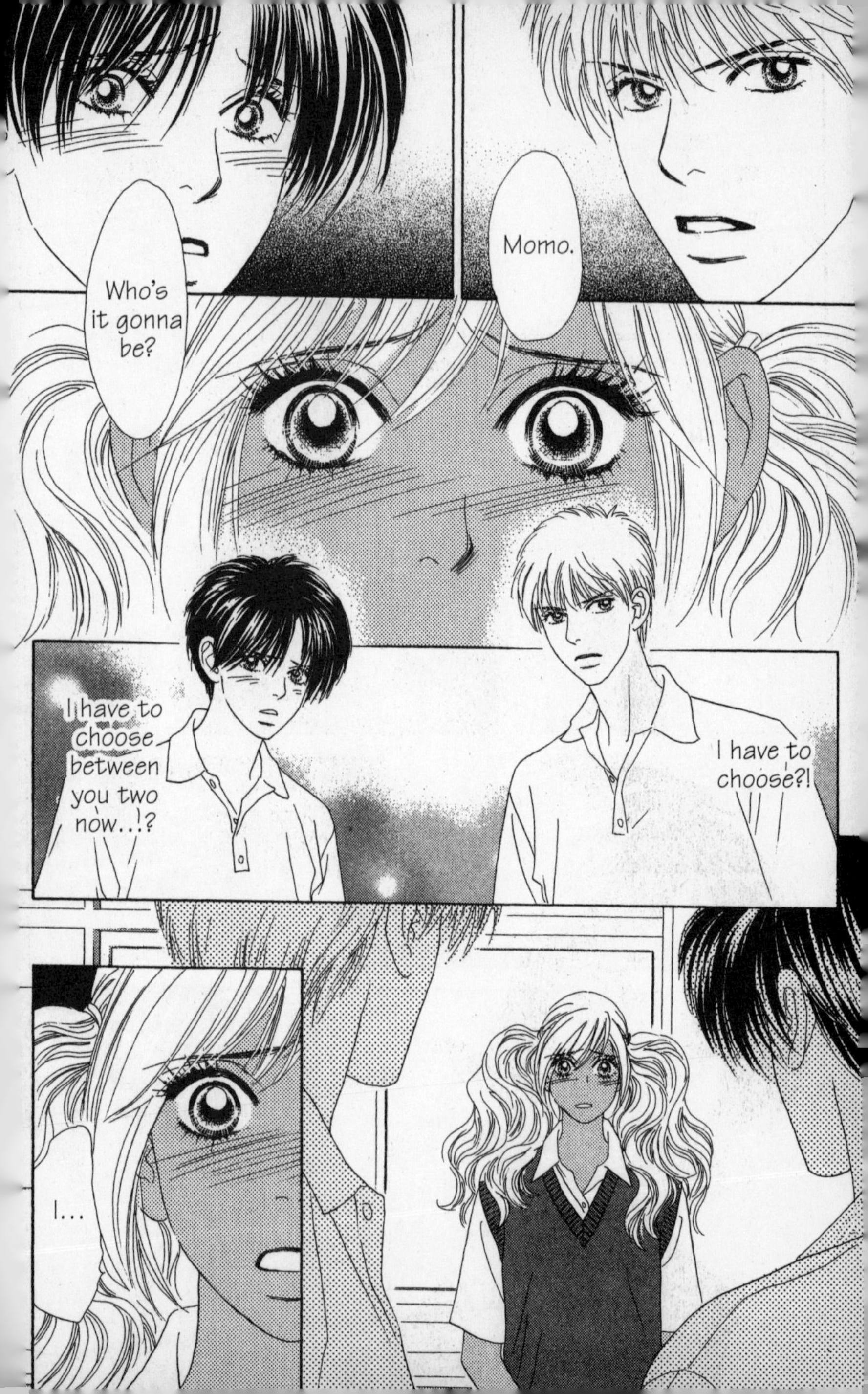
Momo.
Who's it gonna be?
I have to choose?!
I have to choose between you two now...!?
I...

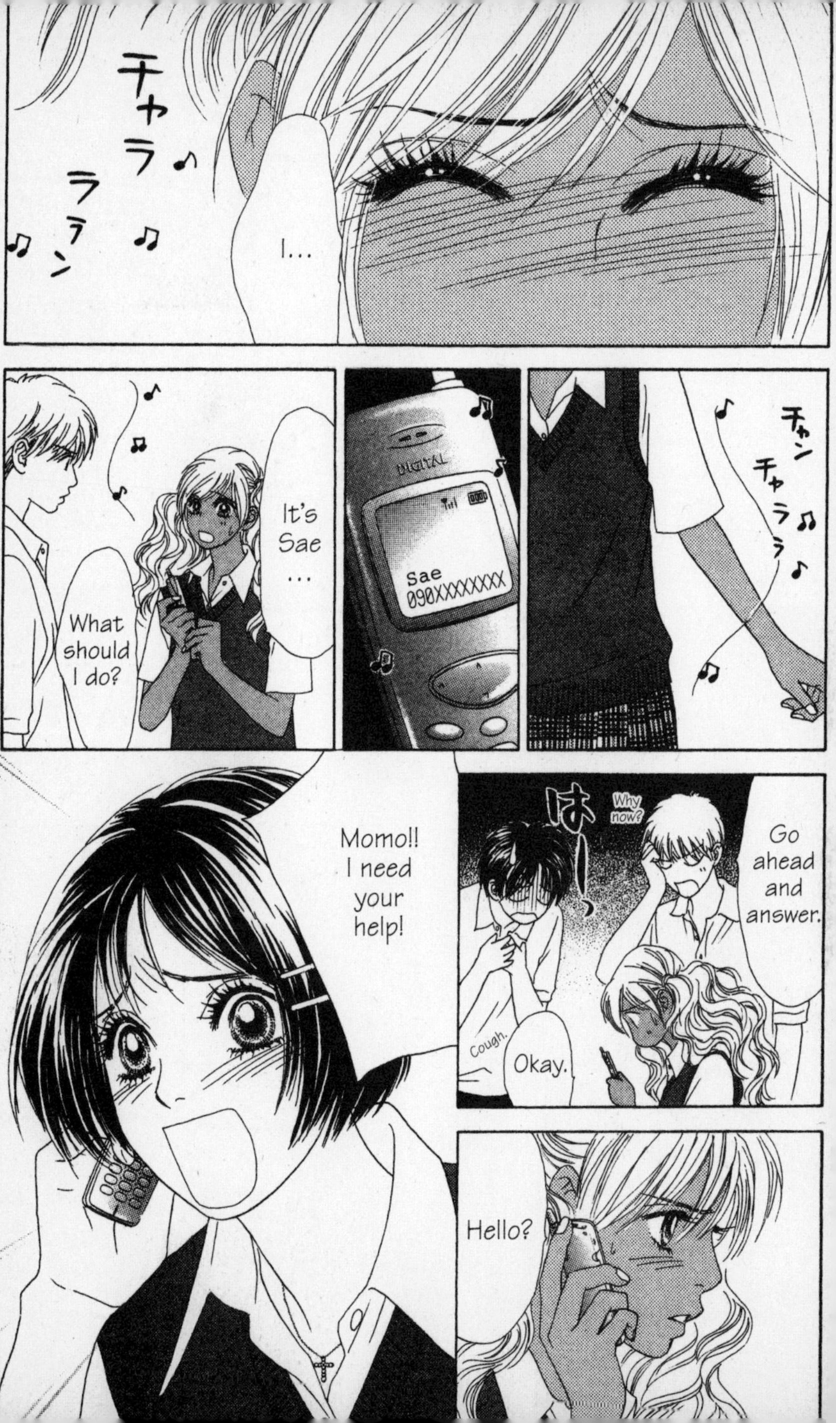
チャラ♪
ララン♪
I...
チャン
チャラララ♪
DIGITAL
Sae
090XXXXXXXX
It's Sae...
What should I do?
Go ahead and answer.
Why now?
はー
Cough.
Okay.
Hello?
Momo!! I need your help!

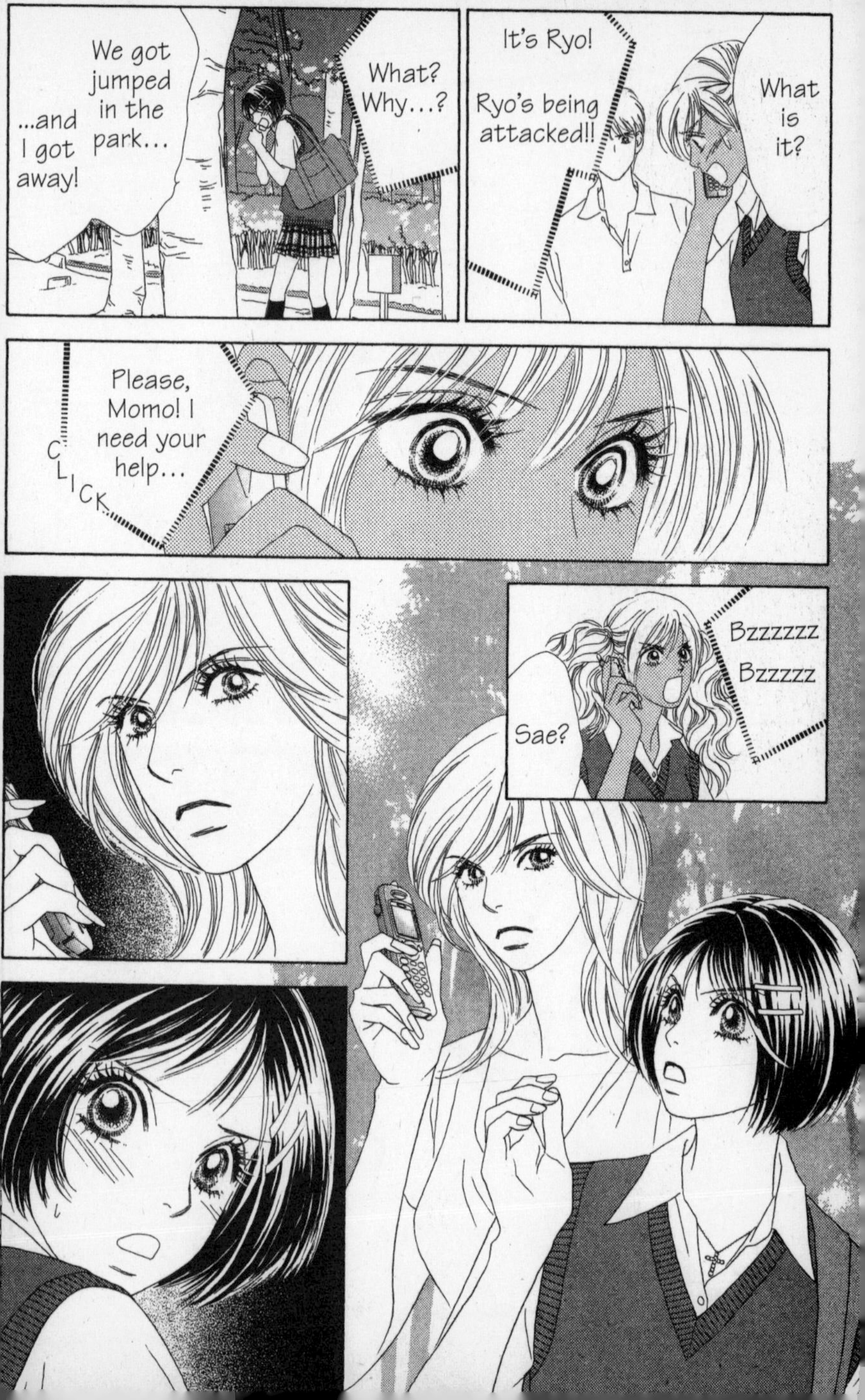
What is it?
It's Ryo!
Ryo's being attacked!!
What? Why...?
We got jumped in the park...
...and I got away!
Please, Momo! I need your help...
CLICK
Bzzzzzz
Bzzzzz
Sae?

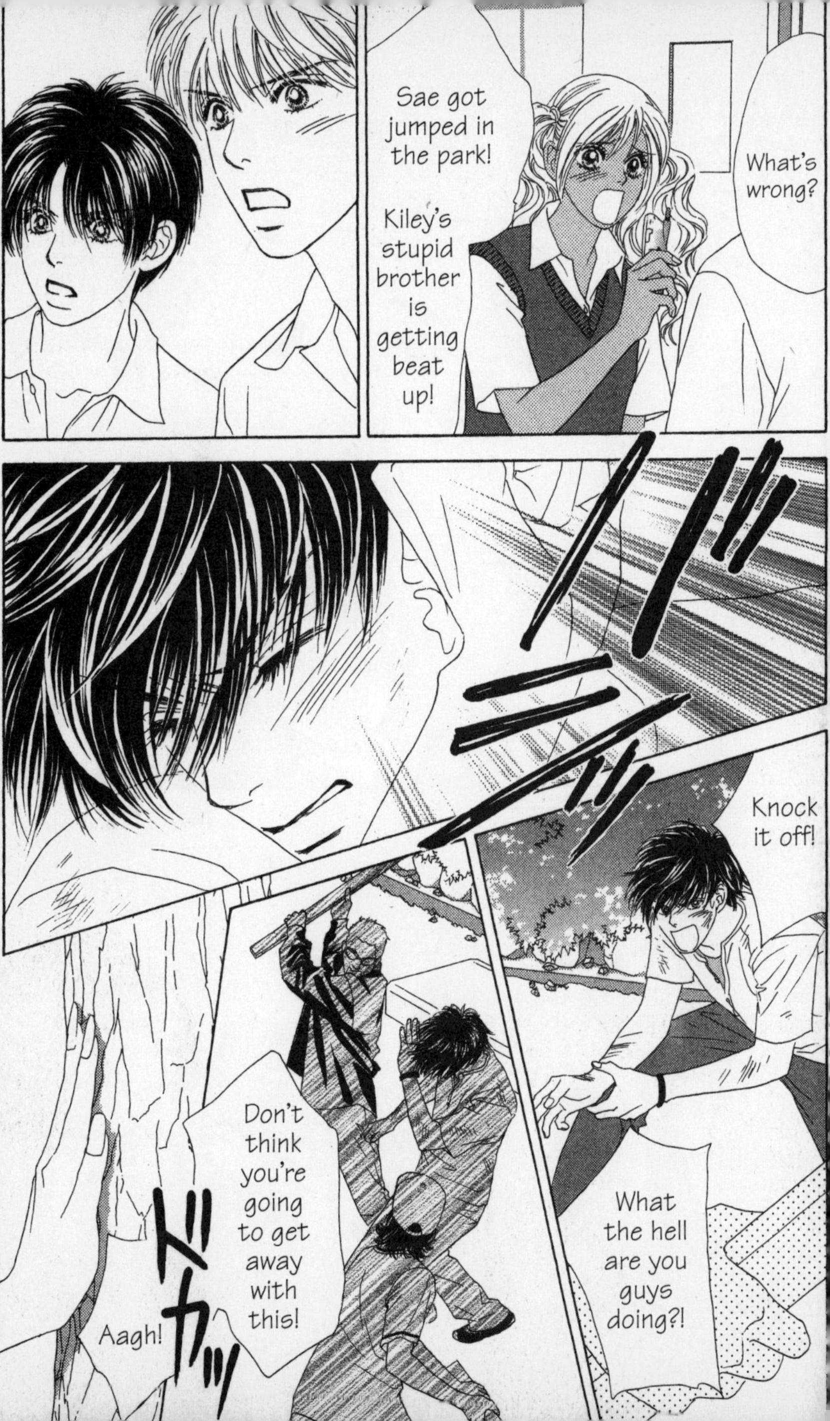
What's wrong?
Sae got jumped in the park!
Kiley's stupid brother is getting beat up!
Knock it off!
What the hell are you guys doing?!
Don't think you're going to get away with this!
ドカッ
Aagh!

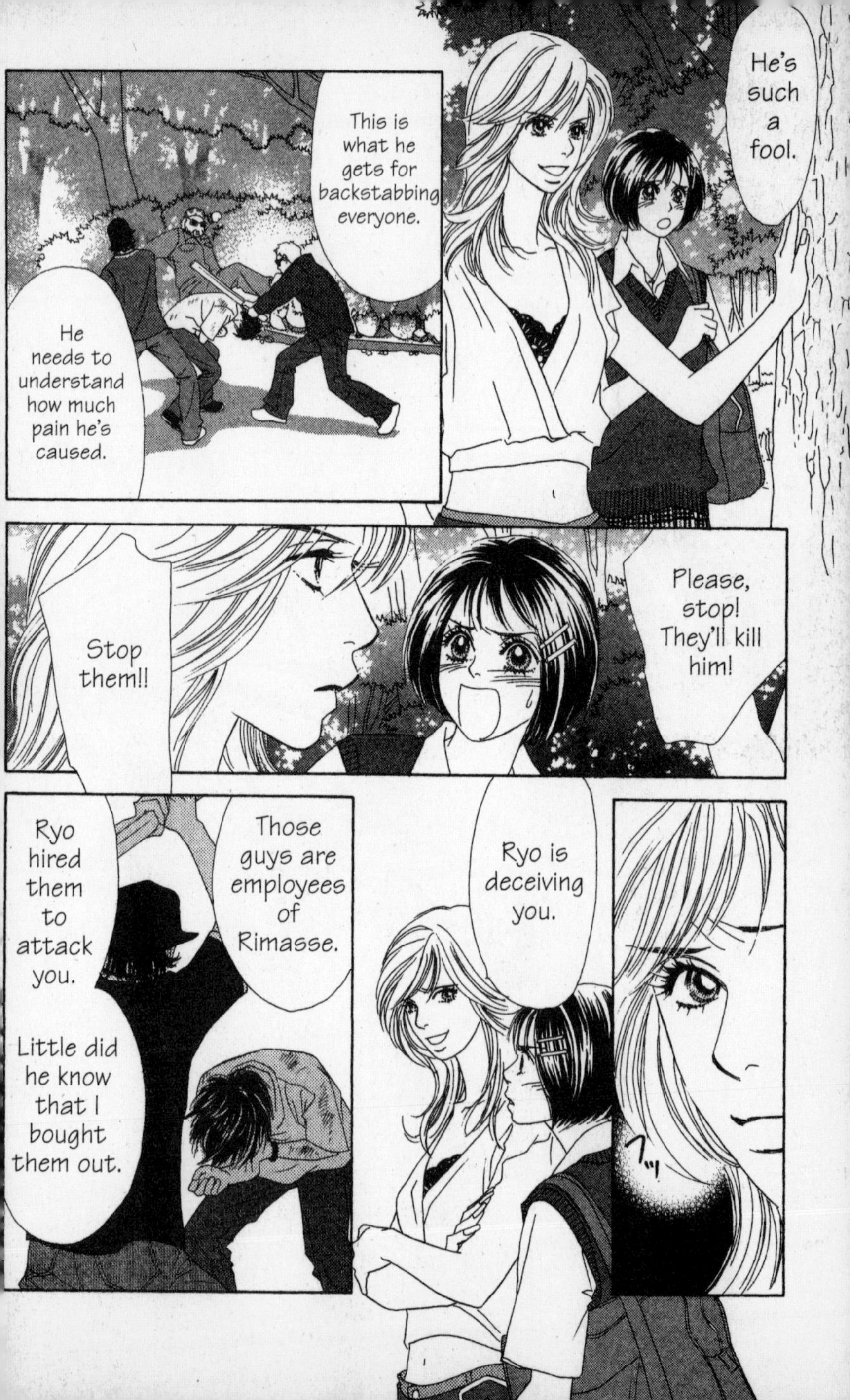
He's such a fool.
This is what he gets for backstabbing everyone.
He needs to understand how much pain he's caused.
Please, stop! They'll kill him!
Stop them!!
Ryo is deceiving you.
Those guys are employees of Rimasse.
Ryo hired them to attack you.
Little did he know that I bought them out.

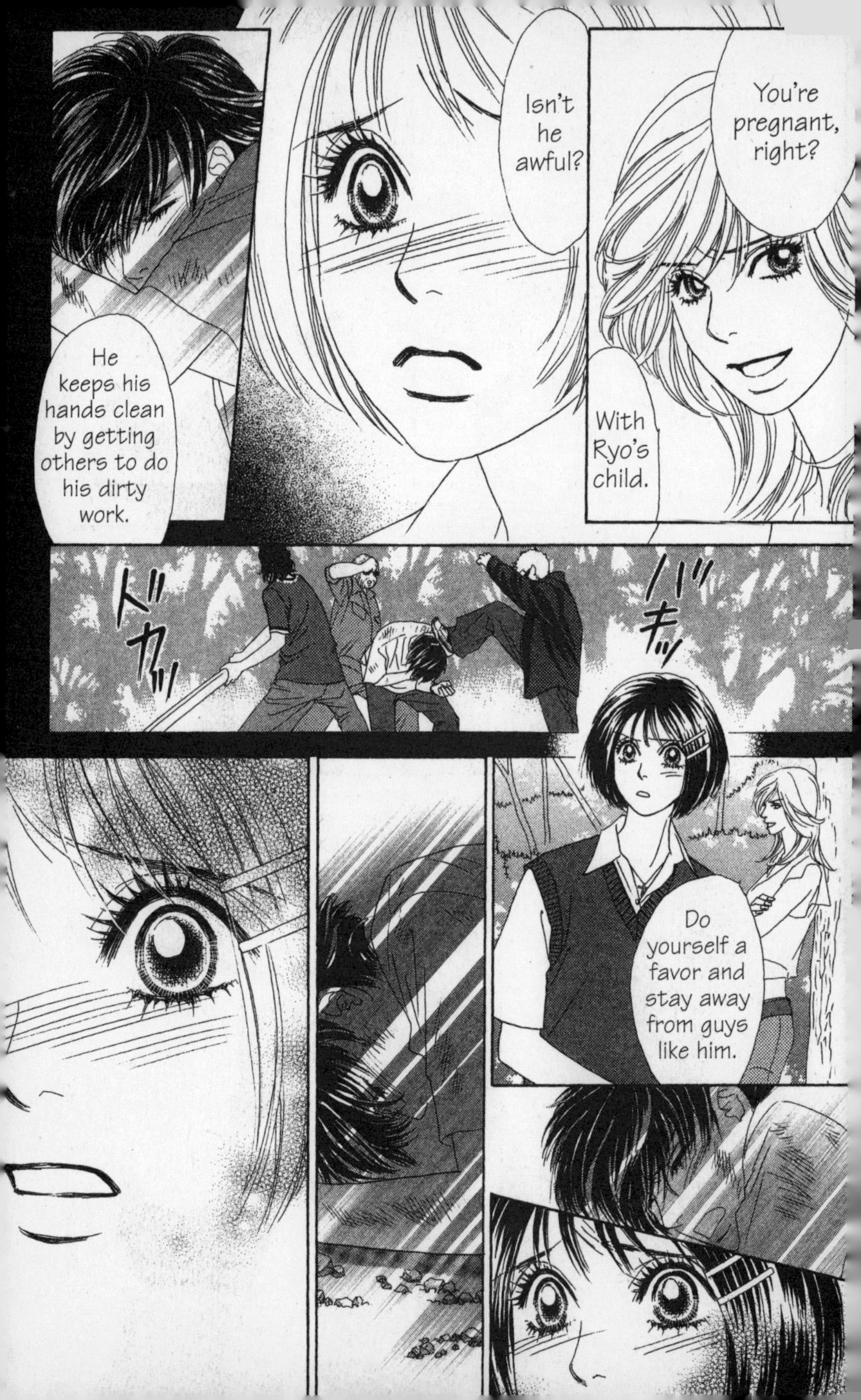
You're pregnant, right?
With Ryo's child.
Isn't he awful?
He keeps his hands clean by getting others to do his dirty work.
バキッ
ドガッ
Do yourself a favor and stay away from guys like him.

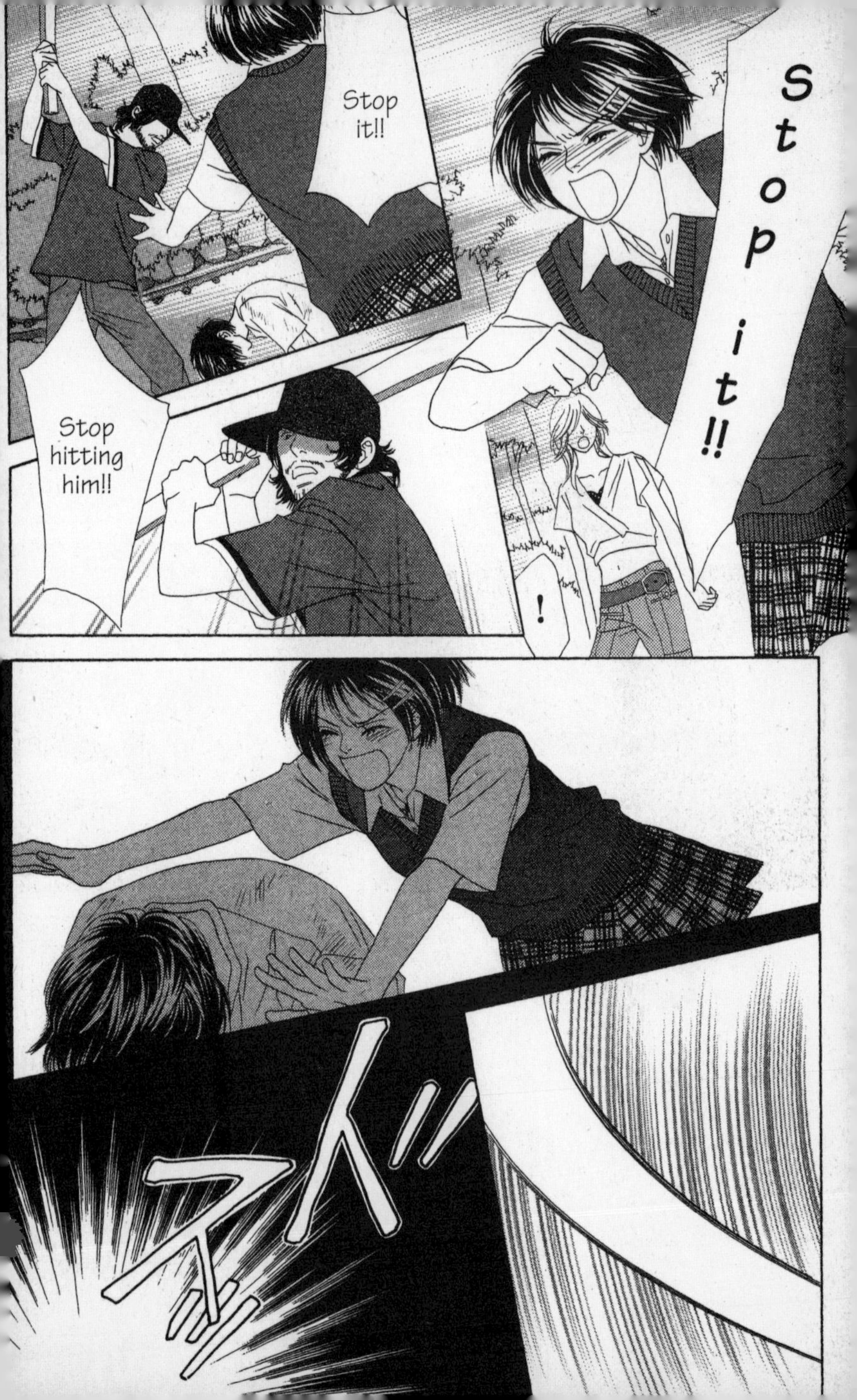
Stop it!!
!
Stop it!!
Stop hitting him!!

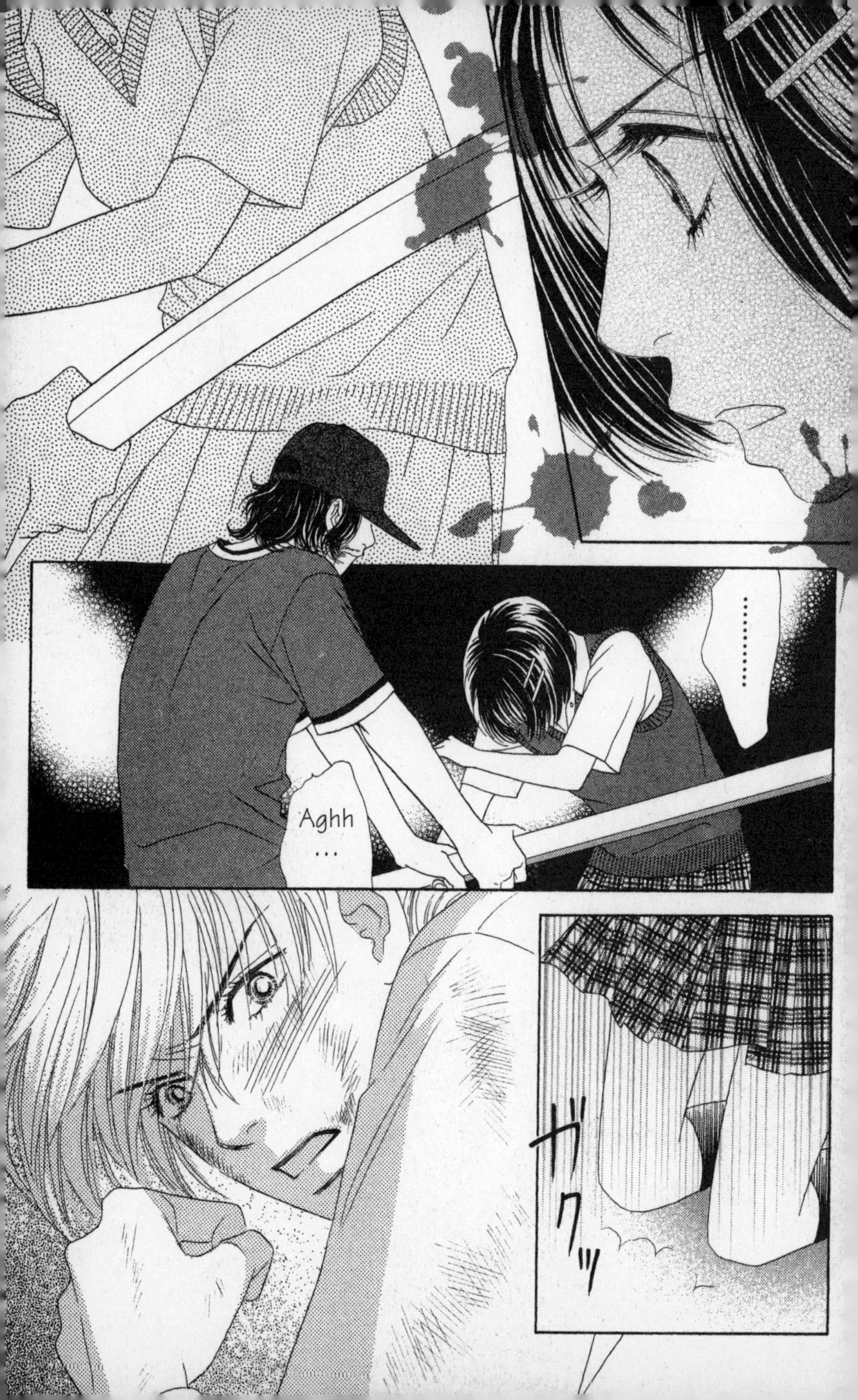
……
Aghh ...
ガクッ

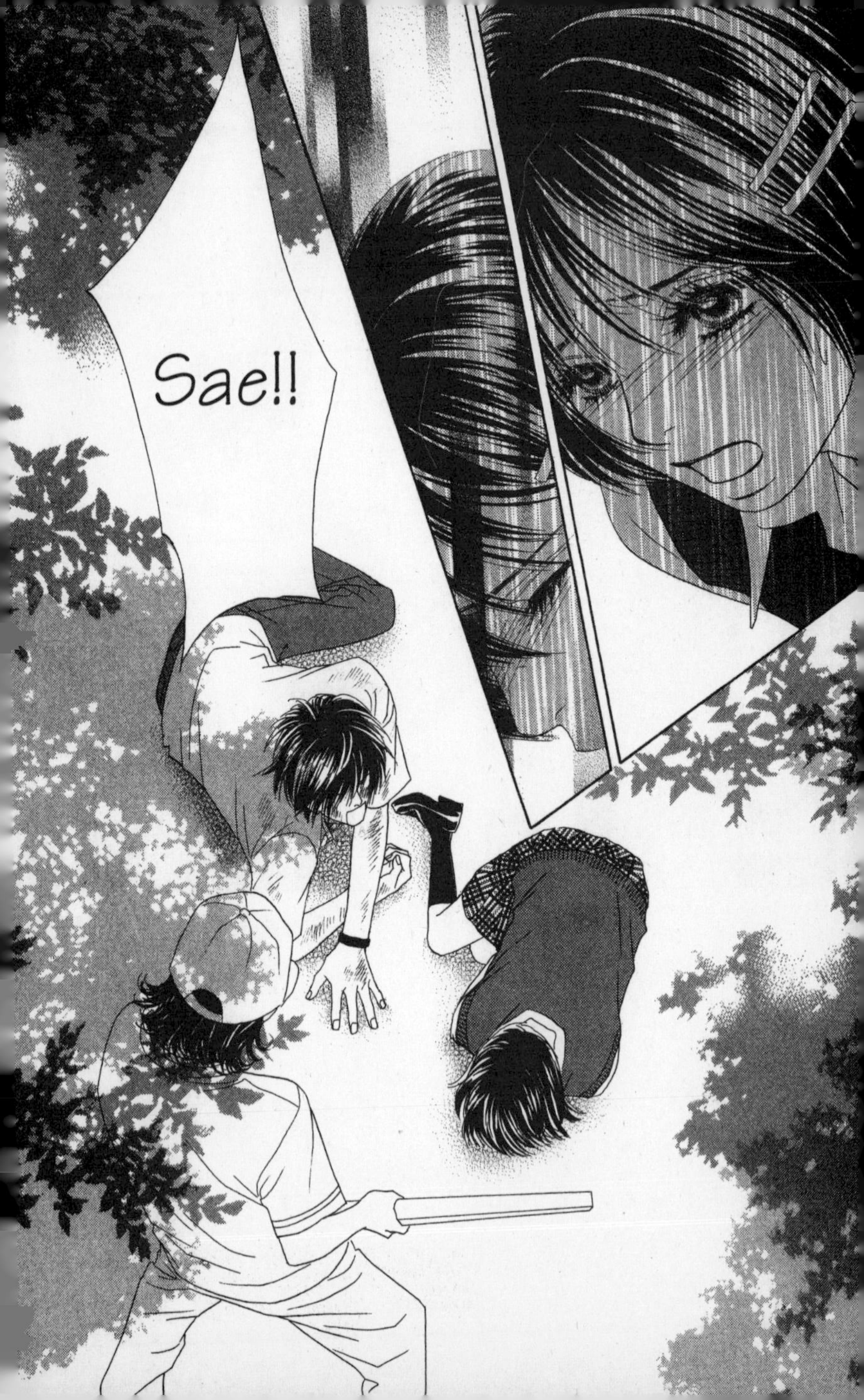
Sae!!

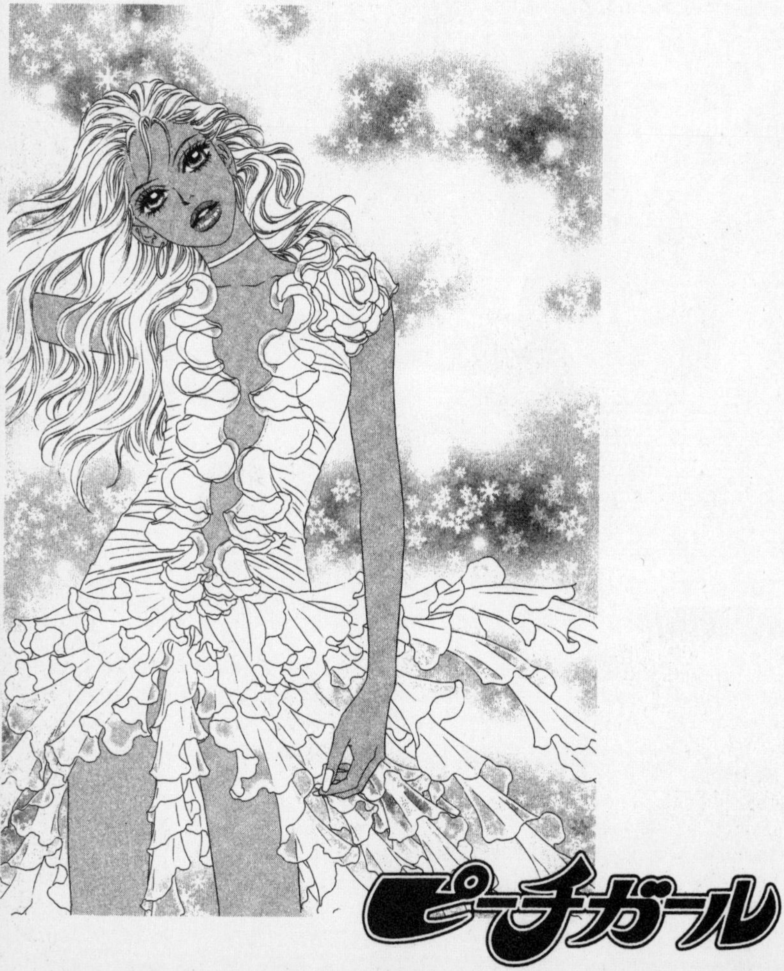
ピーチガール

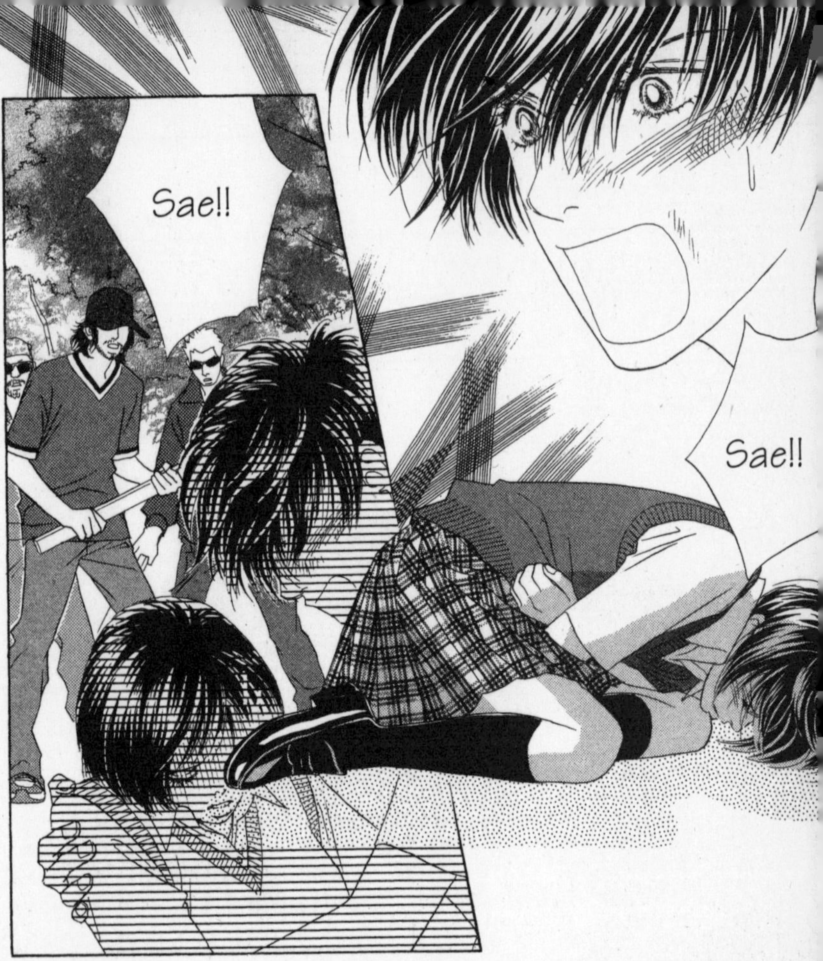
Sae!!
Sae!!

PEACH CLUB

August 7 was my only day off, so I did an Internet search using the keywords "fireworks" and "August 7," and what came up was the Kameoka Peace Festival. I thought to myself, where is Kameoka? Oh yeah! It's a place where you can go rafting on the Horitsu River. I've always wanted to go river rafting, but I never put my plans into action, so this was my chance to finally check out Kameoka. On the day of the Peace Festival, what started off as a light evening drizzle, turned into a major downpour! I thought they might cancel the fireworks, but the city of Kameoka came through! They went on with the show!! I guess fireworks still work even in the rain. It was so beautiful, watching those 7000 fireworks light up the sky. I'm glad I made the trip from Kobe. I was drenched, but it certainly made it a memorable night (ha ha!). It was so fun that I hope I can go again. --Miwa

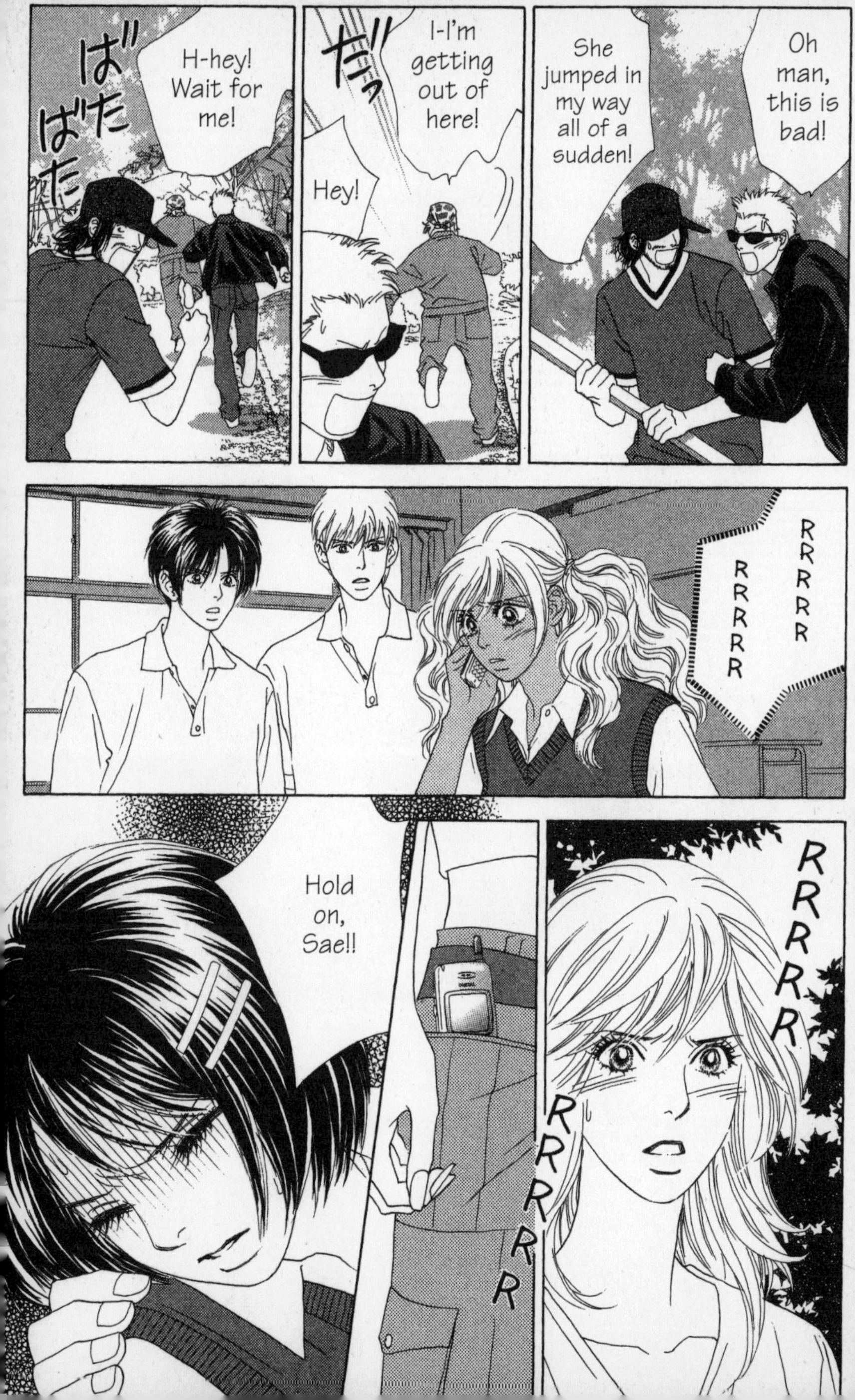
Oh man, this is bad!
She jumped in my way all of a sudden!
だっ
I-I'm getting out of here!
Hey!
H-hey! Wait for me!
ばたばた
RRRRR
RRRRR
RRRRR
RRRRRR
Hold on, Sae!!

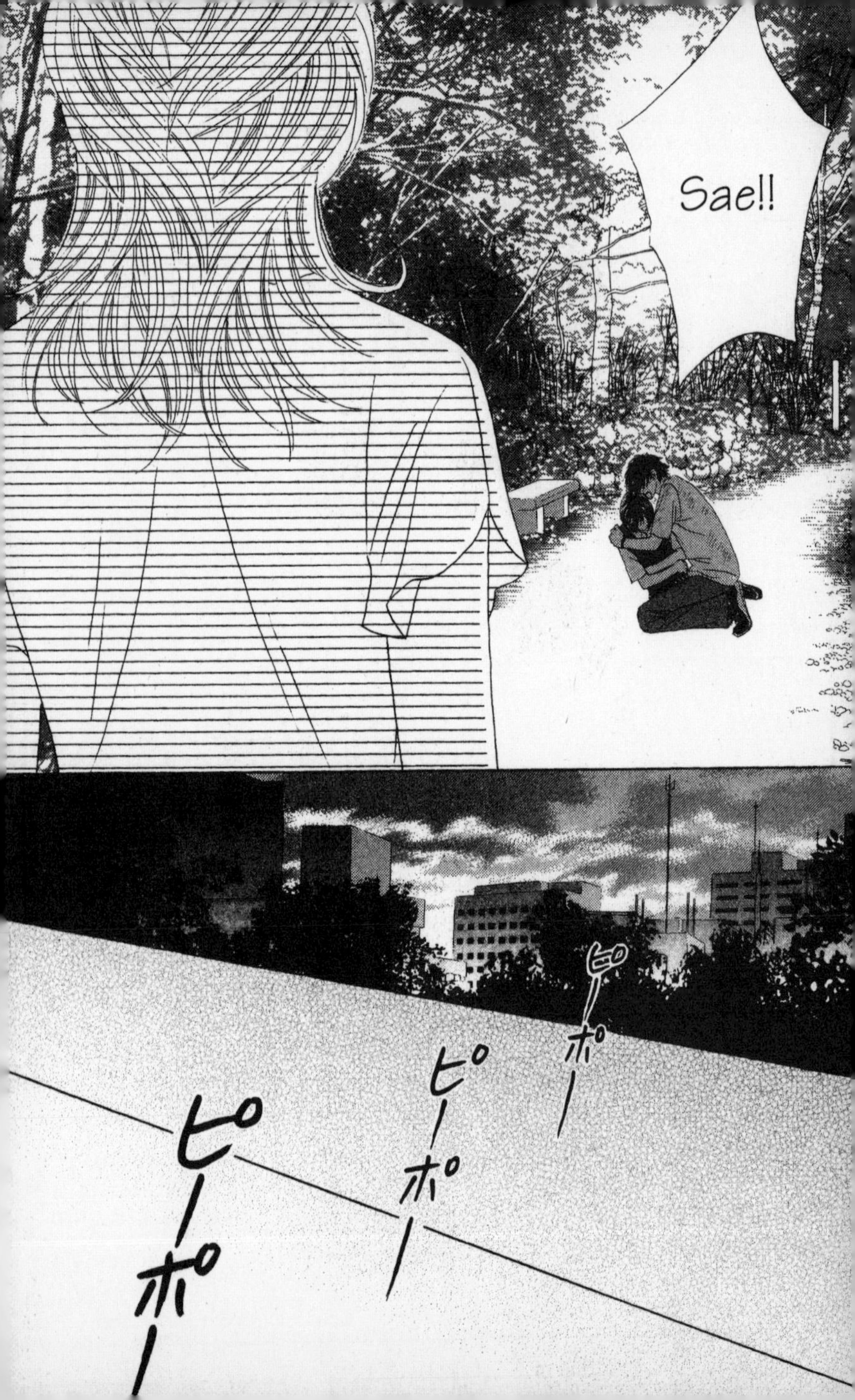
Sae!!
ピーポー
ピーポー
ピーポー

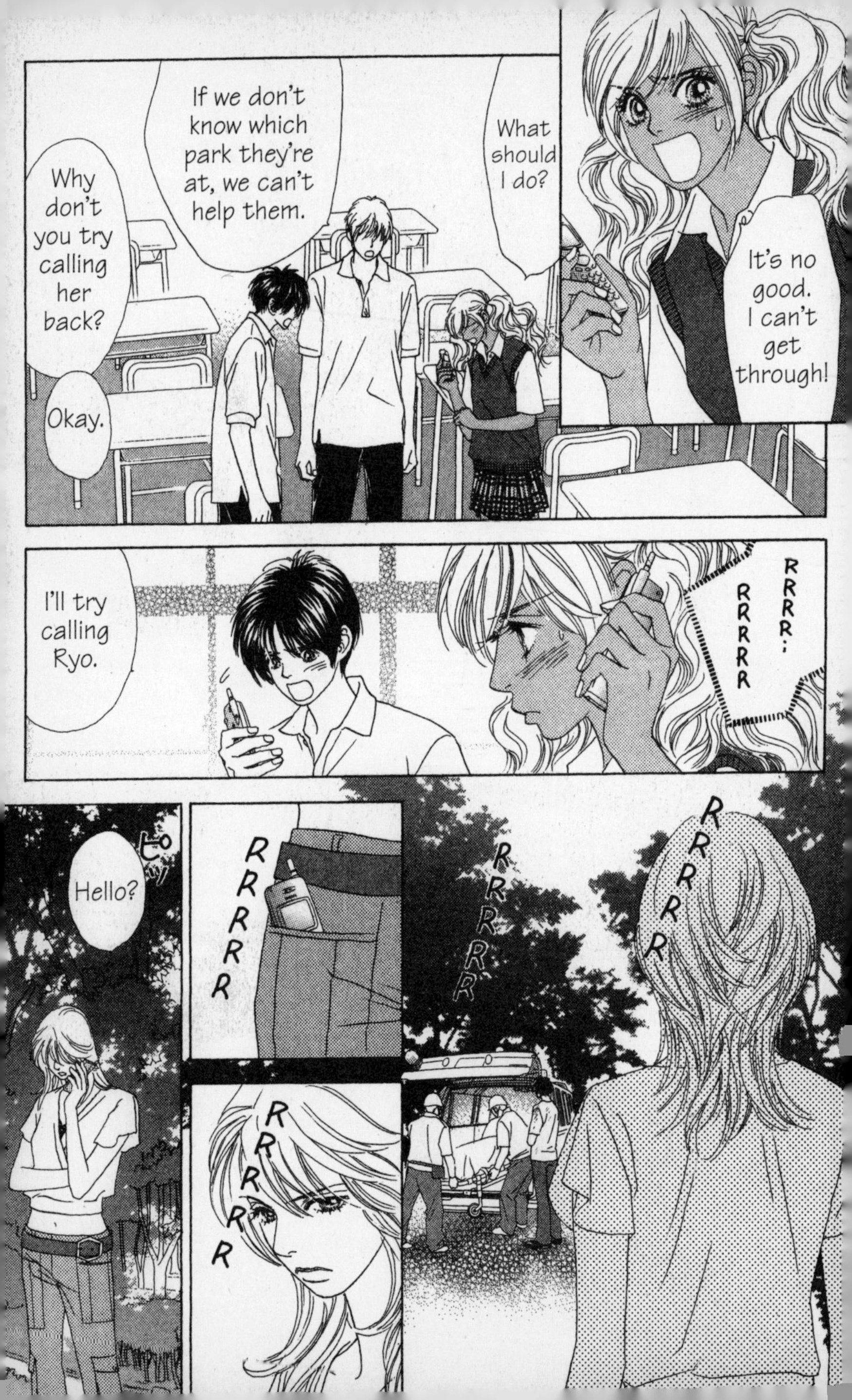
It's no good. I can't get through!
What should I do?
If we don't know which park they're at, we can't help them.
Why don't you try calling her back?
Okay.
RRRR...
RRRRR
I'll try calling Ryo.
RRRRR
RRRRR
RRRRR
RRRRRR
ピッ
Hello?

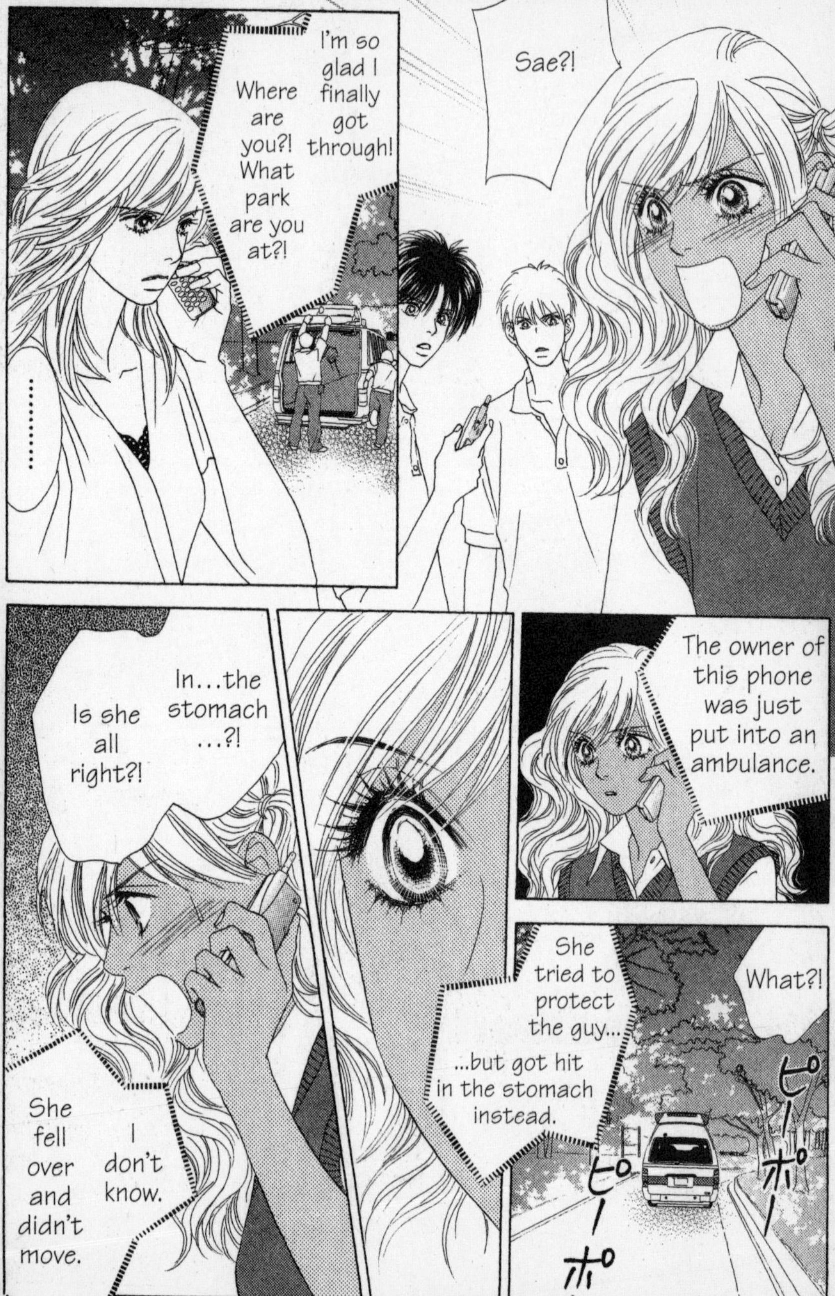
Sae?!
I'm so glad I finally got through!
Where are you?! What park are you at?!
......
The owner of this phone was just put into an ambulance.
What?!
She tried to protect the guy...
...but got hit in the stomach instead.
ピーポーピーポー
In...the stomach ...?!
Is she all right?!
I don't know.
She fell over and didn't move.

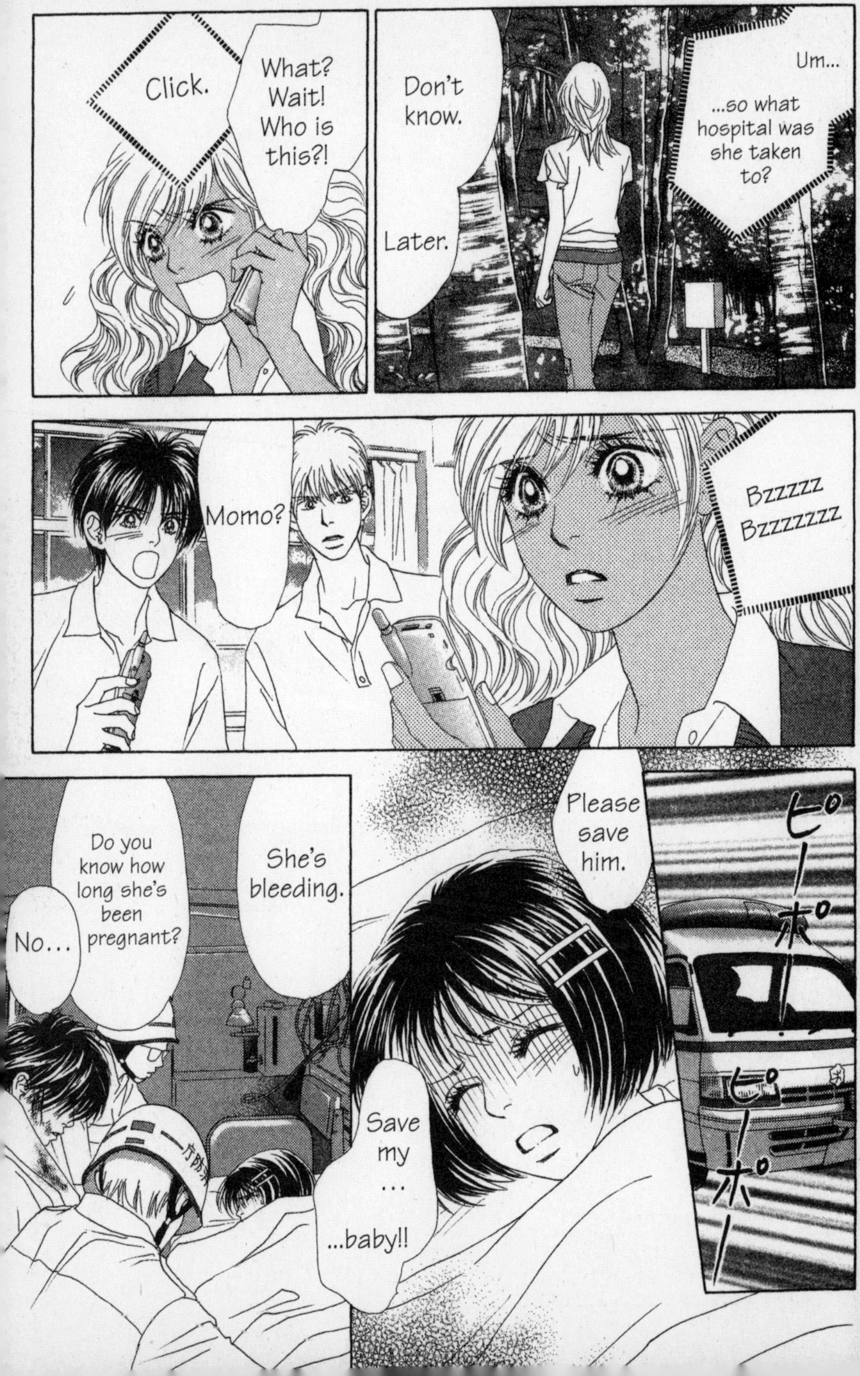
Um...
...so what hospital was she taken to?
Don't know.
Later.
What? Wait! Who is this?!
Click.
Bzzzzz Bzzzzzzz
Momo?
ピーポー
ピーポー
Please save him.
Save my ...
...baby!!
She's bleeding.
Do you know how long she's been pregnant?
No...

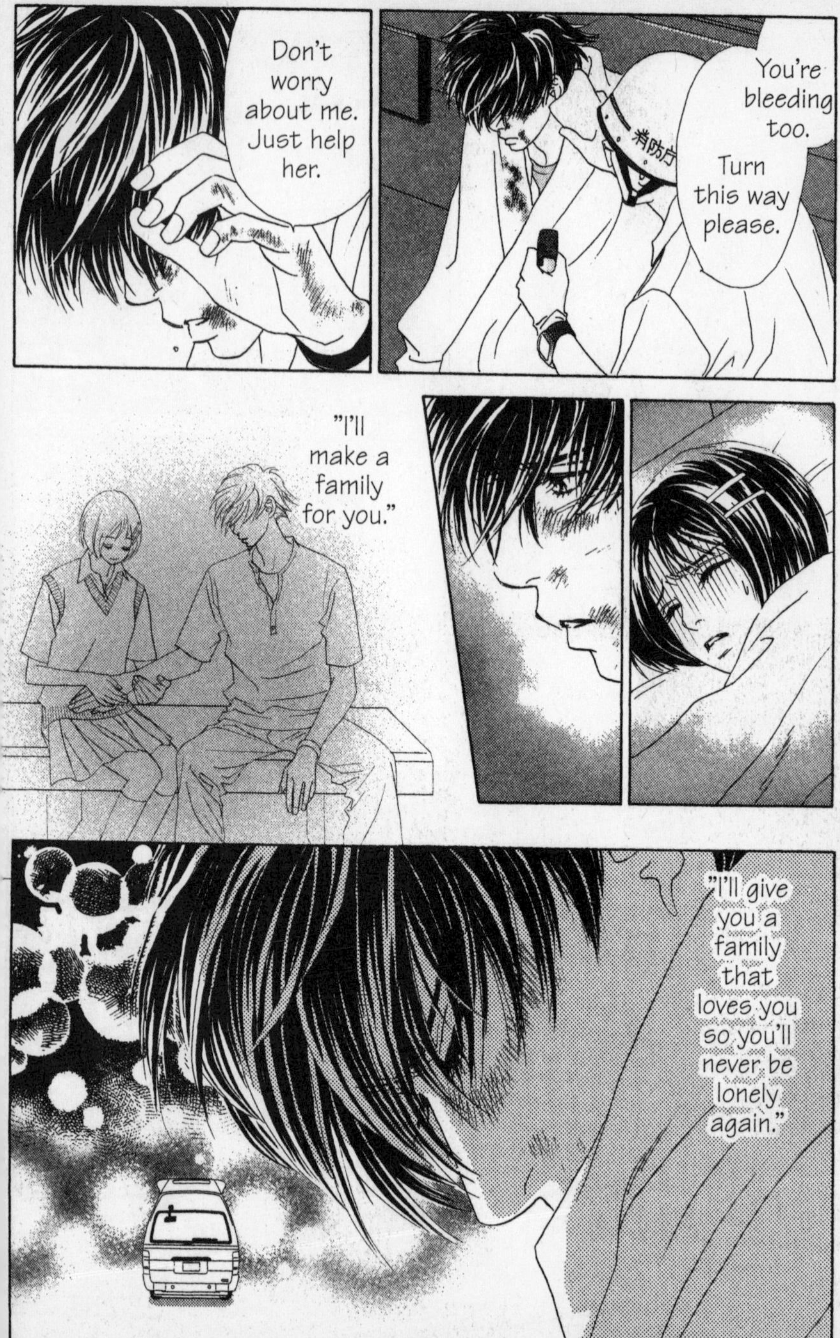
消防庁
You're bleeding too.
Turn this way please.
Don't worry about me. Just help her.
"I'll make a family for you."
"I'll give you a family that loves you so you'll never be lonely again."

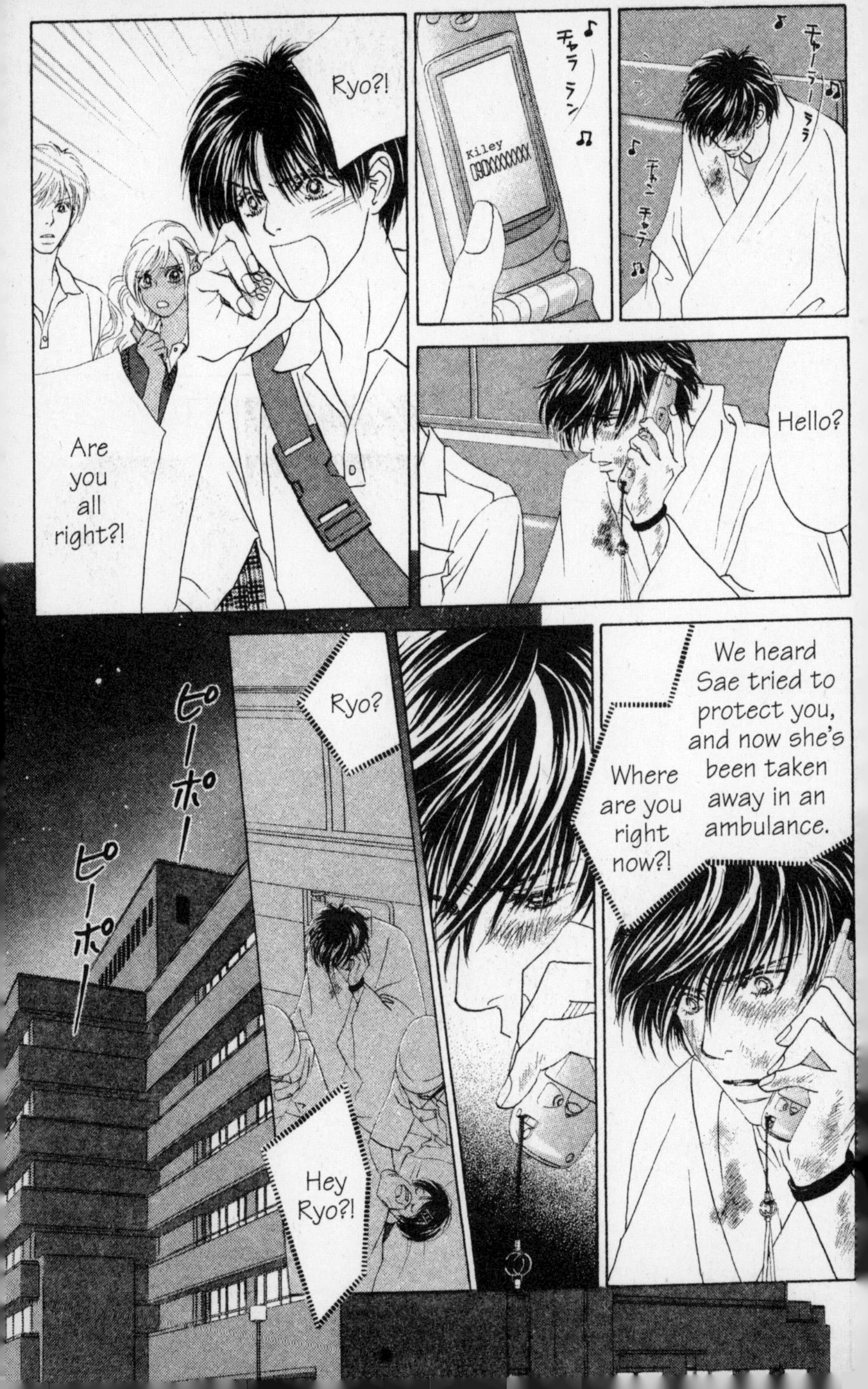
チャーラーララ
チャラ チャラ
チャラ ラン
Kiley
090XXXXXXX
Hello?
Ryo?!
Are you all right?!
We heard Sae tried to protect you, and now she's been taken away in an ambulance.
Where are you right now?!
Ryo?
Hey Ryo?!
ピーポー
ピーポー

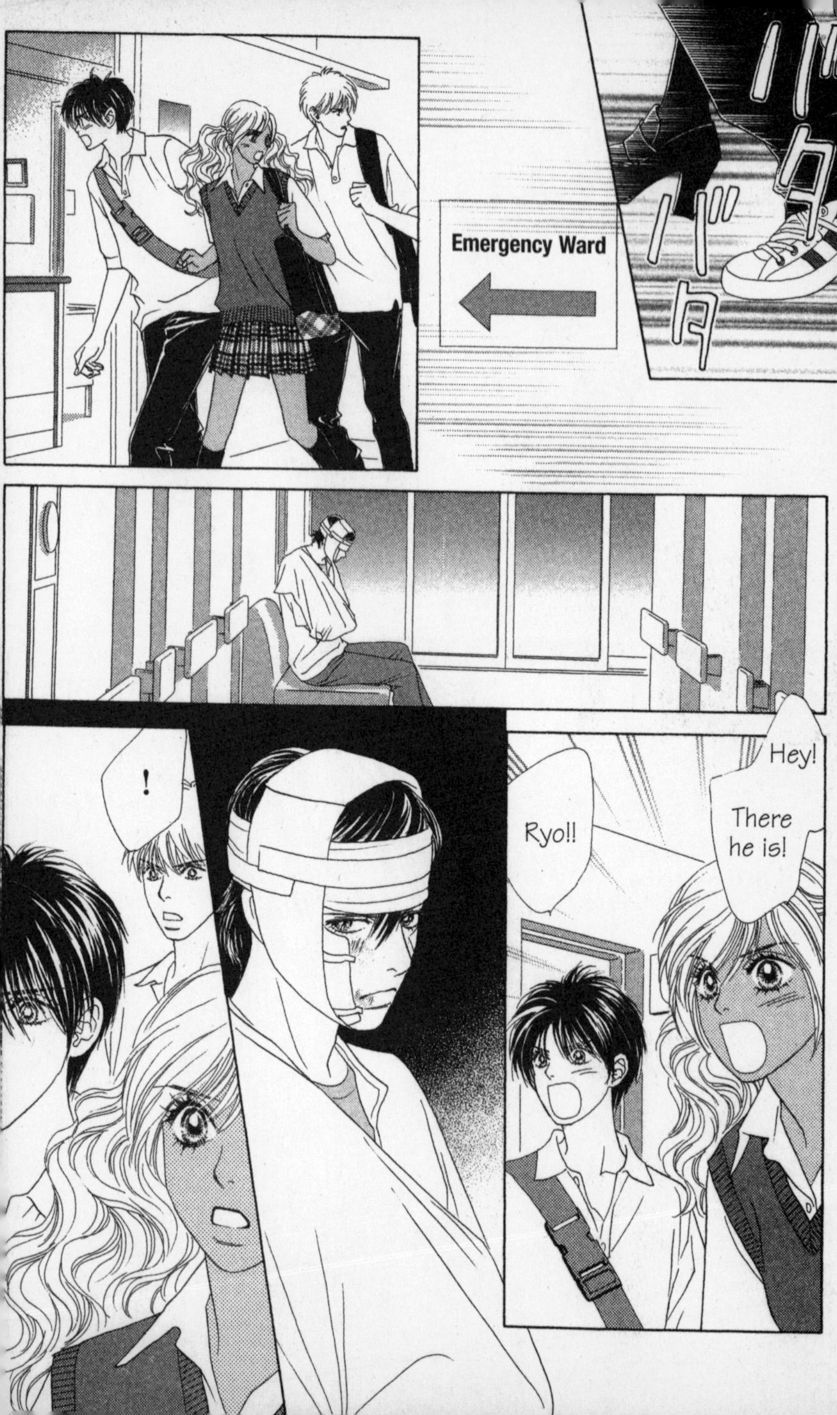

バタバタ
Emergency Ward
Hey!
There he is!
Ryo!!
!

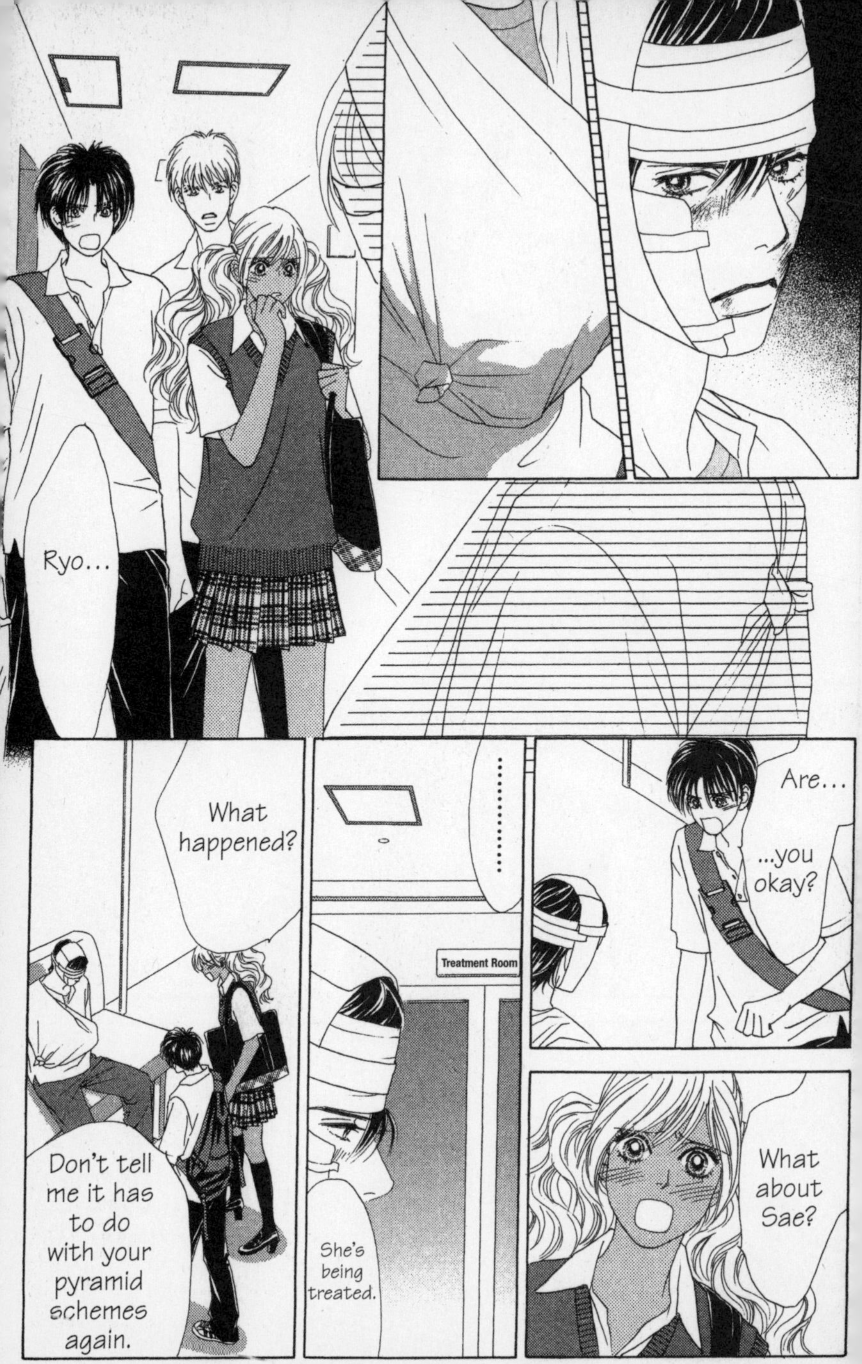
Ryo...
Are...
...you okay?
What about Sae?
......
Treatment Room
She's being treated.
What happened?
Don't tell me it has to do with your pyramid schemes again.

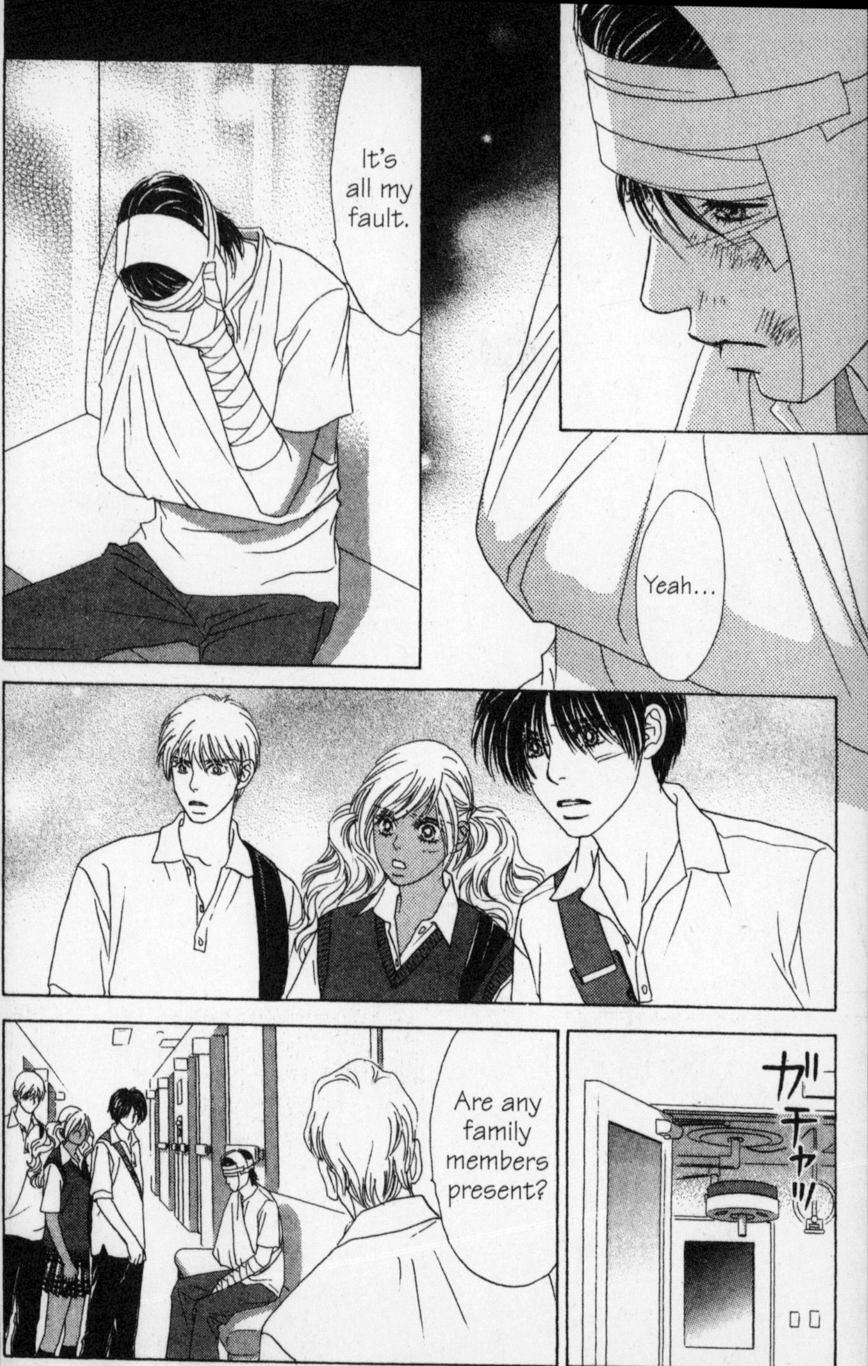
Yeah...
It's all my fault.
ガチャッ
Are any family members present?

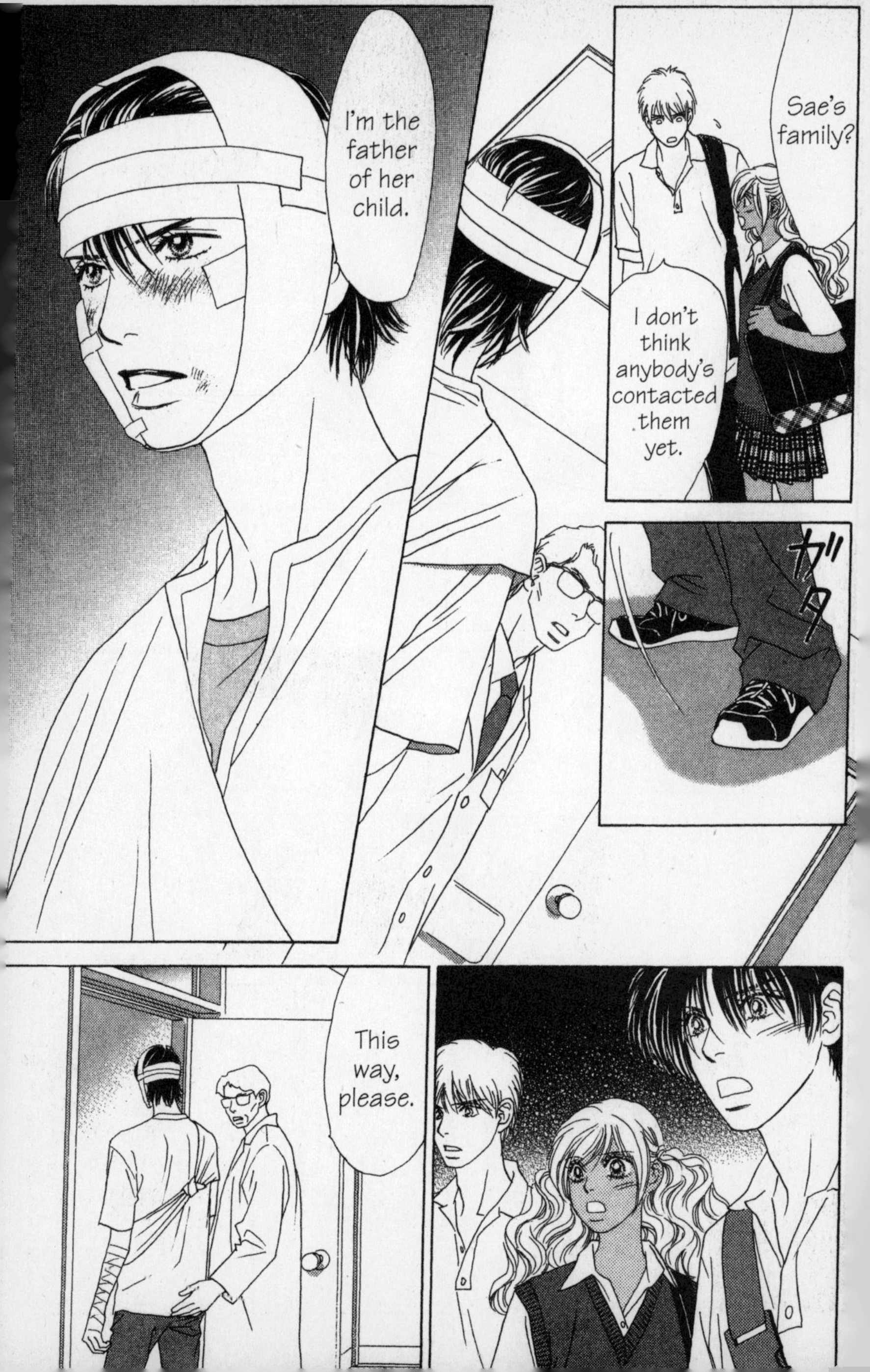
Sae's family?
I don't think anybody's contacted them yet.
ガタ
I'm the father of her child.
This way, please.

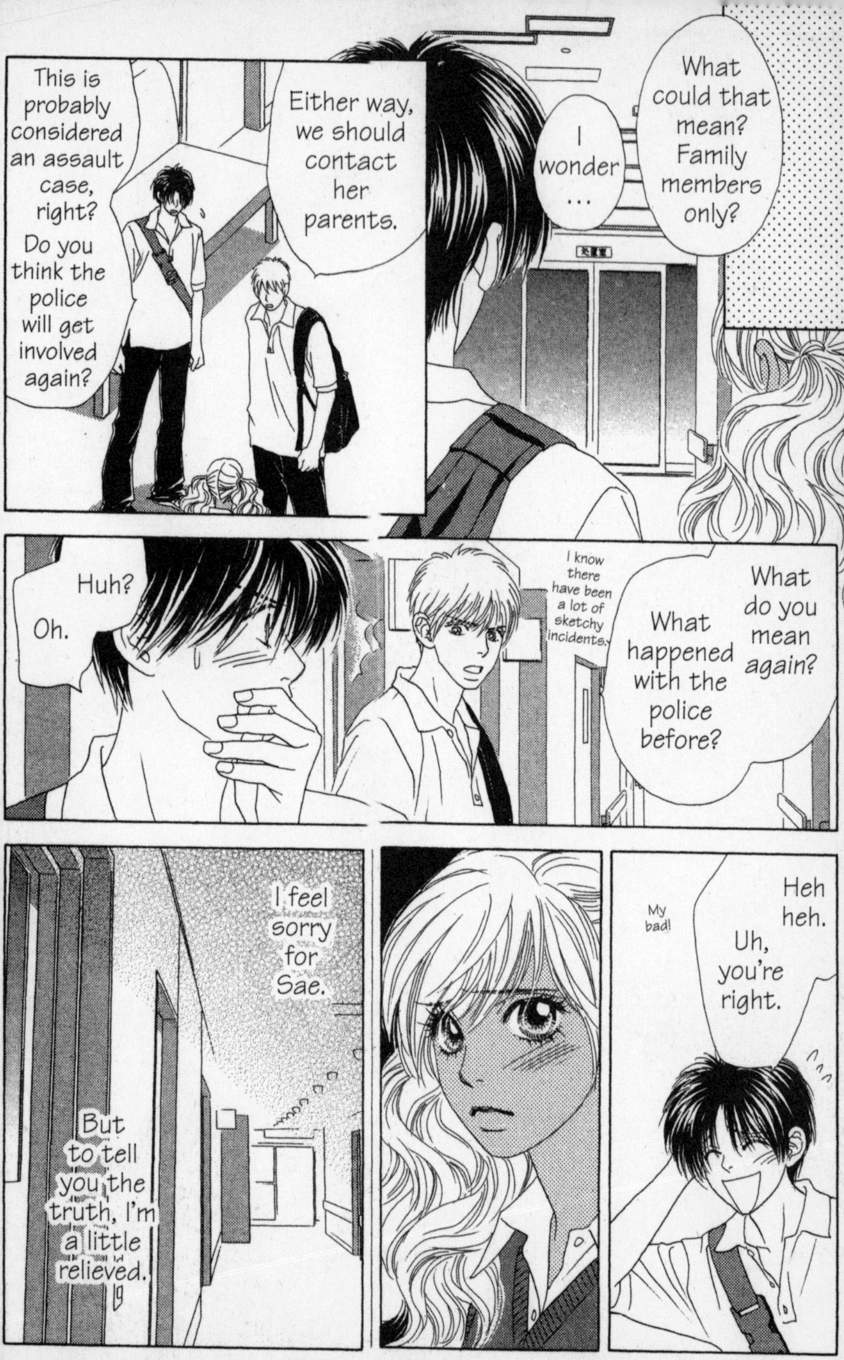

What could that mean? Family members only?
I wonder...
Either way, we should contact her parents.
This is probably considered an assault case, right?
Do you think the police will get involved again?
What do you mean again?
What happened with the police before?
I know there have been a lot of sketchy incidents.
Huh?
Oh.
Heh heh.
Uh, you're right.
My bad!
I feel sorry for Sae.
But to tell you the truth, I'm a little relieved.

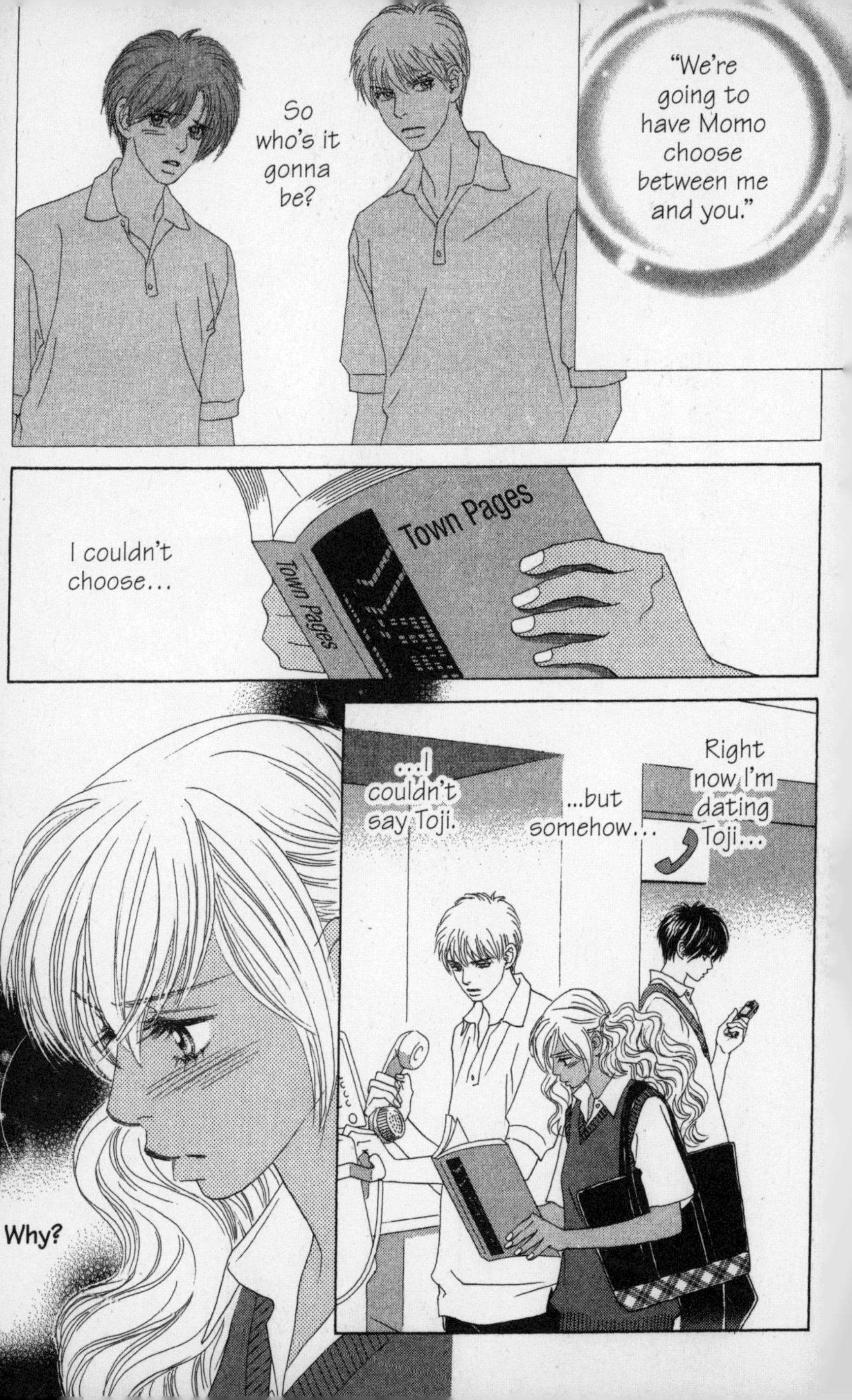
"We're going to have Momo choose between me and you."
So who's it gonna be?
Town Pages
Town Pages
I couldn't choose...
Right now I'm dating Toji...
...but somehow...
...I couldn't say Toji.
Why?

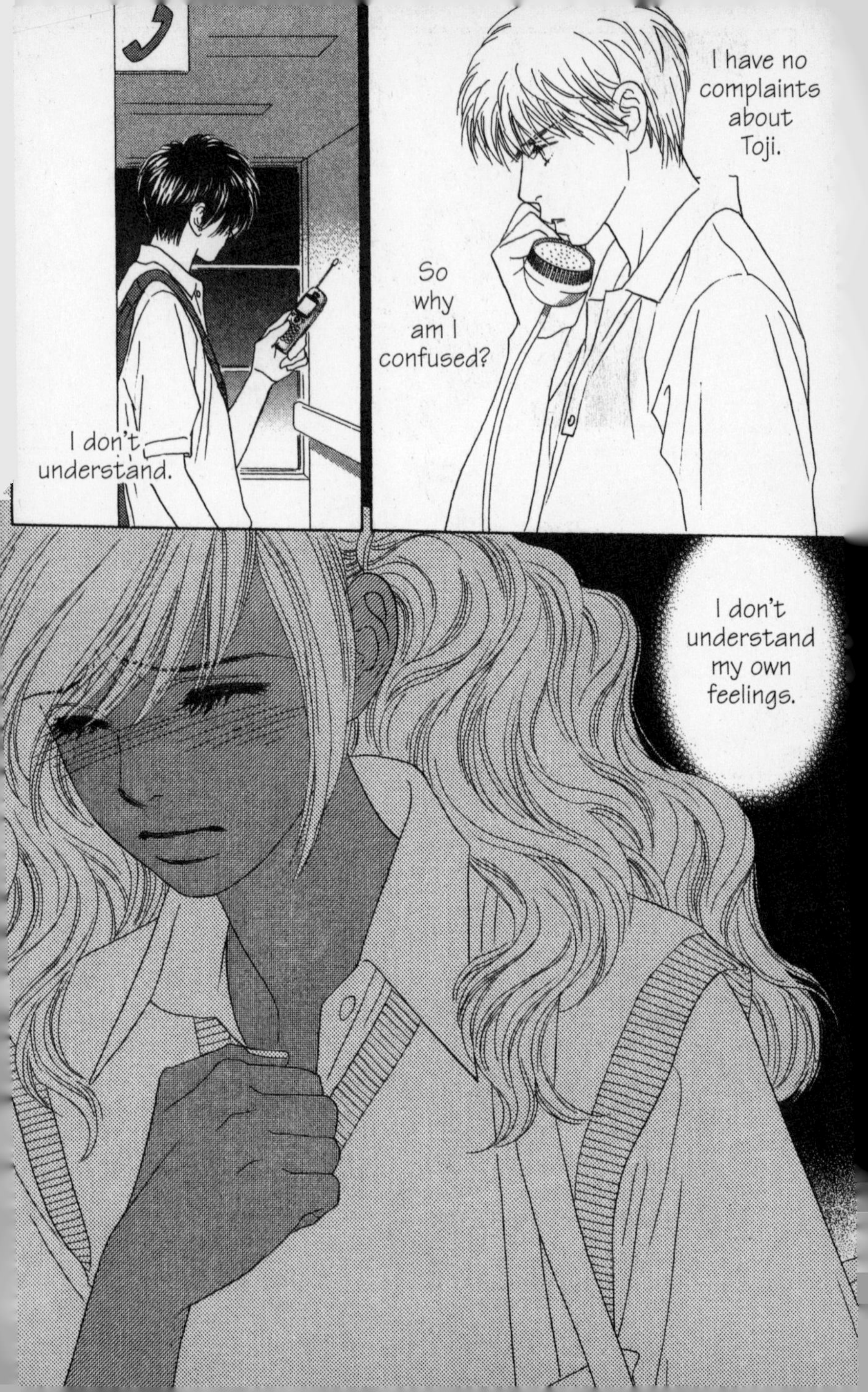
I have no complaints about Toji.
So why am I confused?
I don't understand.
I don't understand my own feelings.

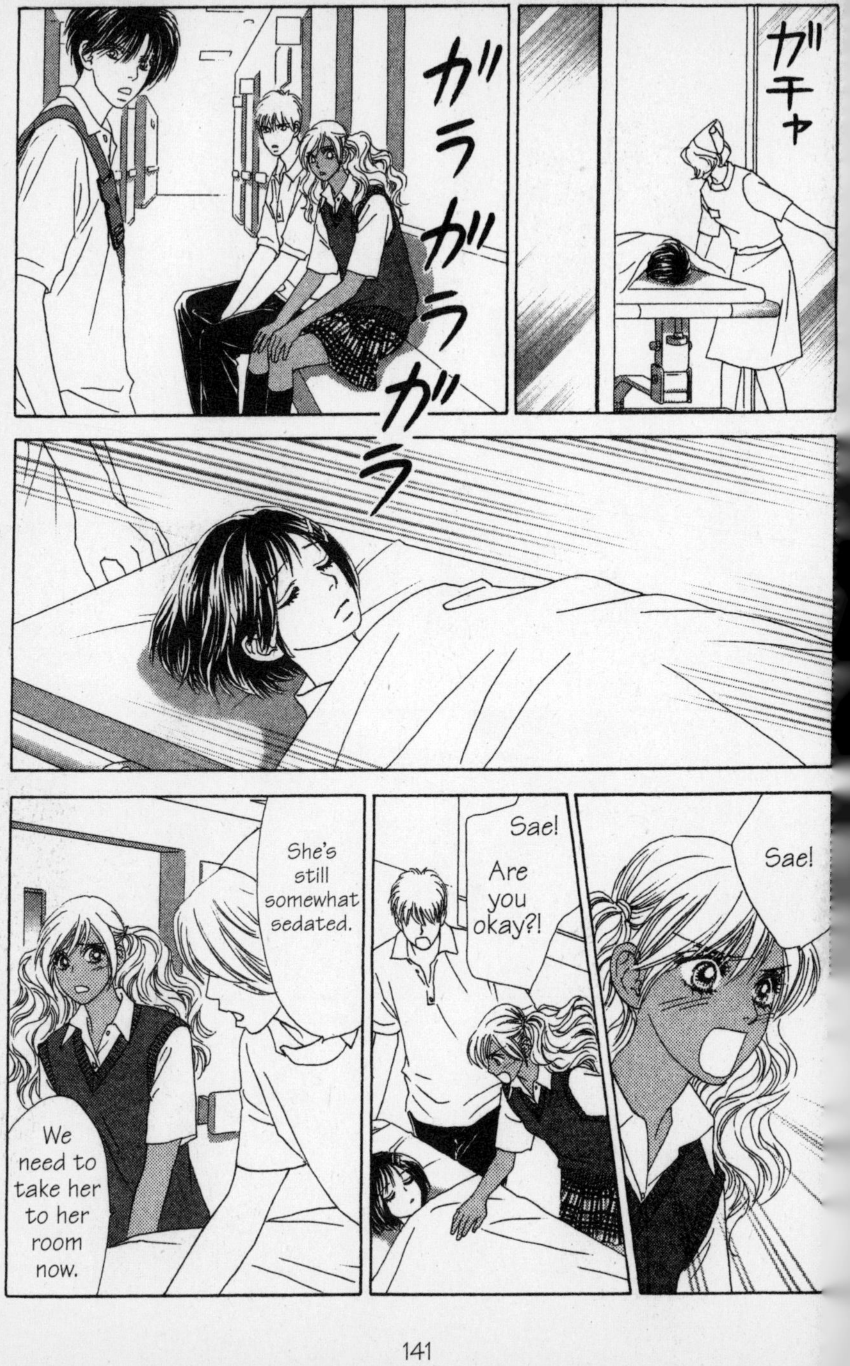
ガチャ
ガラガラガラ
Sae!
Sae!
Are you okay?!
She's still somewhat sedated.
We need to take her to her room now.

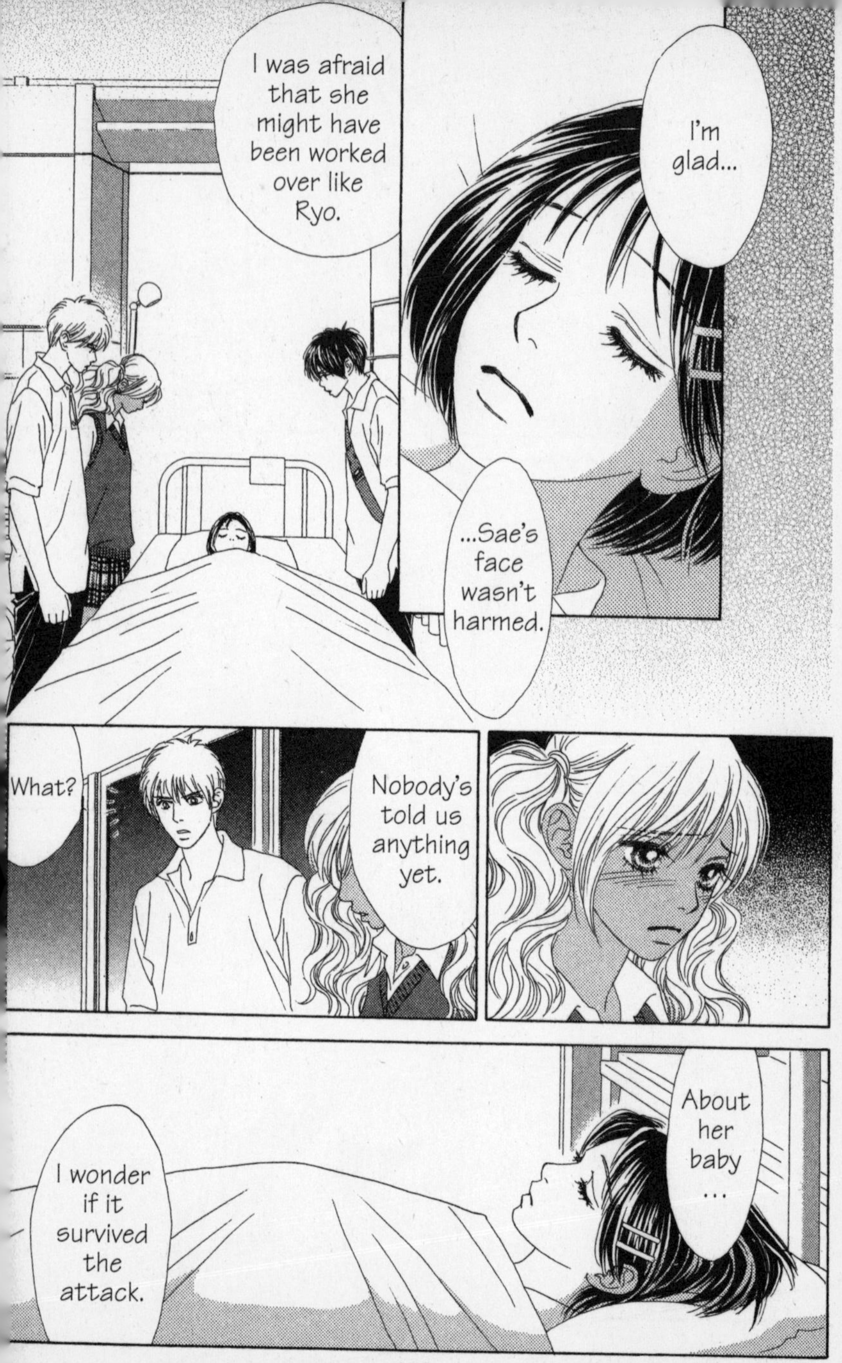
I'm glad...
...Sae's face wasn't harmed.
I was afraid that she might have been worked over like Ryo.
Nobody's told us anything yet.
What?
About her baby...
I wonder if it survived the attack.

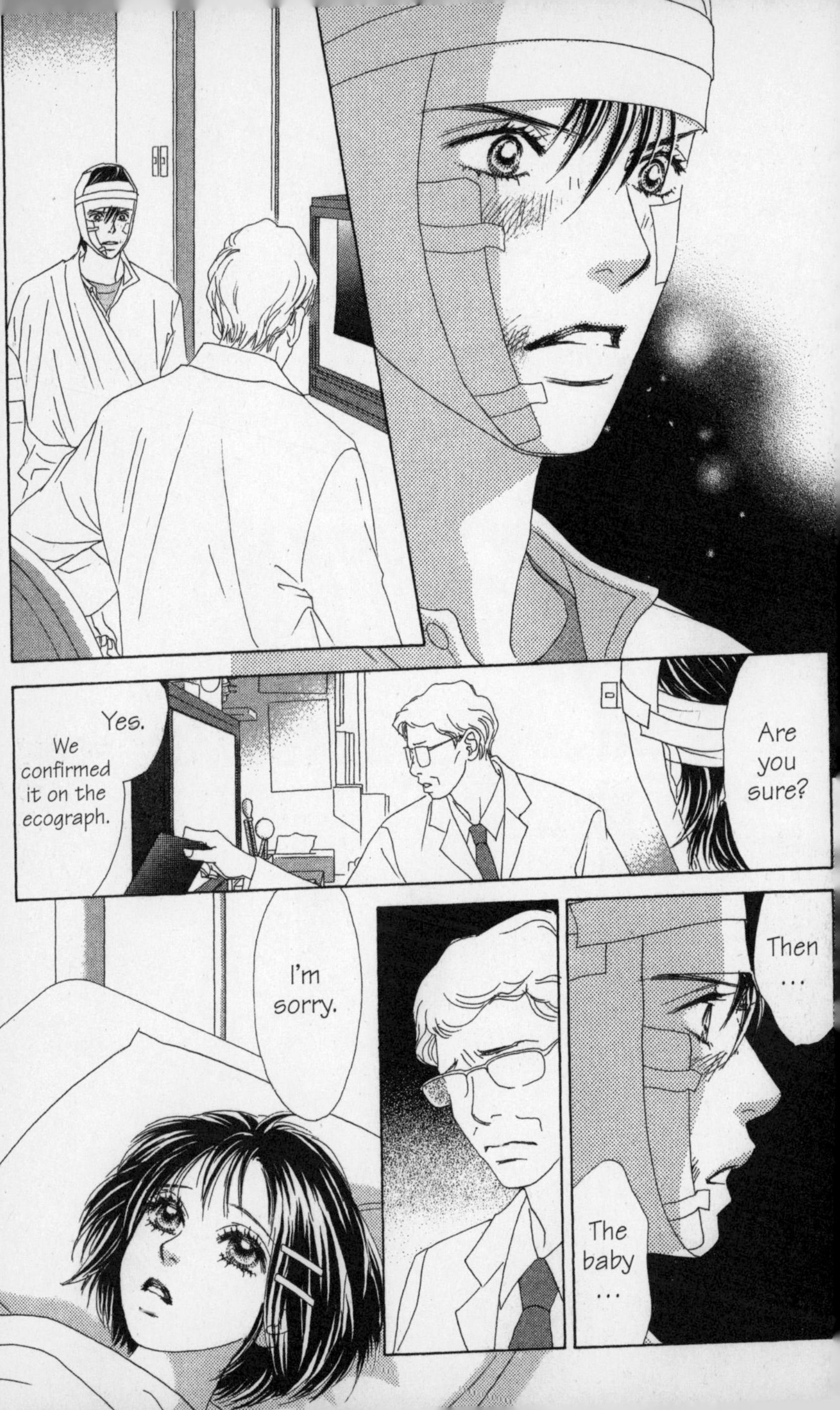
Are you sure?
Yes.
We confirmed it on the ecograph.
Then ...
The baby ...
I'm sorry.

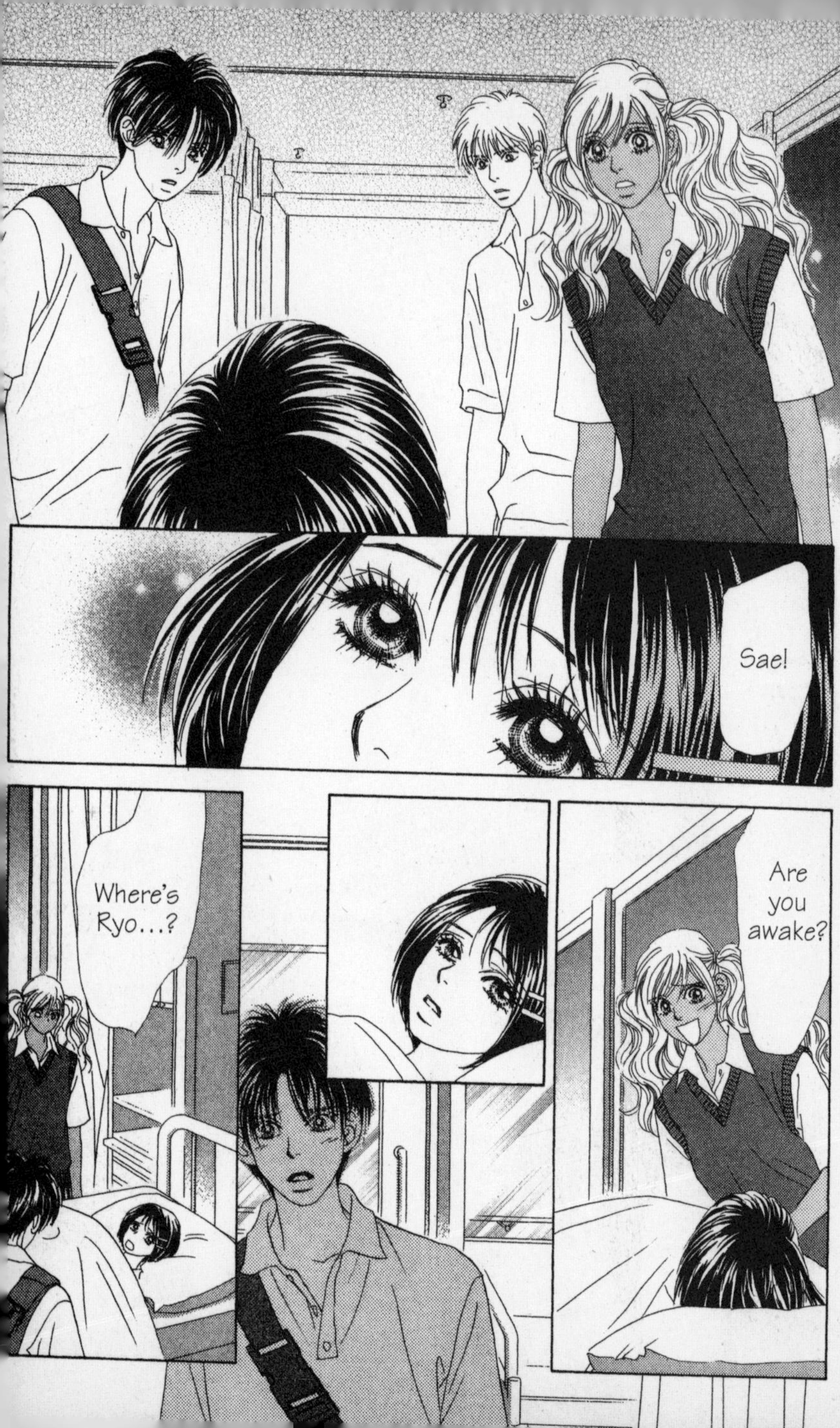
Sae!
Are you awake?
Where's Ryo...?

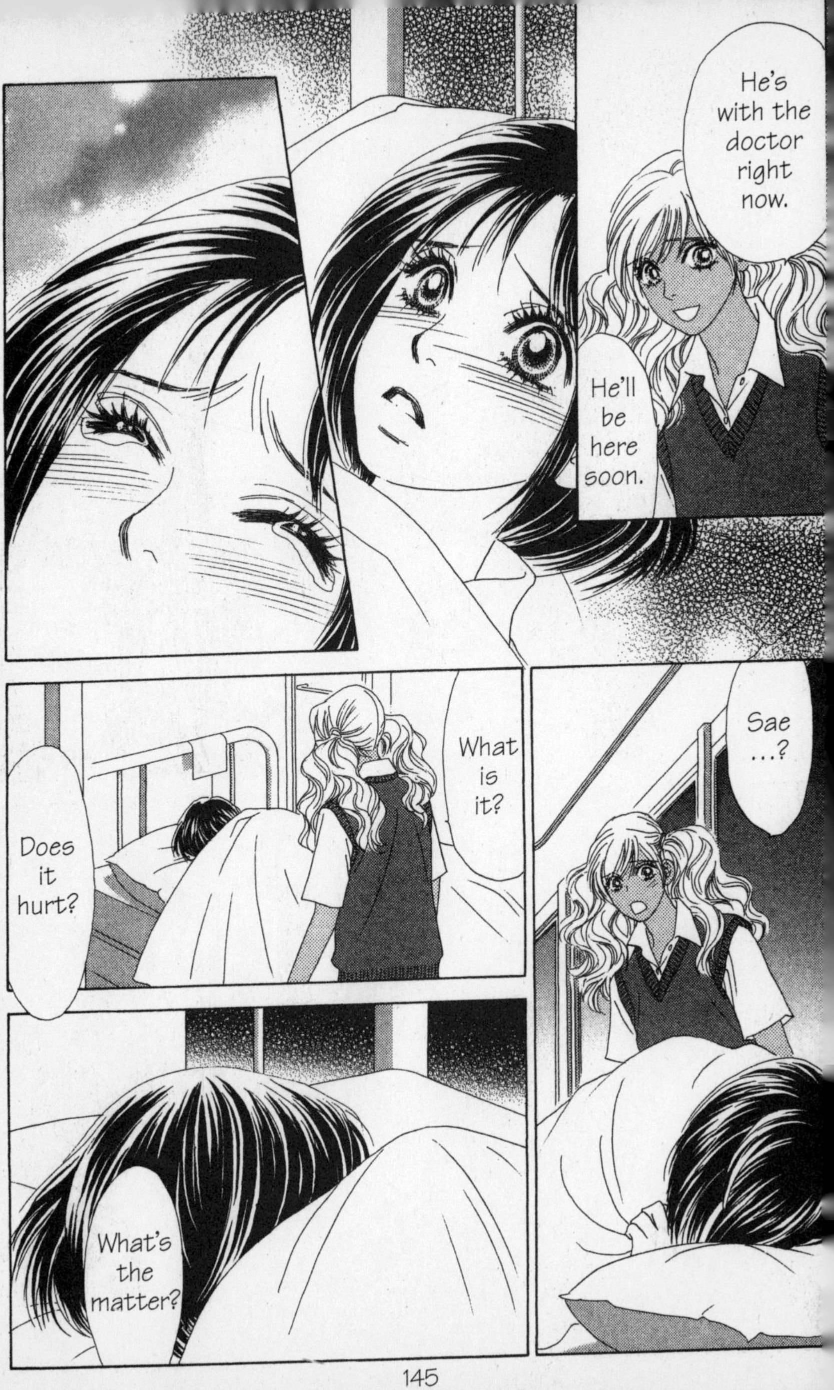
He's with the doctor right now.
He'll be here soon.
Sae ...?
What is it?
Does it hurt?
What's the matter?

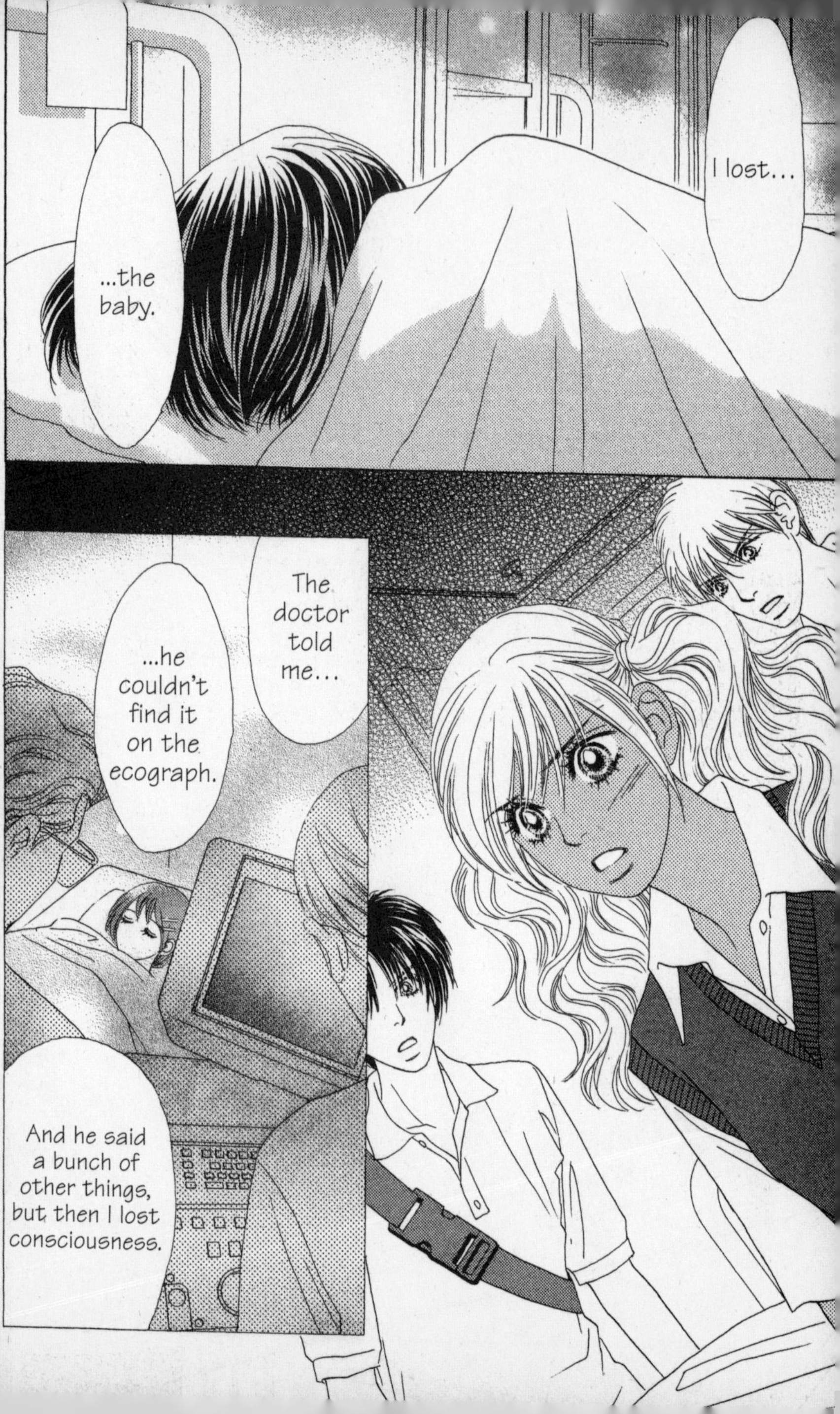
I lost…
...the baby.
The doctor told me…
...he couldn't find it on the ecograph.
And he said a bunch of other things, but then I lost consciousness.

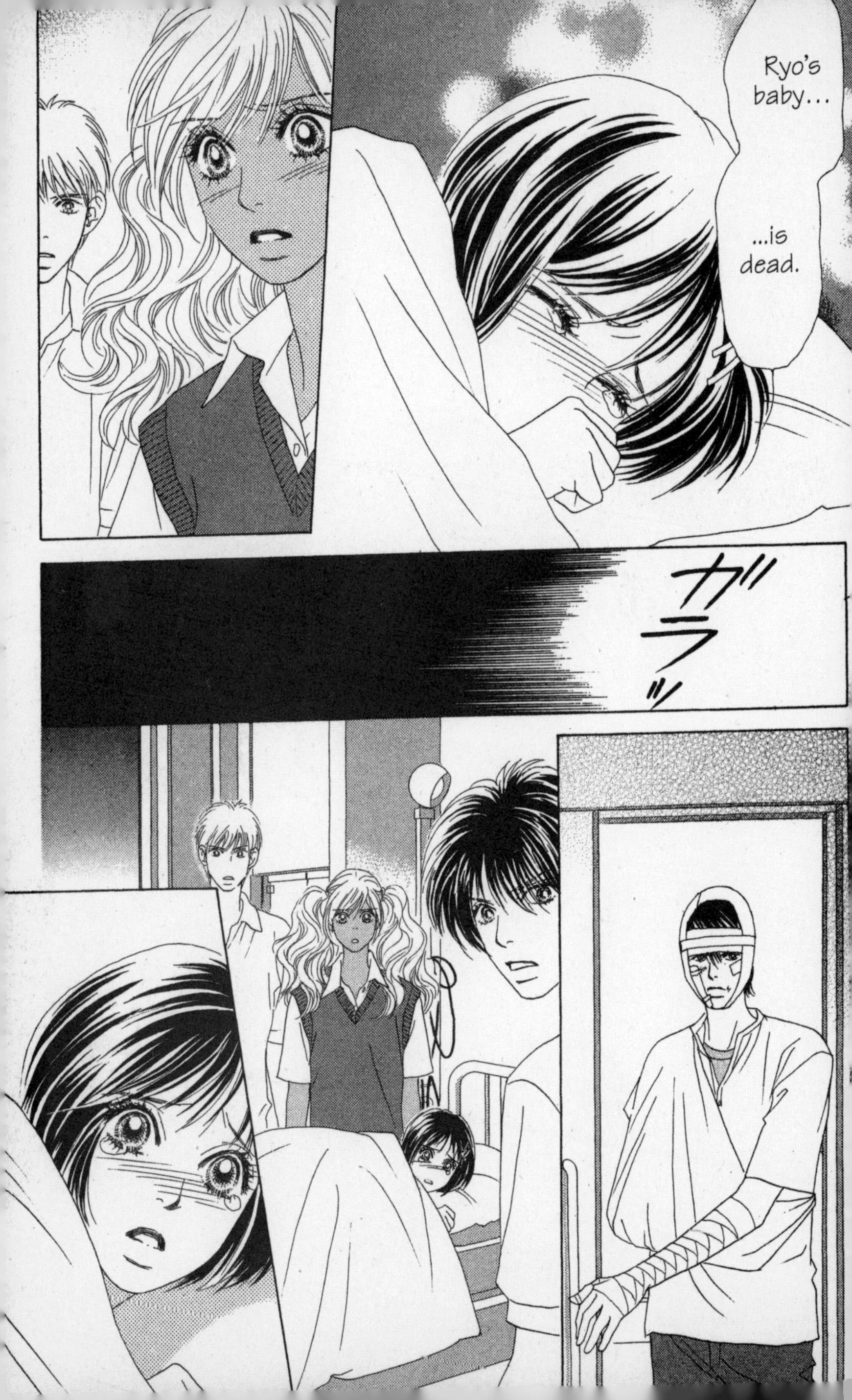
Ryo's baby...
...is dead.
ガラッ

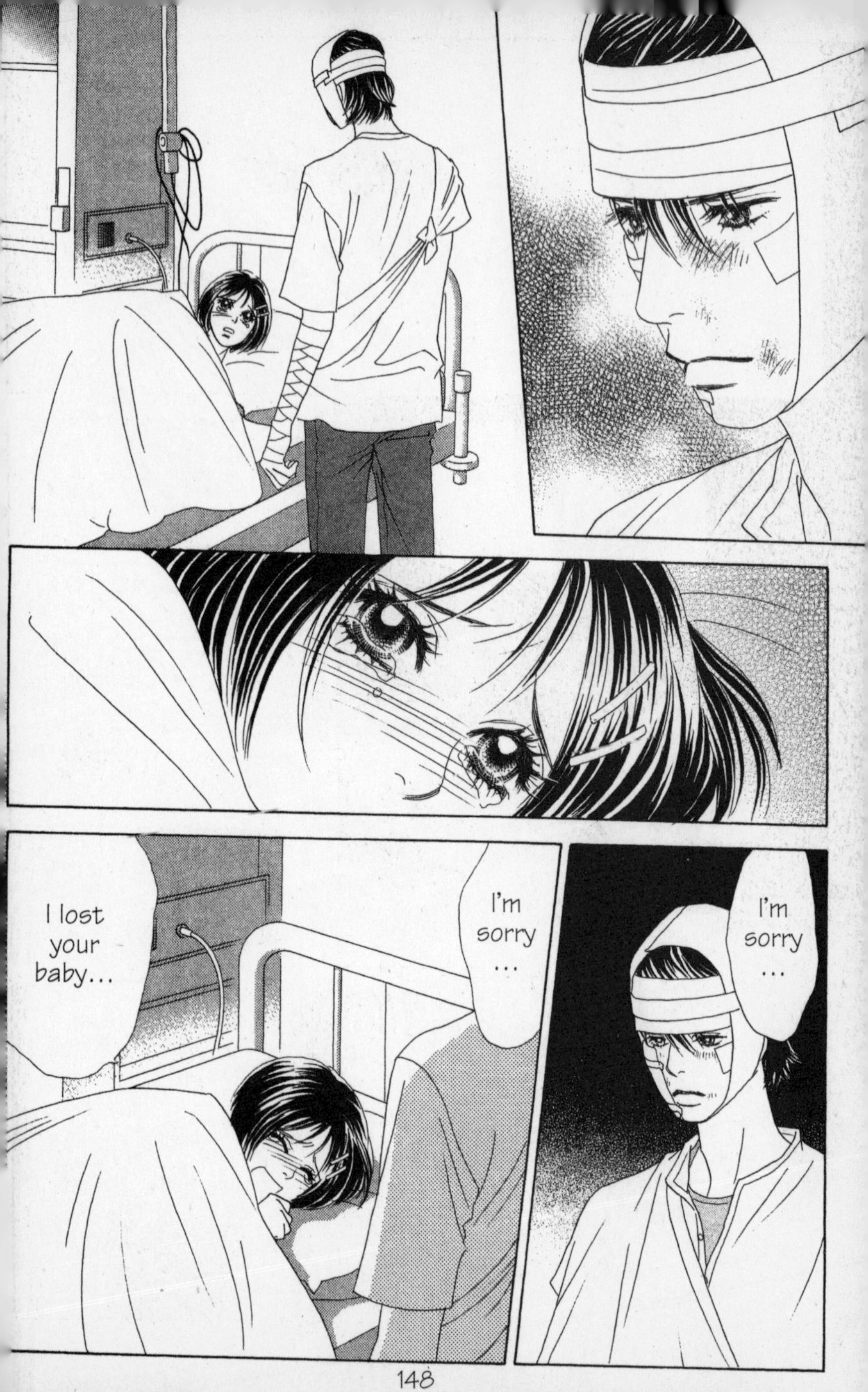
I'm sorry ...
I'm sorry ...
I lost your baby...

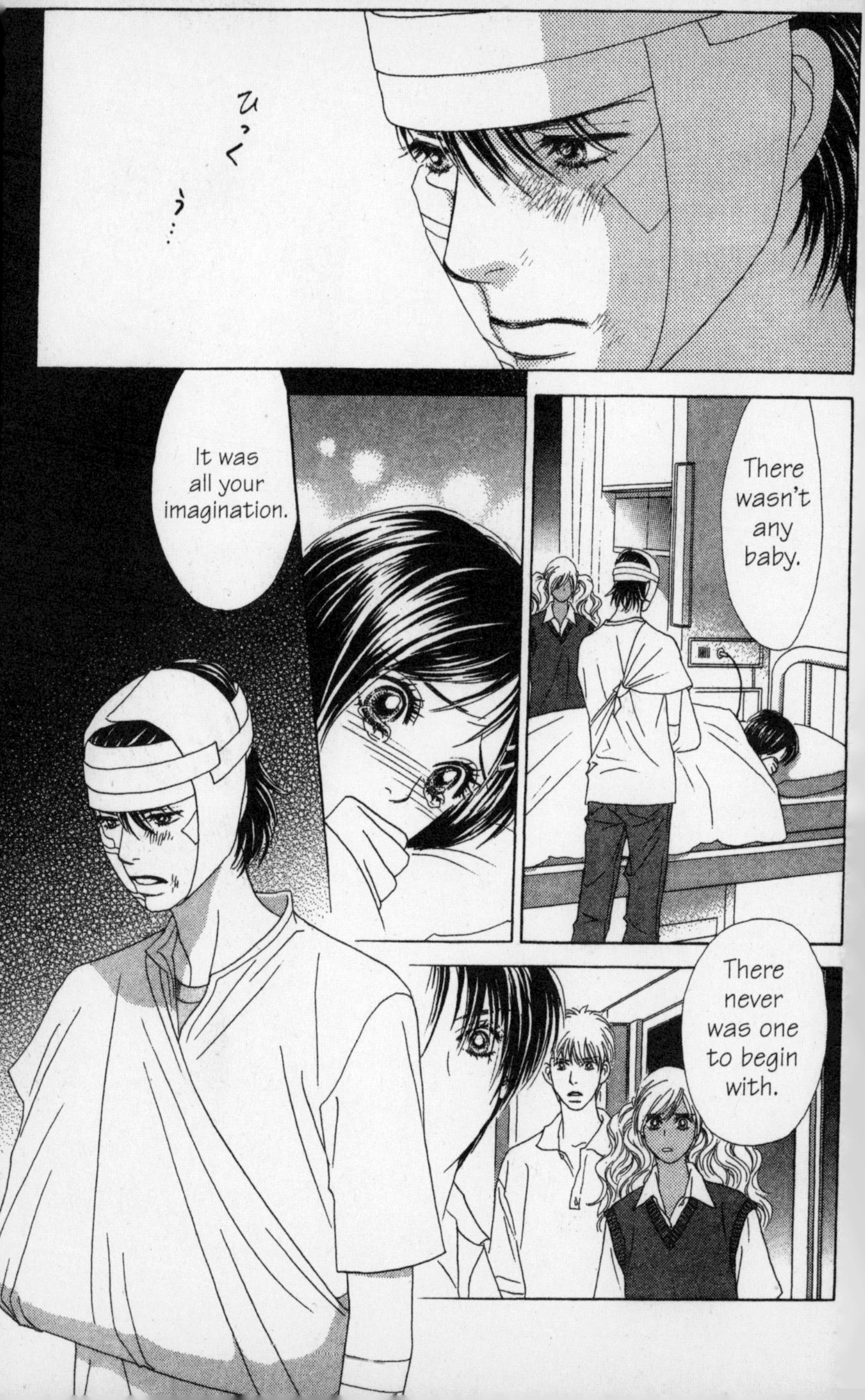
ひっく
う…
There wasn't any baby.
There never was one to begin with.
It was all your imagination.

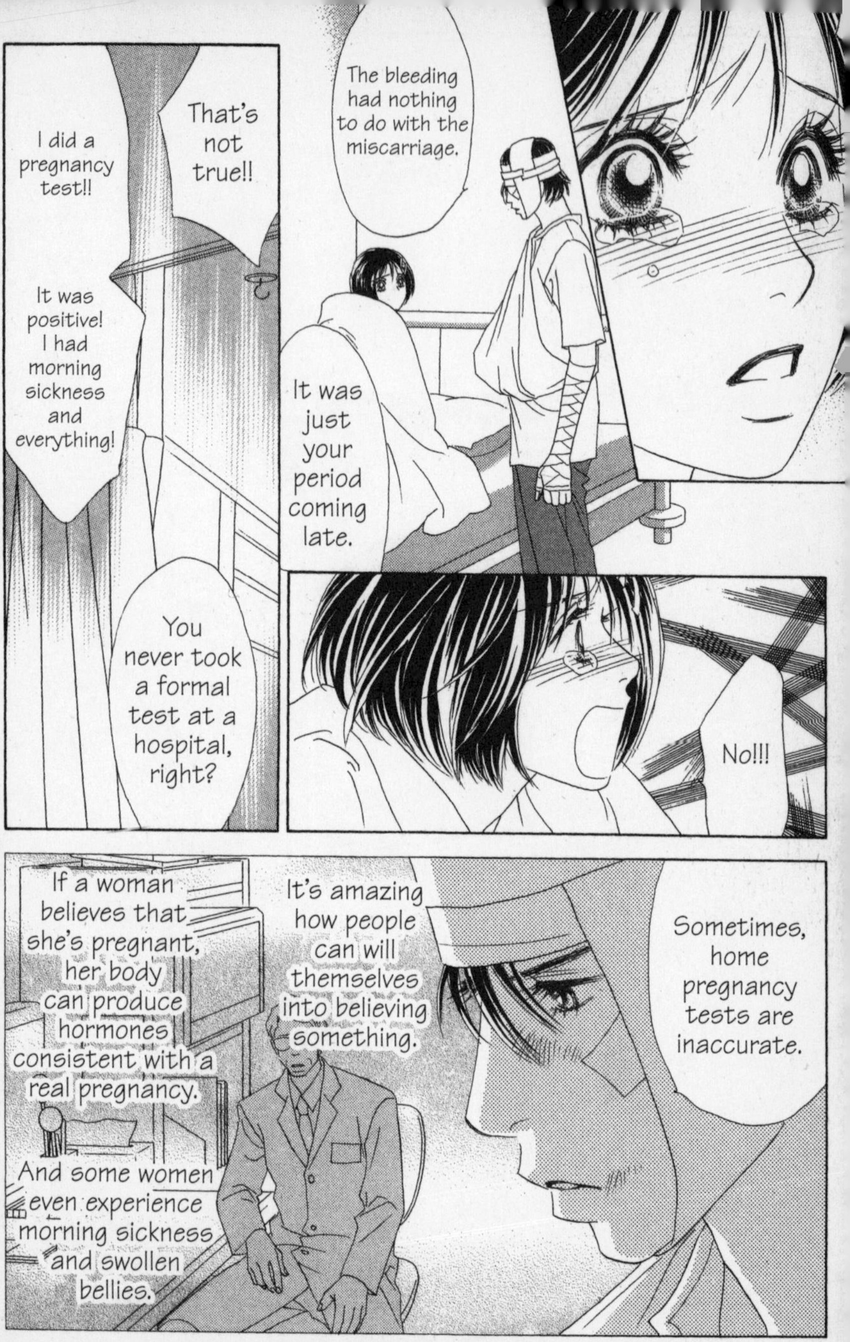
The bleeding had nothing to do with the miscarriage.
It was just your period coming late.
No!!!
That's not true!!
I did a pregnancy test!!
It was positive! I had morning sickness and everything!
You never took a formal test at a hospital, right?
Sometimes, home pregnancy tests are inaccurate.
It's amazing how people can will themselves into believing something.
If a woman believes that she's pregnant, her body can produce hormones consistent with a real pregnancy.
And some women even experience morning sickness and swollen bellies.

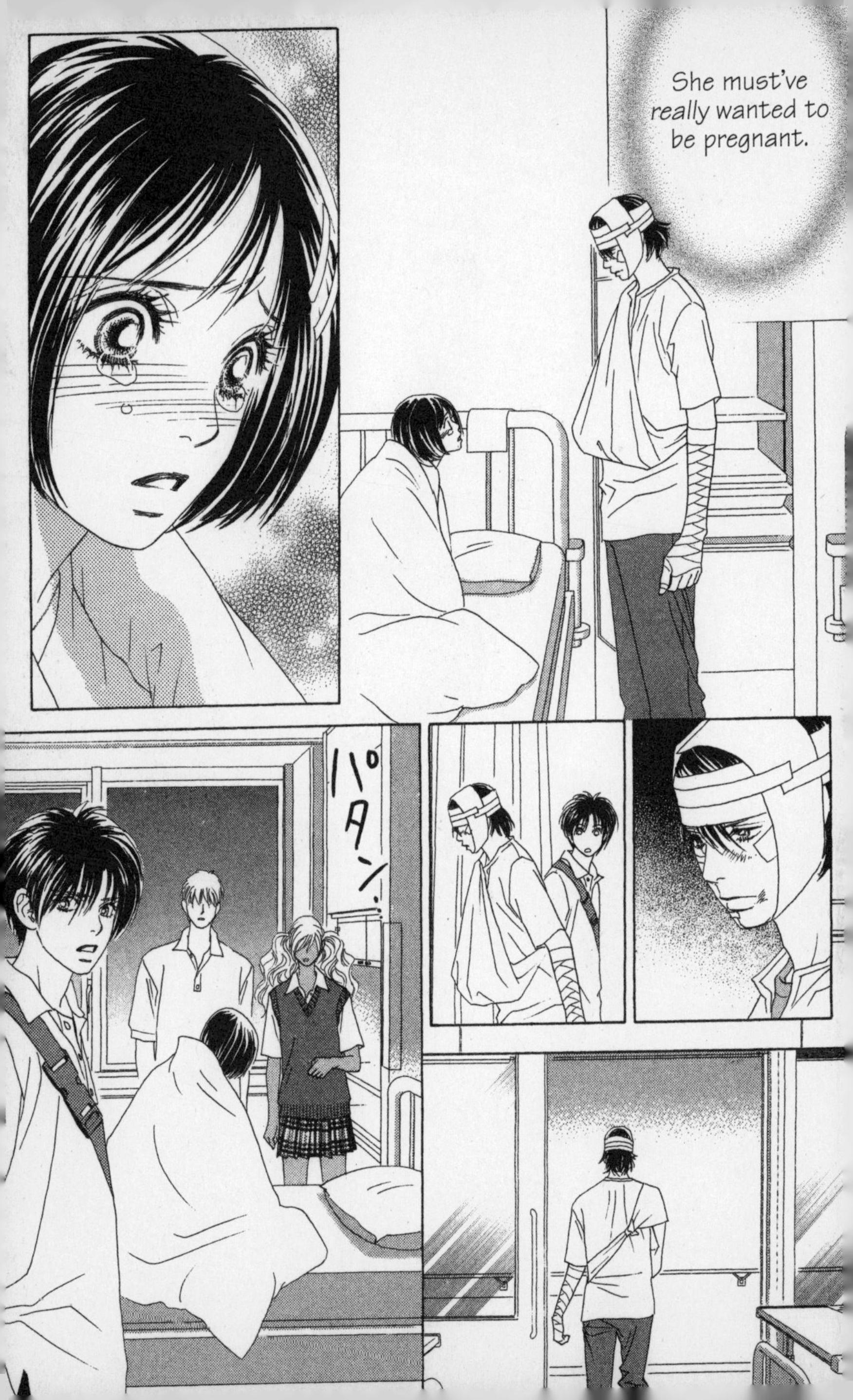
She must've really wanted to be pregnant.
パタン…

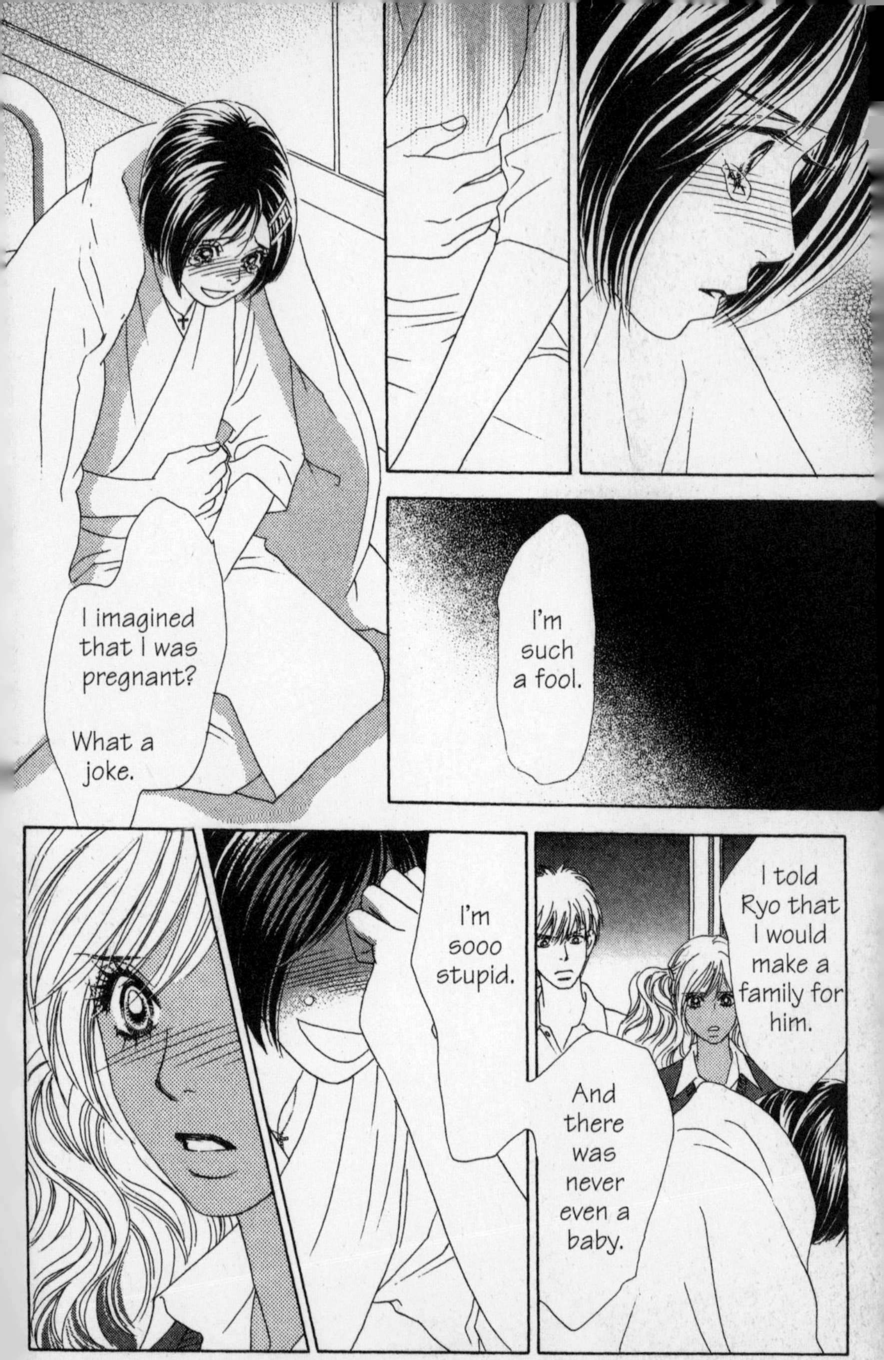
I'm such a fool.
I imagined that I was pregnant?
What a joke.
I told Ryo that I would make a family for him.
And there was never even a baby.
I'm sooo stupid.

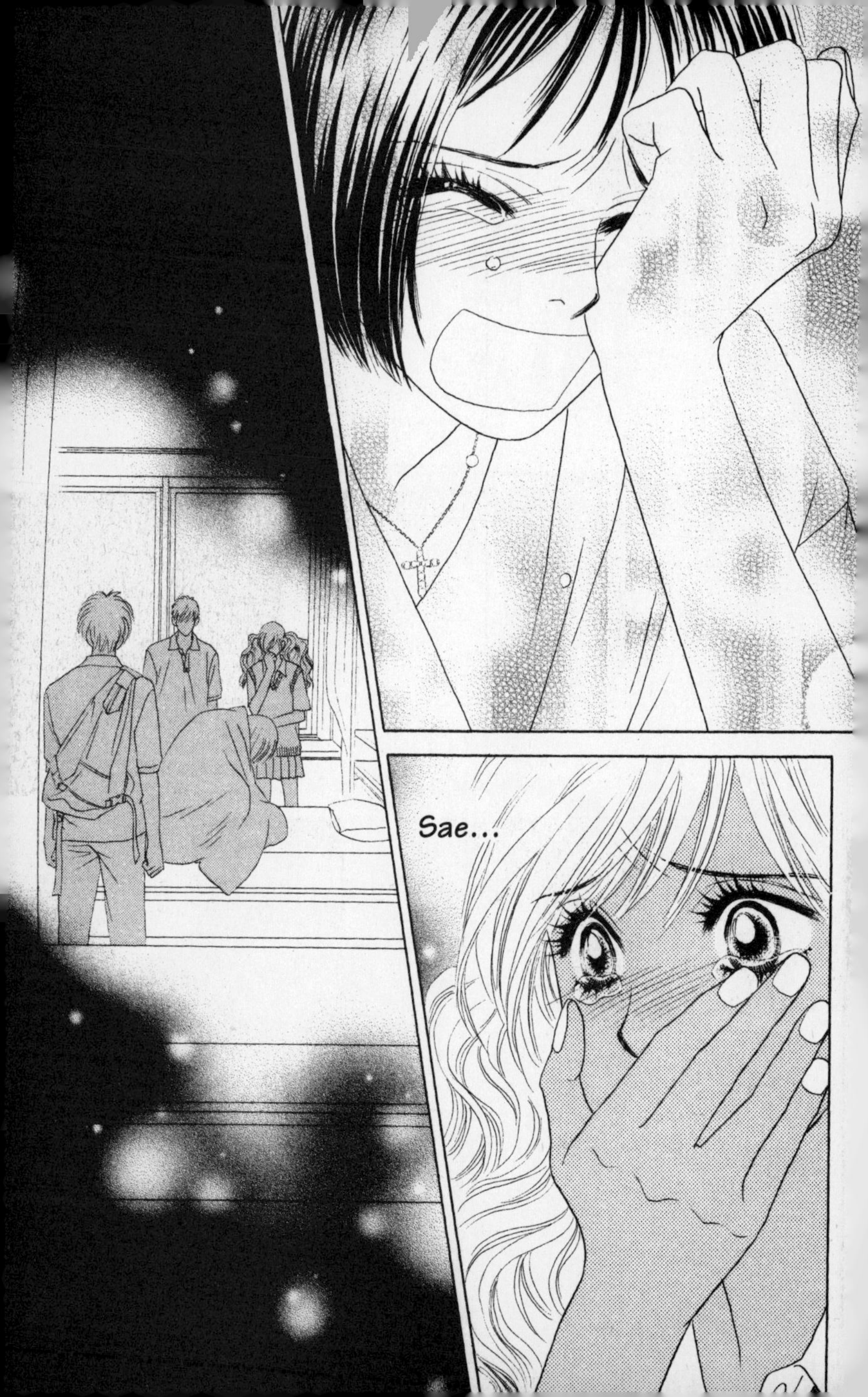
Sae...

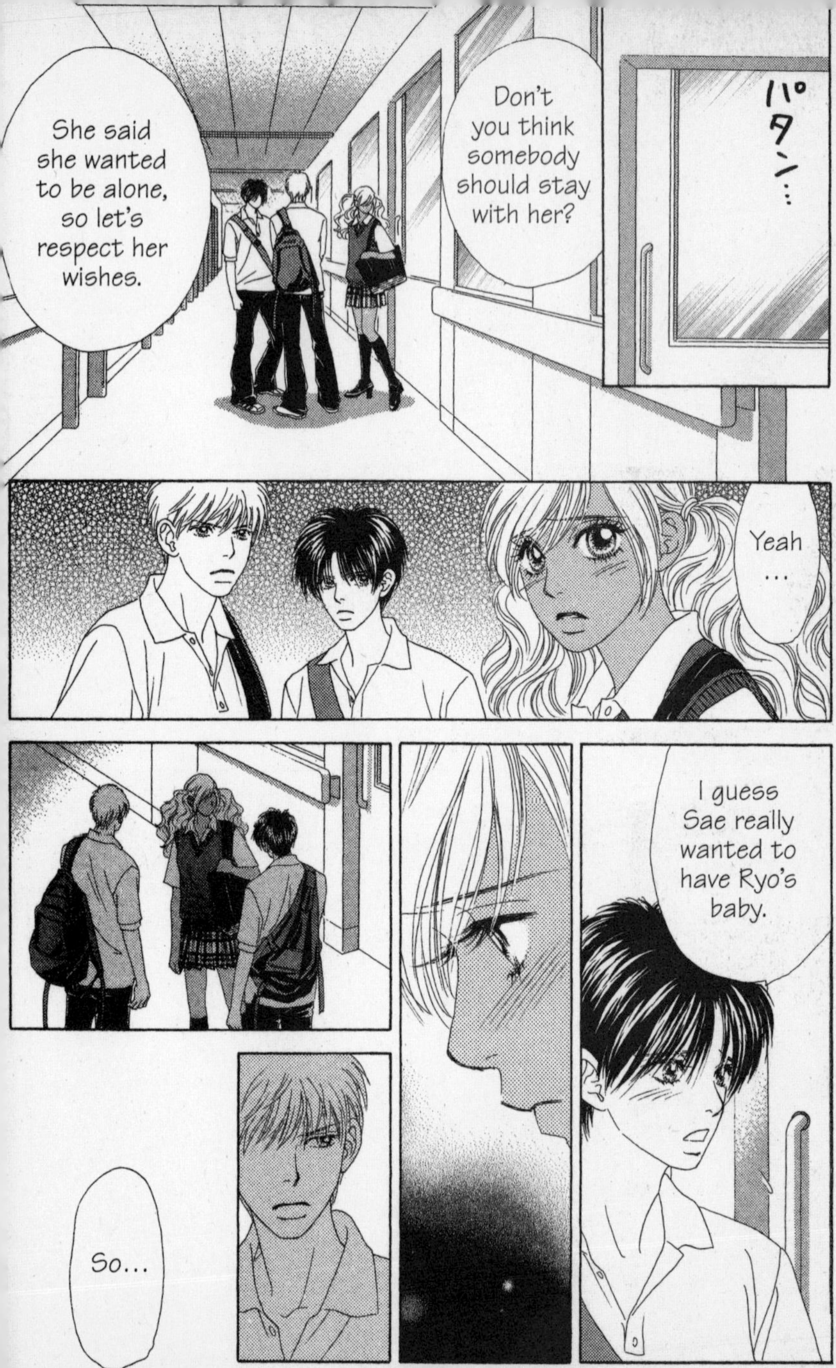
パタン…
Don't you think somebody should stay with her?
She said she wanted to be alone, so let's respect her wishes.
Yeah...
I guess Sae really wanted to have Ryo's baby.
So...

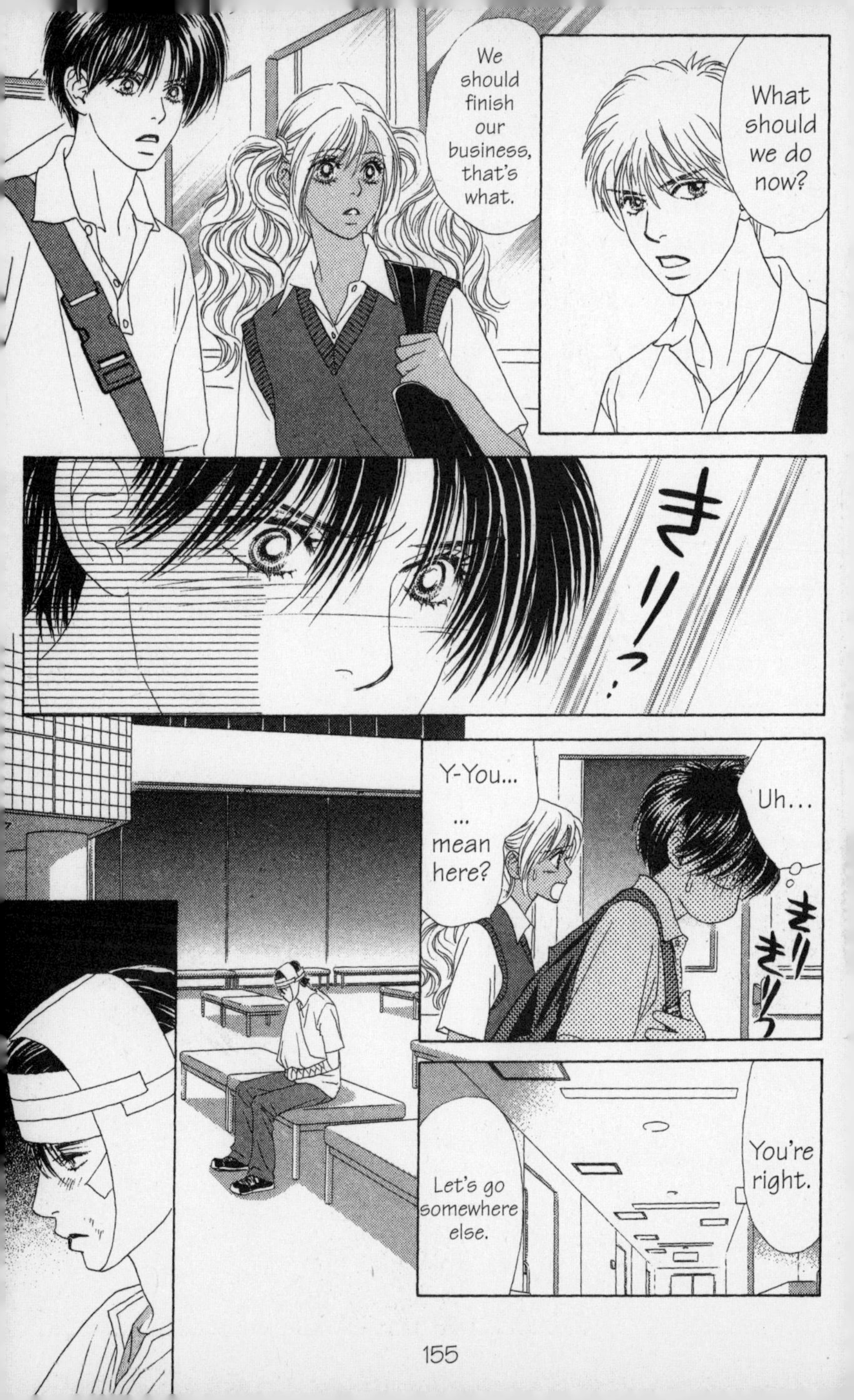
What should we do now?
We should finish our business, that's what.
きりっ
Uh...
Y-You...
... mean here?
きりきりっ
You're right.
Let's go somewhere else.

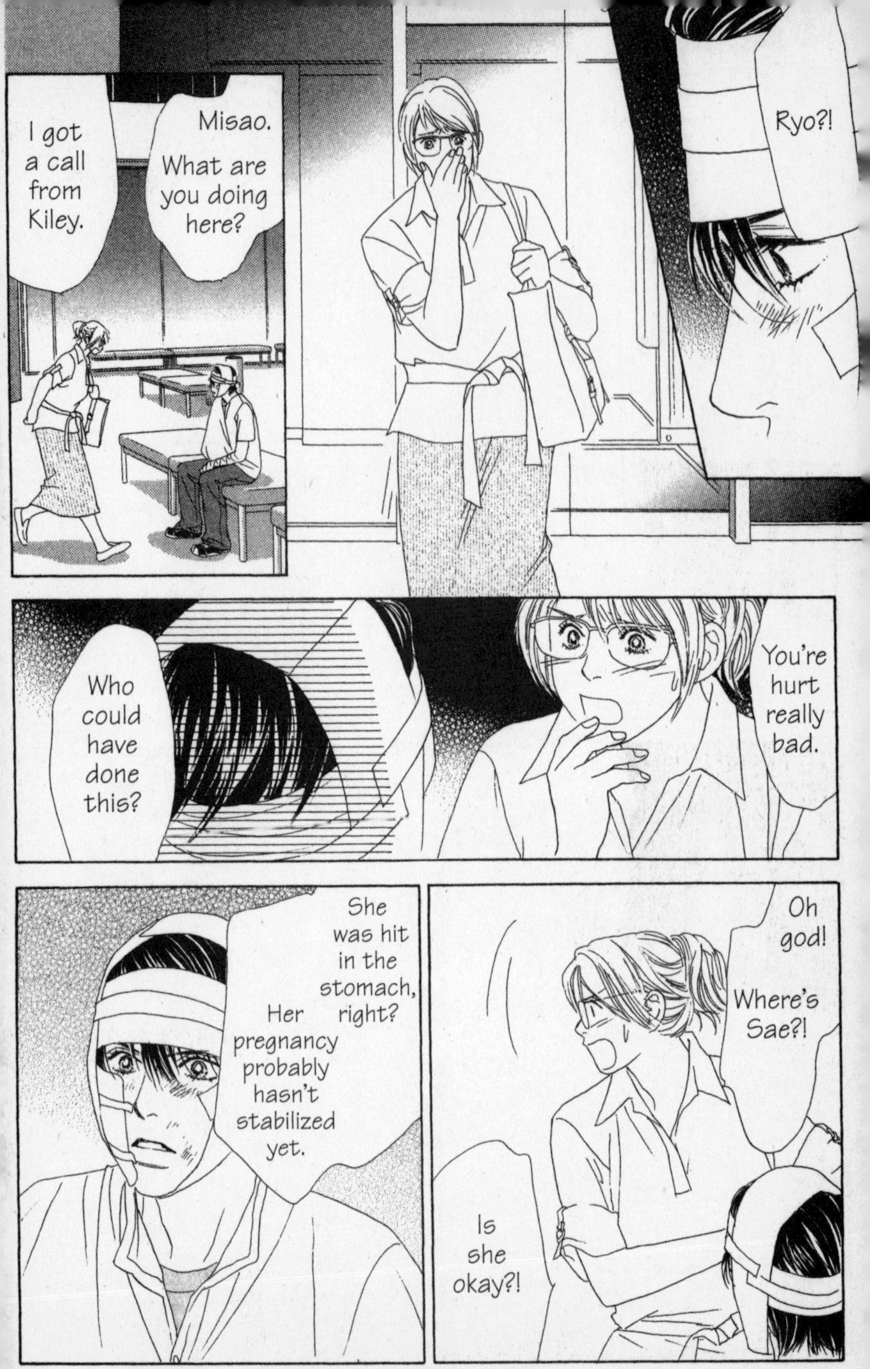
Ryo?!
Misao.
What are you doing here?
I got a call from Kiley.
You're hurt really bad.
Who could have done this?
Oh god!
Where's Sae?!
Is she okay?!
She was hit in the stomach, right?
Her pregnancy probably hasn't stabilized yet.

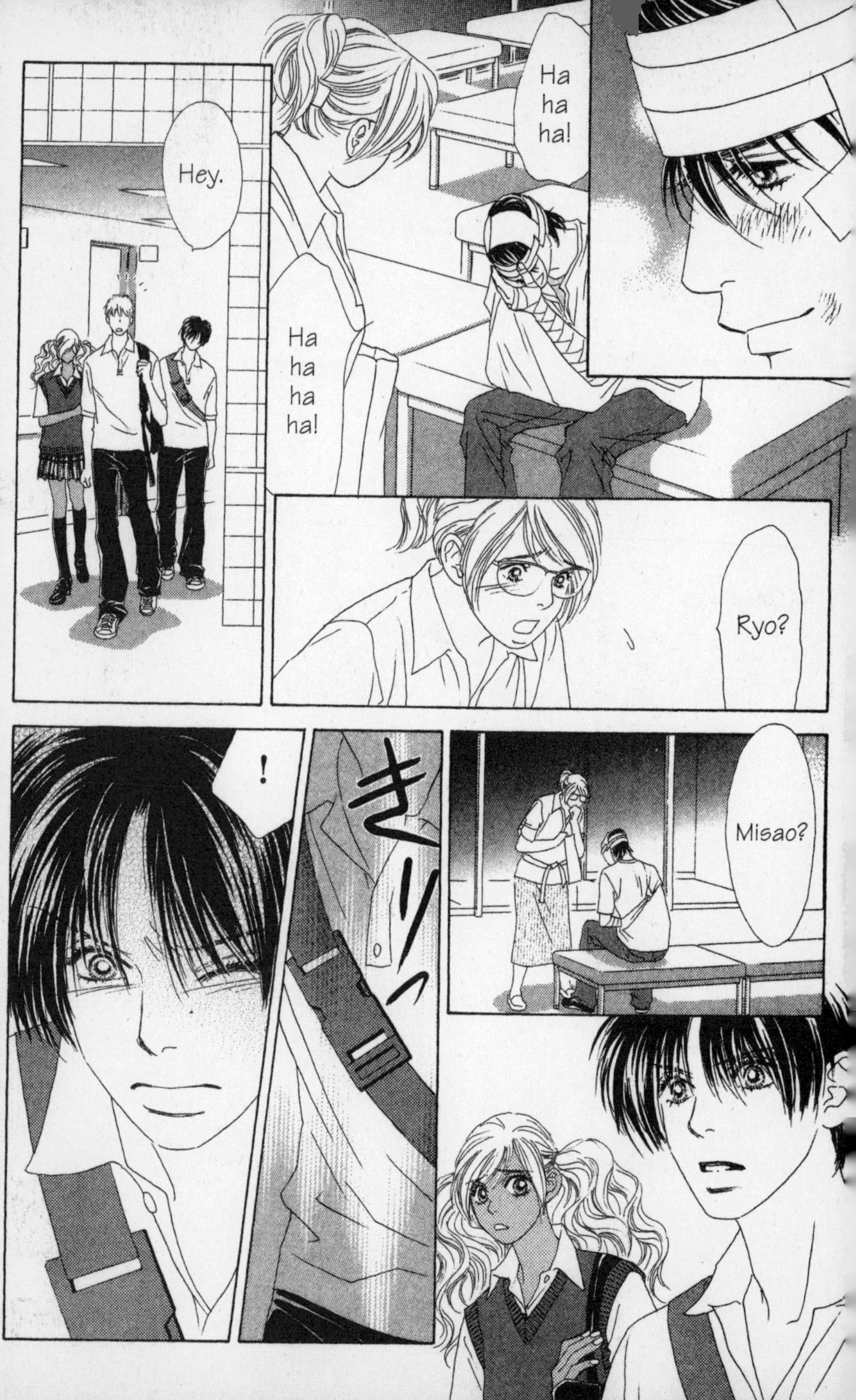
Ha ha ha!
Ha ha ha ha!
Ryo?
Hey.
Misao?
きりっ
!

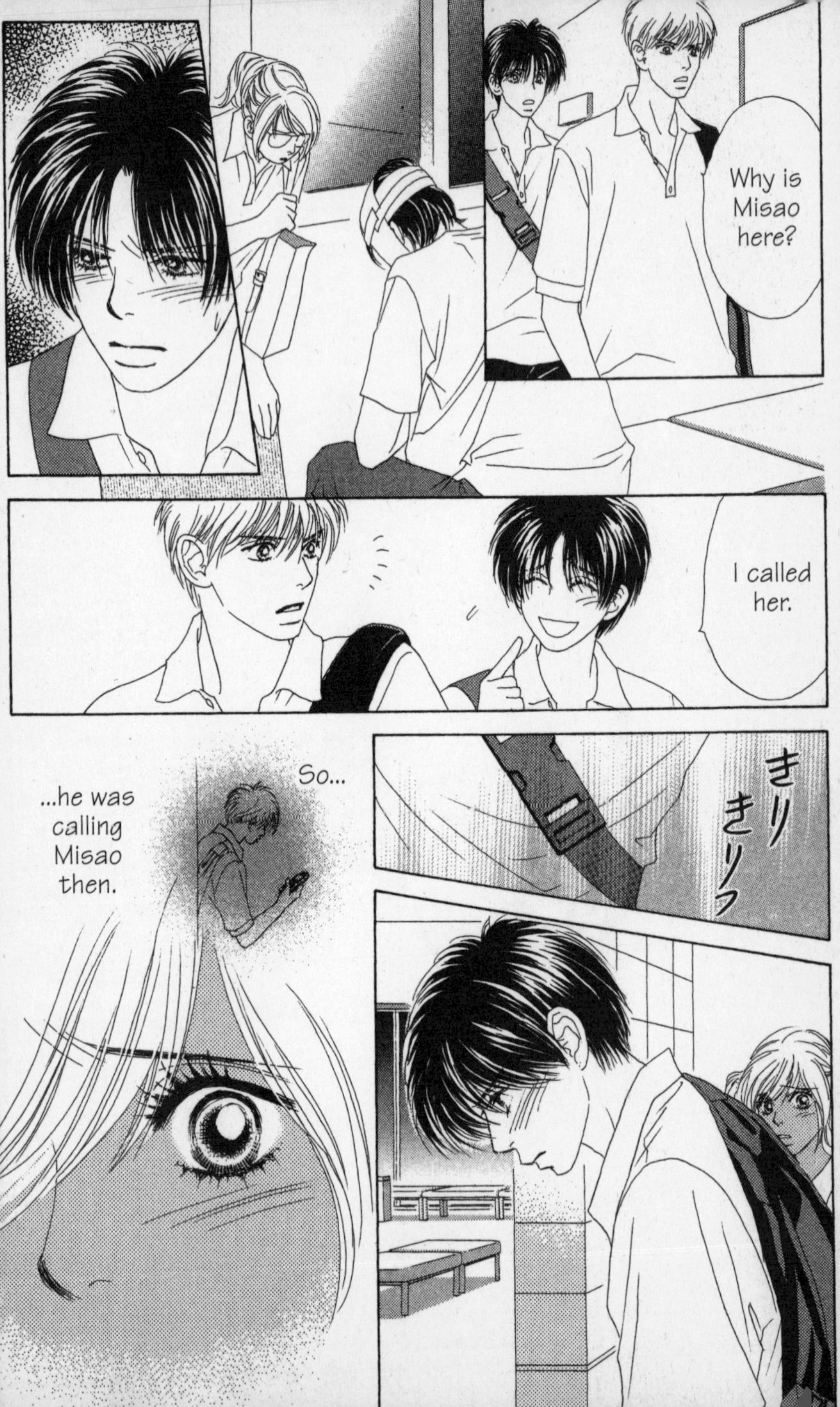

Why is Misao here?
I called her.
きり
きりっ
So...
...he was calling Misao then.

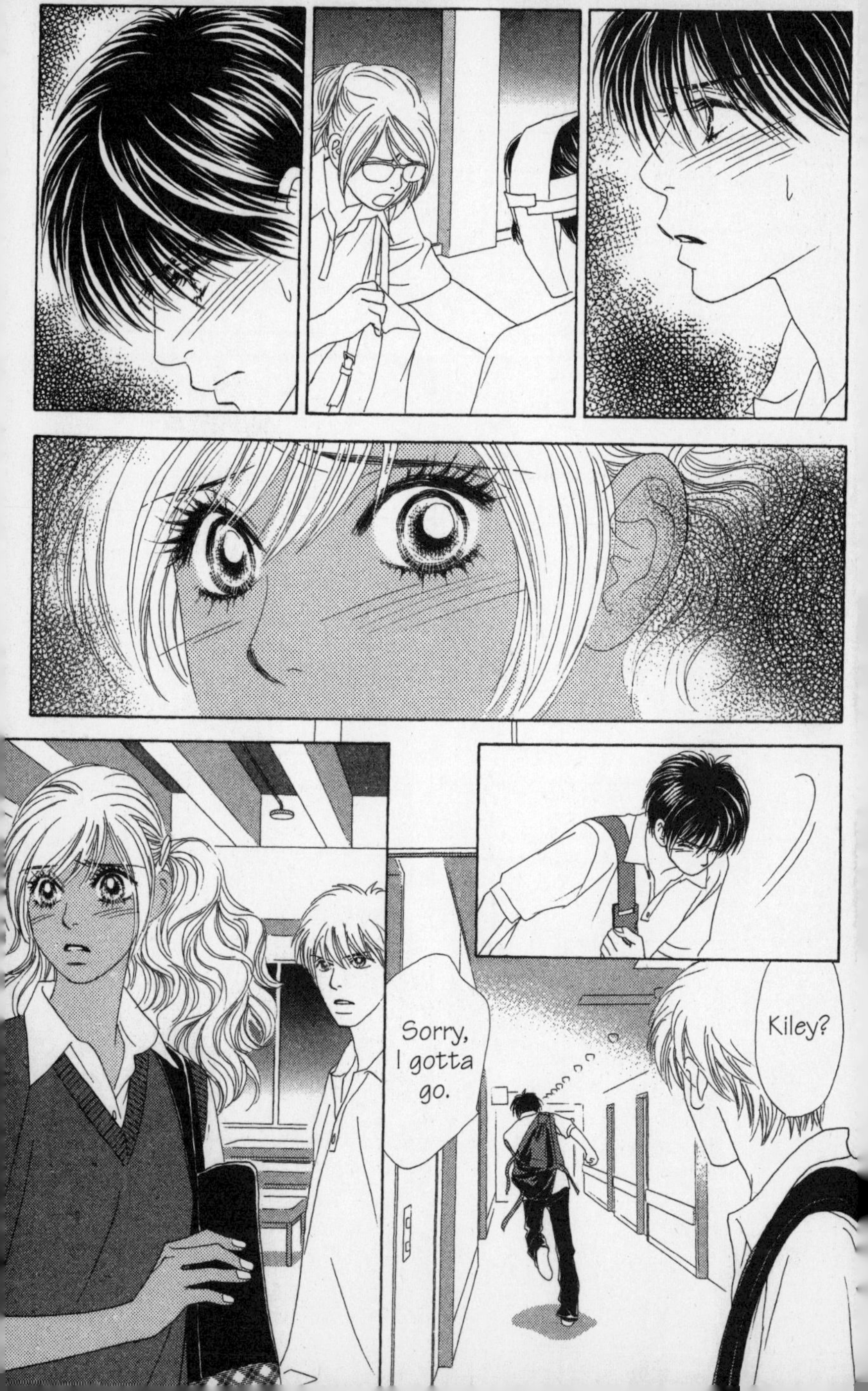
Kiley?
Sorry, I gotta go.

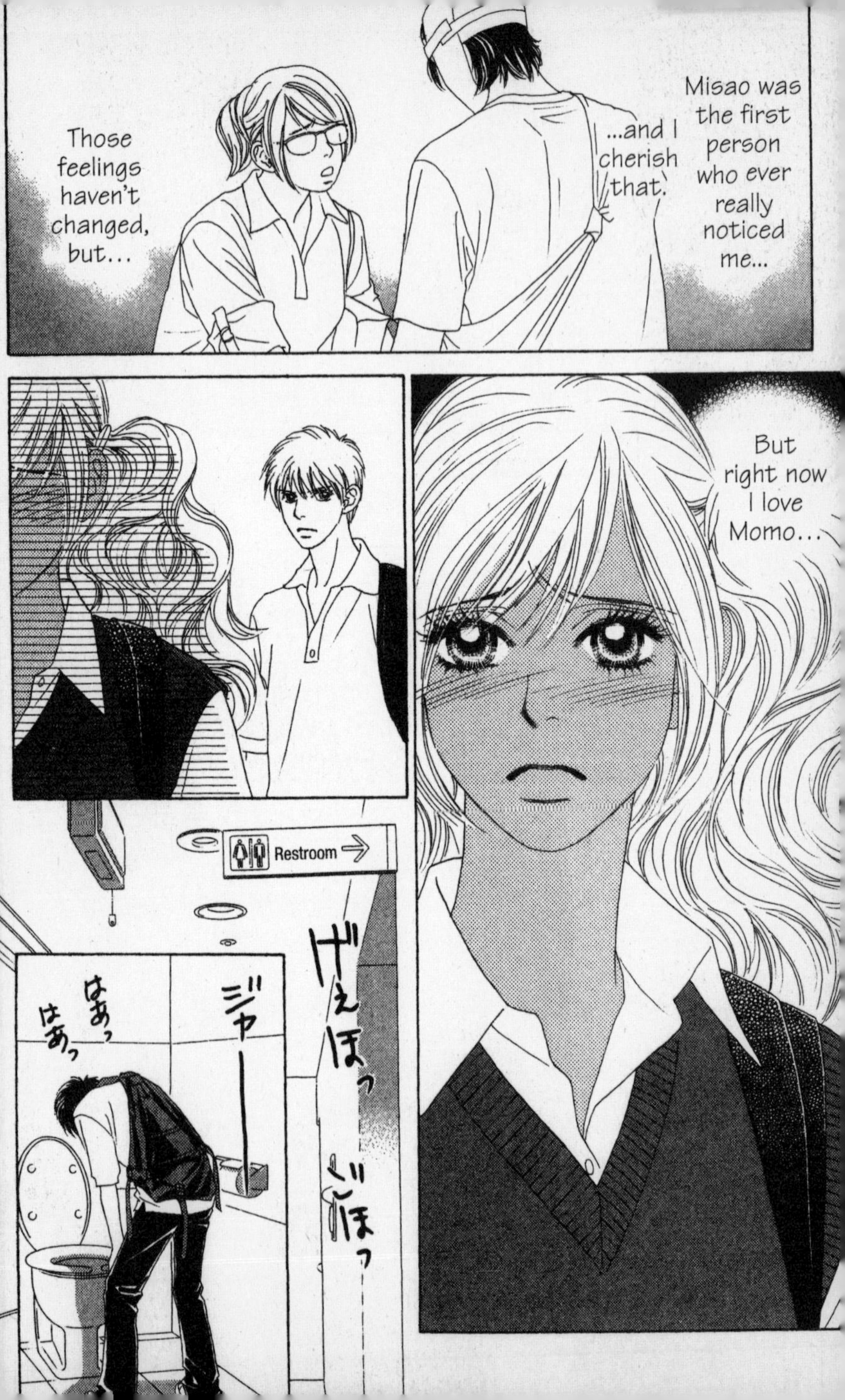
Misao was the first person who ever really noticed me...
...and I cherish that.
Those feelings haven't changed, but...
But right now I love Momo...
Restroom
げぇほっ
ごほっ
ジャー
はあっ
はあっ

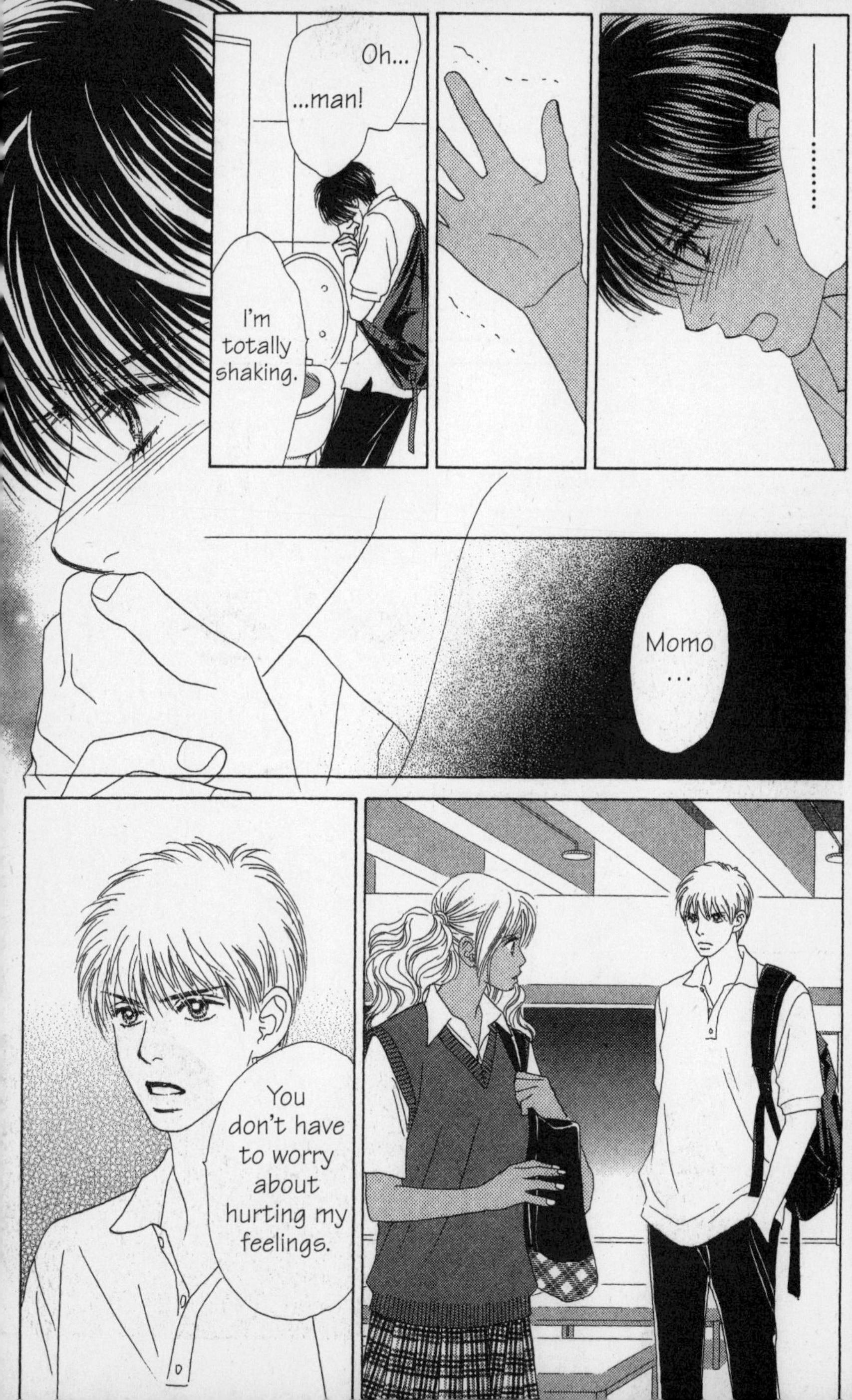
......
Oh...
...man!
I'm totally shaking.
Momo ...
You don't have to worry about hurting my feelings.

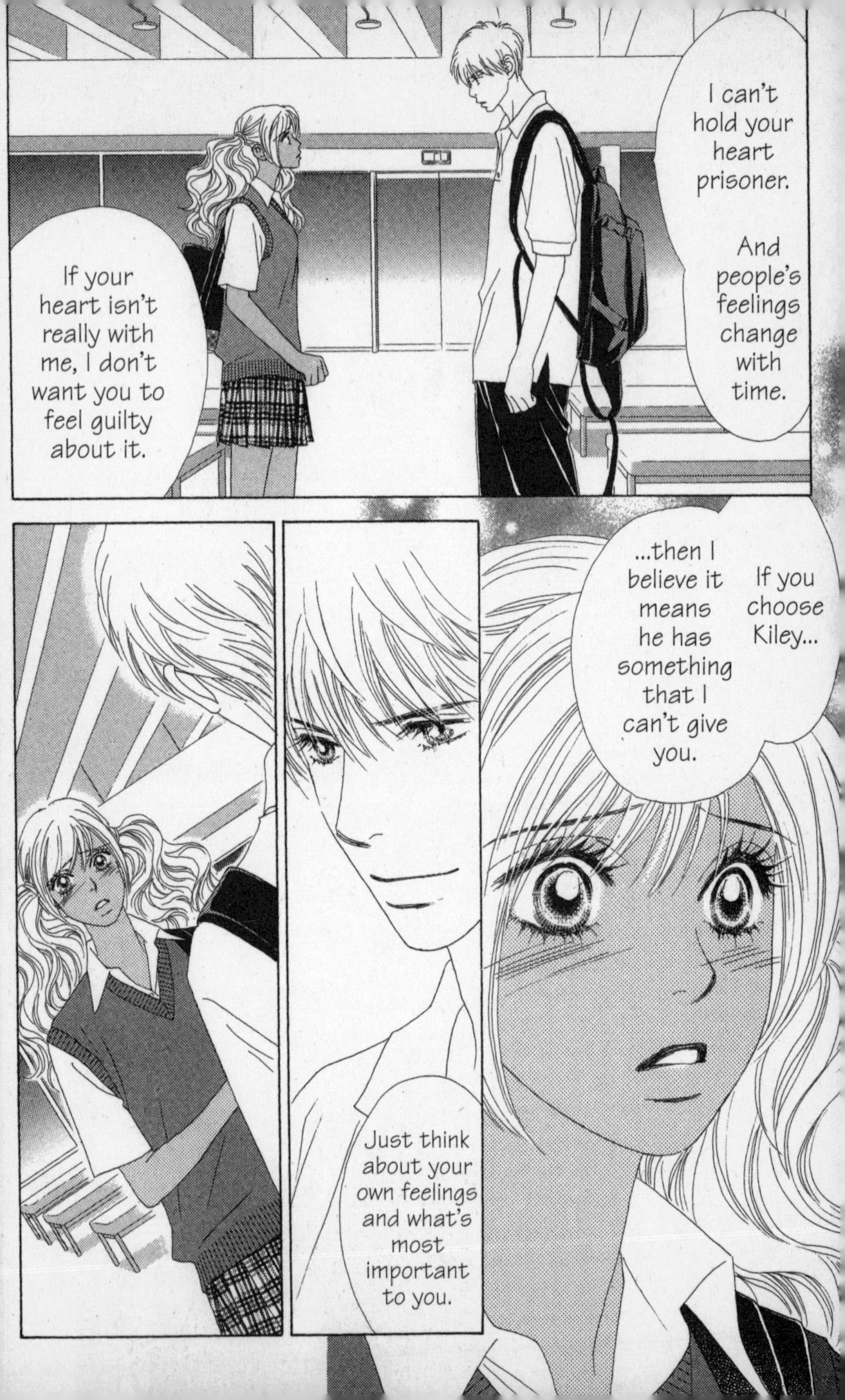
I can't hold your heart prisoner.
And people's feelings change with time.
If your heart isn't really with me, I don't want you to feel guilty about it.
If you choose Kiley...
...then I believe it means he has something that I can't give you.
Just think about your own feelings and what's most important to you.

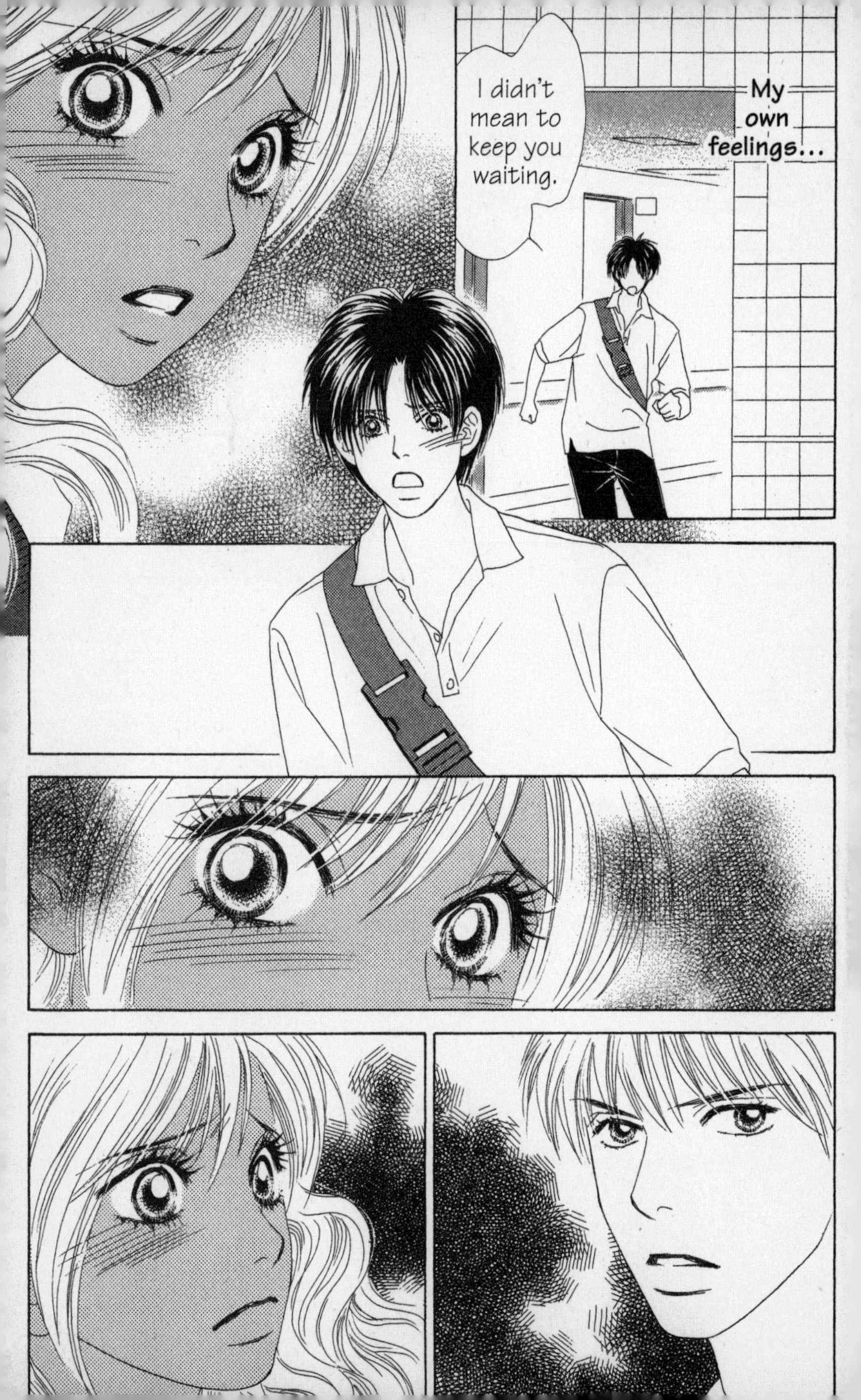
My own feelings...
I didn't mean to keep you waiting.

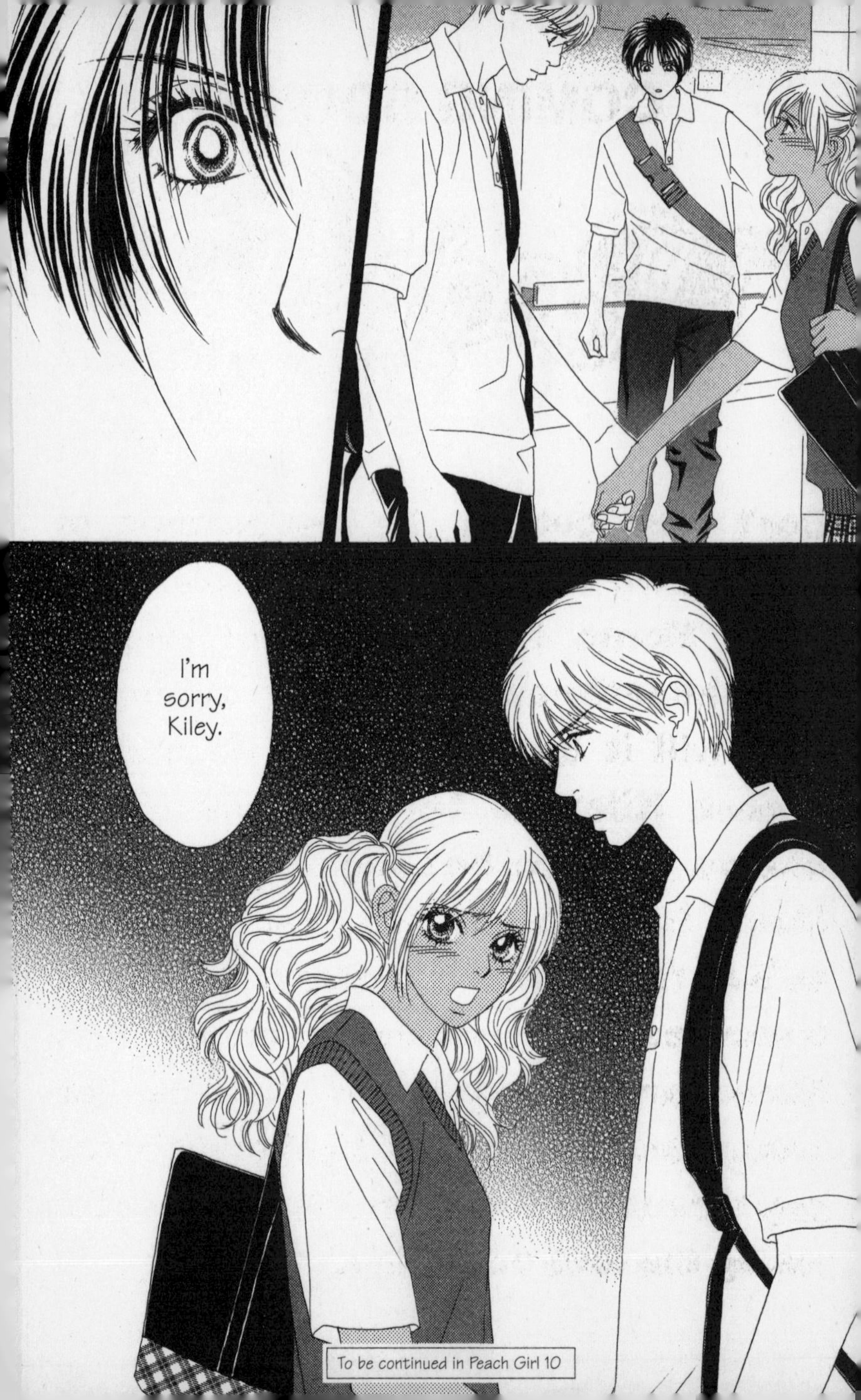
I'm sorry, Kiley.
To be continued in Peach Girl 10

ALSO AVAILABLE FROM  TOKYOPOP®

MANGA

.HACK//LEGEND OF THE TWILIGHT
@LARGE
ABENOBASHI: MAGICAL SHOPPING ARCADE
A.I. LOVE YOU
AI YORI AOSHI
ANGELIC LAYER
ARM OF KANNON
BABY BIRTH
BATTLE ROYALE
BATTLE VIXENS
BRAIN POWERED
BRIGADOON
B'TX
CANDIDATE FOR GODDESS, THE
CARDCAPTOR SAKURA
CARDCAPTOR SAKURA - MASTER OF THE CLOW
CHOBITS
CHRONICLES OF THE CURSED SWORD
CLAMP SCHOOL DETECTIVES
CLOVER
COMIC PARTY
CONFIDENTIAL CONFESSIONS
CORRECTOR YUI
COWBOY BEBOP
COWBOY BEBOP: SHOOTING STAR
CRAZY LOVE STORY
CRESCENT MOON
CROSS
CULDCEPT
CYBORG 009
D•N•ANGEL
DEMON DIARY
DEMON ORORON, THE
DEUS VITAE
DIABOLO
DIGIMON
DIGIMON TAMERS
DIGIMON ZERO TWO
DOLL
DRAGON HUNTER
DRAGON KNIGHTS
DRAGON VOICE
DREAM SAGA
DUKLYON: CLAMP SCHOOL DEFENDERS
EERIE QUEERIE!
ERICA SAKURAZAWA: COLLECTED WORKS
ET CETERA
ETERNITY
EVIL'S RETURN
FAERIES' LANDING
FAKE
FLCL
FLOWER OF THE DEEP SLEEP
FORBIDDEN DANCE
FRUITS BASKET
G GUNDAM

GATEKEEPERS
GETBACKERS
GIRL GOT GAME
GIRLS' EDUCATIONAL CHARTER
GRAVITATION
GTO
GUNDAM BLUE DESTINY
GUNDAM SEED ASTRAY
GUNDAM WING
GUNDAM WING: BATTLEFIELD OF PACIFISTS
GUNDAM WING: ENDLESS WALTZ
GUNDAM WING: THE LAST OUTPOST (G-UNIT)
GUYS' GUIDE TO GIRLS
HANDS OFF!
HAPPY MANIA
HARLEM BEAT
HONEY MUSTARD
I.N.V.U.
IMMORTAL RAIN
INITIAL D
INSTANT TEEN: JUST ADD NUTS
ISLAND
JING: KING OF BANDITS
JING: KING OF BANDITS - TWILIGHT TALES
JULINE
KARE KANO
KILL ME, KISS ME
KINDAICHI CASE FILES, THE
KING OF HELL
KODOCHA: SANA'S STAGE
LAMENT OF THE LAMB
LEGAL DRUG
LEGEND OF CHUN HYANG, THE
LES BIJOUX
LOVE HINA
LUPIN III
LUPIN III: WORLD'S MOST WANTED
MAGIC KNIGHT RAYEARTH I
MAGIC KNIGHT RAYEARTH II
MAHOROMATIC: AUTOMATIC MAIDEN
MAN OF MANY FACES
MARMALADE BOY
MARS
MARS: HORSE WITH NO NAME
MINK
MIRACLE GIRLS
MIYUKI-CHAN IN WONDERLAND
MODEL
MY LOVE
NECK AND NECK
ONE
ONE I LOVE, THE
PARADISE KISS
PARASYTE
PASSION FRUIT
PEACH GIRL
PEACH GIRL: CHANGE OF HEART
PET SHOP OF HORRORS

An ordinary student
with an extraordinary gift...

Eerie Queerie!

He's there for you in spirit.

kare kano

his and her circumstances

Story by Masami Tsuda

Life Was A Popularity Contest For Yukino. Somebody Is About To Steal Her Crown.

Available Now At Your Favorite Book And Comic Stores!

Rank	Name	Class	Points
1	???		
2	???		
3	Tomohiko Ta	B	
4	Takumi	A	
5	Mieko Ta	E	
6	Nijo Watanab	C	
7	Akemi Imafuku		
8	Mizue Tanaka		
9	Yuki Honj		
10	Reiko Yokoo		
11	Hiroki Sato		
12	Akira Oshima		
13	Eri Yugawa		
14	Aiko Yamac		
15	Shogo Ka		
16	Masami Ha		
17	Mizuho On		

100% AUTHENTIC MANGA

T TEEN AGE 13+

forbidden Dance ™

by Hinako Ashihara

Dancing was her life...

Her dance partner might be her future...

Available Now

On the edge of high fashion and hot passion.

Ai Yazawa's
Paradise Kiss

FROM JAPAN'S #1 SHOJO CREATOR